Preface Books

A series of scholarly and critical studies of major writers intended for those needing modern and authoritative guidance through the characteristic difficulties of their work to reach an intelligent understanding and enjoyment of it.

General Editor: JOHN PURKIS
Founding Editor: MAURICE HUSSEY

A Preface to Wordsworth (*Revised edn*)	JOHN PURKIS
A Preface to Donne (*Revised edn*)	JAMES WINNY
A Preface to Jane Austen (*Revised edn*)	CHRISTOPHER GILLIE
A Preface to Lawrence	GAMINI SALGADO
A Preface to Forster	CHRISTOPHER GILLIE
A Preface to Dickens	ALLAN GRANT
A Preface to Shelley	PATRICIA HODGART
A Preface to Keats	CEDRIC WATTS
A Preface to Orwell	DAVID WYKES
A Preface to Milton (*Revised edn*)	LOIS POTTER
A Preface to the Brontës	FELICIA GORDON
A Preface to T.S. Eliot	RON TAMPLIN
A Preface to Shakespeare's Tragedies	MICHAEL MANGAN
A Preface to Hopkins (*Second edn*)	GRAHAM STOREY
A Preface to James Joyce (*Second edn*)	SYDNEY BOLT
A Preface to Hardy (*Second edn*)	MERRYN WILLIAMS
A Preface to Conrad (*Second edn*)	CEDRIC WATTS
A Preface to Samuel Johnson	THOMAS WOODMAN
A Preface to Pope (*Second edn*)	I. R. F. GORDON
A Preface to Yeats (*Second edn*)	EDWARD MALINS with JOHN PURKIS
A Preface to Shakespeare's Comedies: 1594–1603	MICHAEL MANGAN
A Preface to Ezra Pound	PETER WILSON

Pound as an old man, Venice 1971.

A Preface to Ezra Pound

Peter Wilson

Longman
London and New York

Addison Wesley Longman
Edinburgh Gate
Harlow
Essex CM20 2JE
England
and Associated Companies throughout the world.

*Published in the United States of America
by Addison Wesley Longman Inc., New York.*

First published 1997

ISBN 0 582 25868 5   CSD
ISBN 0 582 25867 7   PPR

British Library Cataloguing-in-Publication Data

A catalogue record of this book is
available from the British Library

Library of Congress Cataloging-in-Publication Data

Wilson, Peter, 1945–
    A preface to Ezra Pound / Peter Wilson.
        p. cm. — (Preface books)
    Includes bibliographical references and index.
    ISBN 0–582–25868–5 (hardcover). — ISBN 0–582–25867–7 (pbk.)
    1. Pound, Ezra, 1885–1972—Criticism and interpretation.
PS3531.O82Z894   1996
811'.52—dc20   96–21679
                                                         CIP

Set by 35 in 10½/11pt Mono Baskerville
Produced by Longman Singapore Publishers (Pte) Ltd.
Printed in Singapore

Contents

Contents

List of illustrations

Acknowledgements

We are grateful to the following for permission to reproduce copyright material:

Text:

Faber and Faber Ltd for extracts from *ABC of Reading* by Ezra Pound (1961), *The Cantos* by Ezra Pound (1987), *Personae: Collected Shorter Poems of Ezra Pound* (1984), *Selected Prose 1909–1965* by Ezra Pound (edited by William Cookson) (1973), *Literary Essays of Ezra Pound* (edited by T S Eliot) (1954), *The Classic Anthology as Defined by Confucius* by Ezra Pound (1954), *Sophocles: Women of Trachis: A Version* by Ezra Pound (1969); Faber and Faber Ltd and New Directions Publishing Corp. for extracts from *Selected Letters of Ezra Pound* (1971). Copyright © 1950 by Ezra Pound; Oxford University Press for an extract from the poem 'On the Fly-leaf of Pound's Cantos' from *Collected Poems* by Basil Bunting (1978).

Illustrations:

Frontispiece © Horst Tappe; *Ezra Pound in a dressing gown, Kensington 1916* Courtesy of the Bodleian Library: shelfmark 28001 e 1557; *Cover of the second issue of Blast (Before Antwerp, Wyndham Lewis)* © Estate of Mrs G A Wyndham Lewis; *Manuscript page from Pound's opera Le Testament de Villon, 1921* © New Directions and Faber & Faber Ltd; *Pound with his daughter, Mary, and his father, Homer, Italy 1929* © Mary de Rachewiltz; *Heiratic Head of Ezra Pound by Henri Gaudier-Brzeska, 1914* from the collection of Raymond D Nasher, Dallas. Courtesy of the Anthony D'Offay Gallery, London; *Gaudier-Brzeska working on the Heiratic Head of Ezra Pound, 1914* Courtesy of the Bodleian Library: shelfmark 1720.c.19; *Line drawing of Pound by Henri Gaudier-Brzeska, 1914* Courtesy of Kettle's Yard, Cambridge.

Introduction

Like other volumes in the Preface series, this book is an attempt to introduce a major writer under the broad headings of life, background and work. The biographical section is rather longer and more detailed than is usual in the series. Pound's life was long and full, a *commedia humana* in the spirit of Dante, one of his most important mentors. His contacts were many and significant, both in human and literary or artistic terms. This life, these contacts, are integral to Pound's work, in its provenance, its development and its content: a biographical outline needs sufficient scope to reflect this. I have also used this section to introduce and discuss briefly some of Pound's work not mentioned in the critical survey, such as some of his major translations, prose works and musical compositions, as they relate to his life. The critical survey is entirely concerned with the poetry, though not without reference to the translations, prose work and letters by which it is both informed and illuminated. The largest part of this critical survey is given to *The Cantos*, reflecting their size, complexity and significance in the history of twentieth-century poetry. They are a literary mountain range whose foothills and peaks have proved difficult to negotiate for many potential readers. This survey provides a map that should allow at least an initial exploration of the territory. In between, a section of background presents a selective view of some literary, cultural and political issues relevant to Pound and his work. The selection reflects, to some extent, my own sense of what is of most concern for readers of Pound in the present climate of theoretical and academic debate.

Throughout his life Pound was a contentious and controversial figure. Since his death in 1972, theoretical, literary, political and biographical commentators have perpetuated on a large scale the contentions and controversies that surrounded him when alive. The quality of his poetry has always been subject to fairly partisan evaluation and the status of *The Cantos* continues to arouse debate. Interestingly though, many, if not most, practising poets acknowledge his work as a model of excellence and a spur to poetic achievement. There have been notable exceptions, however, such as Philip Larkin, for whom Pound's modernist poetics were anathema. Pound's polyglot range of reference and allusion is also negatively judged as an elitist obstacle to the reader. On the other hand, he is heralded as someone whose work is an education in itself. His range of interests, mediated through quotations and translations, opens up a vast window on the art, literature and culture of classical, European and oriental civilizations in a way that no other poet does. However, it is his political associations that still cause the most polarized argument.

For those whose first encounter with Pound is his poetry, getting to know something of Pound the person can be a perplexing and, in some ways, an upsetting experience. On the one hand there are instances of amazing generosity to friends and fellow writers, a seemingly inexhaustible energy in promoting their work and, most impressively, a lack of envy at their talent coupled with genuine joy at their success. On the other hand the energy and obsessiveness which were exercised for the good of the literary causes he espoused were also given over to economic theories. In so far as I understand them, these theories seem reasonable in themselves, since they appear to be partly about the redistribution of wealth. However, Pound's ideas on economics were not only compatible with fascism as a political philosophy, but also led to his support for the fascist cause during the Second World War. This allegiance was also underpinned by a racism that had its most objectionable manifestation in overtly anti-Semitic remarks, some of which tainted his poetry.

The problem posed by Pound is not a new one, since there are plenty of artists, writers, musicians whose work achieves moments of perfection and sublimity, while their lives exhibit opinions, attitudes and actions which dismay and disappoint. Indeed, this disparity is a salutary reminder that artistic endeavour is a very human enterprise undertaken by individuals with flaws similar to our own. Pound epitomizes this problem for the twentieth century, in my view, not just because his opinions, attitudes and actions in this respect were antipathetic, but because the quality of his finest work triggers a kind of literary grief that such a poet should spend so much energy not writing poetry. In addition there is the question of motive: what personal and historical factors compel someone of Pound's gifts to follow the course he took? Motives are always 'Confused, whirled in a tangle', but they are, I think, worth trying to understand. Two major points follow on from this aspect of Pound's life and work. Firstly, the politically incorrect elements should never be tacitly glossed over, as a selective representation would allow: the need to understand and learn from them seems as imperative as ever. On the other hand, misguided notions of political correctness should never result in Pound's work being unread and unstudied or becoming less generally available: as I have already indicated, reading Pound is too important an educative process to be lost.

My primary aim in writing this Preface book is to expose the reader to Pound's poems, their wonderful images, the skilled cadence of their lines. In trying to do so I have employed certain insights and analytical techniques that stem from linguistics and stylistics where these seemed appropriate. However, these techniques are used in the context of what might be called a literary critical approach which seeks to explore how the poems relate to and reflect Pound's 'life and contacts'. In his reaction to what he saw as late Romantic sentimentality, Pound adopted all sorts of personae in order to mask the authorial self, to render the poet invisible and, as a result, invisibly modernist. Ultimately, however, he remained 'master of his lays', the accountable author, responsible for his own words, and suffered accordingly. In a brilliantly concise discussion of the ethical issues surrounding the concept of authorship, Sean Burke suggests that 'questions of the signature are among the first to be raised in the context of an ethically troublesome text: "Who wrote this discourse?" "At what point in history?" "Under what circumstances?"' (Burke, 1995, p. 289). Some of Pound's texts are ethically troublesome and, like those of great writers in general, most of them entail ethical concerns. To the extent that Burke's questions need to be asked about Pound, or any writer for that matter, the author is never dead in the sense that Barthes argues for in his 'Death of the Author' theory. Nevertheless, my chief concern is with the poetry. Without it Pound would still be, among other things, the most significant literary talent scout of the twentieth century, a fine editor of other writers' work, a critic and literary theorist of considerable significance and an obsessive political activist. With it, he is what he is: 'il miglior fabbro'.

Part One
The Writer and His Setting

Chronological table

	POUND'S LIFE	OTHER EVENTS
1885	Born 30 October in Hailey, Idaho.	D.H. Lawrence born.
1887		Alfred Krupp, German industrialist and arms manufacturer, dies.
1888		T.S. Eliot born.
1889		Robert Browning dies. Adolf Hitler born.
1890		Idaho becomes a state of the United States.
1892	Family finally settled in Wyncote, a suburb of Philadelphia.	Walt Whitman dies. Alfred Lord Tennyson dies.
1894		Aubrey Beardsley's drawings for Oscar Wilde's *Salome*.
1895		W.B. Yeats's *Poems* published.
1898	First European tour, visiting London, Paris and Venice.	Ernest Hemingway born. Paris Metro opened.
1900		The Wallace Collection opened in London. John Ruskin dies.
1901–06	Student at University of Pennsylvania and Hamilton College: B Phil and MA degrees.	

	POUND'S LIFE	OTHER EVENTS
1901		Wigmore Hall opened in London.
1902	Begins lifelong friendship with William Carlos Williams.	
1902 and 1906	Further visits to Europe, including London, Venice, Spain and Paris.	
1903		Henry James's *The Ambassadors* published. James Whistler dies.
1905		F.T. Marinetti's *Futurist Manifesto* published. Jacob Epstein settles in London.
1905–07	Intensely romantic friendship with Hilda Doolittle, writes the poems collected in *Hilda's Book*.	
1907	Teaching post at Wabash College, Crawfordsville, Indiana, terminated because of a minor 'scandal'.	
1908	Leaves for Europe. William Brooke Smith, Pound's 'first friend', dies, aged 25. *A Lume Spento* published in Venice. Settles in London.	Lord Northcliffe buys *The Times* newspaper.
1909	Meets and begins literary associations with W.B. Yeats, Ford	A.C. Swinburne dies. Wassily Kandinsky paints first abstract paintings.

POUND'S LIFE	OTHER EVENTS
Madox Ford and Wyndham Lewis. *Personae* and *Exultations* published.	

1910	*The Spirit of Romance* published.	H.G. Wells's *The History of Mr Polly* published. The first Post-Impressionist Exhibition is mounted in London.
1911	*Canzoni* published.	Marie Curie wins Nobel Prize for Chemistry.
1912	Influenced by T.E. Hulme. First reference to 'Imagistes' in *Ripostes*.	Woodrow Wilson wins US presidential election. Amy Lowell's *A Dome of Many-Colored Glass* published.
1913	Poems by 'H.D. Imagiste' first appear in *Poetry*. Begins friendship and artistic association with Henri Gaudier-Brzeska.	Suffragette demonstrations in London: Mrs Pankhurst imprisoned. Rabindranath Tagore wins Nobel Prize for Literature. John D. Rockefeller founds the Rockefeller Institute.
1913–16	Spends three consecutive winters at Stone Cottage with Yeats, working on Fenollosa manuscripts, Japanese Noh plays and the early cantos.	
1914	The first imagist anthology, *Des Imagistes*, published. Marries Dorothy Shakespeare. Meets and begins literary association with	James Joyce's *Dubliners* published. Outbreak of First World War.

5

	POUND'S LIFE	OTHER EVENTS
	T.S. Eliot. Vorticism and the first issue of *Blast*. Promotes the serialization of Joyce's *A Portrait of the Artist as a Young Man* in *The Egoist*.	
1915	*Cathay* published.	Henri Gaudier-Brzeska killed in the trenches.
1916	*Lustra* published.	James Joyce's *A Portrait of the Artist as a Young Man* published. Henry James dies.
1917	*Three Cantos* published.	America enters the war against Germany. The Russian Revolution takes place. T.S. Eliot's *Prufrock and Other Observations* published. T.E. Hulme killed at the front.
1918	Promotes the serialization of Joyce's *Ulysses* in the *Little Review*.	Women over 30 get the vote in Britain. Rebecca West's *The Return of the Soldier* published. Wyndham Lewis's *Tarr* published. Armistice between Allies and Germany ends First World War. Claude Debussy dies.
1919	*Homage to Sextus Propertius* published in full. Discovers the economic theories of Major C.H. Douglas.	Benito Mussolini founds Italian Fascist Party. Thomas Hardy's *Collected Poems* published. Treaty of Versailles signed.
1920	*Hugh Selwyn Mauberley* published. Meets Joyce for the first time.	

POUND'S LIFE	OTHER EVENTS
Leaves London for good.	

1921	Settles in Paris. Writes an opera, *Le Testament de Villon*. Musical association with American composer, George Antheil.	

1922	Helps to raise money for the first publication of *Ulysses* in book form. Gives Eliot substantial editorial help with the manuscript of *The Waste Land*.	Mussolini marches on Rome and forms fascist government in Italy. Eliot's *The Waste Land* published. Joyce's *Ulysses* published. Marcel Proust dies.

1923	Begins a lifelong relationship with the violinist Olga Rudge.	Yeats wins Nobel Prize for Literature. Katherine Mansfield dies.

1924		Lenin dies. Sigmund Freud's *Collected Writings* published.

1924–25	Moves to Italy and eventually settles in Rapallo.	

1925	*A Draft of XVI Cantos* published. Mary, daughter of Pound and Olga Rudge, born.	Hitler's *Mein Kampf* published. Amy Lowell dies.

1926	Omar, son of Dorothy Pound, born. *Personae: The Collected Poems of Ezra Pound* published.	General Strike followed by miners' strike in Britain.

1926 onwards	The 'Ezuversity' at Rapallo: new literary associations with Basil	

	POUND'S LIFE	OTHER EVENTS
	Bunting, Louis Zukofsky, James Laughlin and others.	
1928	Pound's parents, Homer and Isabel, settle in Rapallo.	Thomas Hardy dies. Lawrence's *Lady Chatterley's Lover* published. Virginia Woolf's *Orlando* published. Mussolini's *My Autobiography* published.
1929		George Antheil's opera *Transatlantic* first performed. Hemingway's *A Farewell to Arms* published.
1930	*A Draft of XXX Cantos* published.	
1932	Major work on Cavalcanti, resulting in the publication of *Guido Cavalcanti Rime*.	
1933	Audience with Mussolini. *ABC of Economics* published. Begins innovative series of yearly musical concerts in Rapallo.	Hitler appointed Chancellor of Germany. Franklin D. Roosevelt becomes president of the USA. Gertrude Stein's *The Autobiography of Alice B Toklas* published.
1934	*Eleven New Cantos XXXI–XLI*, *Make It New* and *ABC of Reading* published.	
1935	*Jefferson and/or Mussolini* published.	Italy invades Abyssinia.
1936		Outbreak of Spanish Civil War.

	POUND'S LIFE	OTHER EVENTS
1937	*The Fifth Decad of Cantos* published.	Pablo Picasso's *Guernica* exhibited in Paris. Maurice Ravel dies.
1938	*Guide to Kulchur* published.	
1939	Visits America to promote economic theories and prevent American involvement in a future European war.	Joyce's *Finnegans Wake* published. Yeats dies. Freud dies. Outbreak of Second World War.
1940	*Cantos LII–LXXI* published.	Winston Churchill becomes British prime minister. F.D. Roosevelt elected president of the US for a third term. Italy declares war on the Allies.
1941	Begins to broadcast on Rome Radio.	Germany invades the Soviet Union. Japan bombs Pearl Harbor and America enters the war against the Axis powers. James Joyce dies. Virginia Woolf dies.
1942	Homer Pound dies.	
1943	Indicted for treason by the United States government for broadcasting what is judged to be Axis propaganda.	Mussolini overthrown. Italy surrenders and declares war on Germany. Eliot's *Four Quartets* published in full.
1944	Wartime circumstances force Pound, Dorothy and Olga to live together in Sant'Ambrogio, above Rapallo.	

	POUND'S LIFE	OTHER EVENTS
1945	Arrested by Italian partisans and transferred to Detention Training Centre, Pisa. Writes *Pisan Cantos*. Flown to Washington for trial, but found unfit to stand on grounds of insanity. Begins confinement in St Elizabeth's Hospital for the insane.	Mussolini executed. F.D. Roosevelt dies. Second World War ends with the surrender of Germany and Japan.
1946	Charles Olson becomes the first of many regular visitors Pound has throughout his incarceration.	H.D.'s *Trilogy* published.
1948	Isabel Pound dies. The *Pisan Cantos* finally published.	T.S. Eliot wins Nobel Prize for Literature.
1949	Awarded the Bollingen Prize for the *Pisan Cantos*.	
1951		Marianne Moore's *Collected Poems* wins the Pulitzer Prize.
1954	*The Classic Anthology defined by Confucius* and *The Women of Trachis* published.	Ernest Hemingway wins the Nobel Prize for Literature.
1955	*Section: Rock-Drill de los cantares* published.	
1956		Allen Ginsberg's *Howl* published.
1957		Wyndham Lewis dies.

POUND'S LIFE	OTHER EVENTS
1958	Indictment for treason dismissed, thirteen years after his first imprisonment in Pisa. Returns to Italy, initially to live with his daughter.	
1959	*Thrones de los cantares XCVI–CIX* published.	Jacob Epstein dies.
1959–62	A period of restlessness, domestic tension and illness at the end of which he begins to live with Olga Rudge for the rest of his life.	
1961		Ernest Hemingway dies.
1963		William Carlos Williams dies.
1964		Hemingway's *A Moveable Feast* published posthumously.
1965	Visits London for Eliot's memorial service and Dublin to see Yeats's widow.	T.S. Eliot dies. Winston Churchill dies.
1967	Visits Joyce's grave in Zürich.	
1969	*Drafts and Fragments of Cantos CX–CXVII* published. Visits America for the last time.	
1971		Mary de Rachewiltz's *Discretions* published.
1972	Dies in Venice on 1 November.	

1 *Biographical background*

'*A man on whom the sun has gone down*'

It is customary for epics to begin *in medias res*. Since Pound's life was in many ways as much of an epic as *The Cantos*, his vast 'poem including history', I begin this outline of his life at the Detention Training Centre, Pisa, in 1945, where Pound was to spend his 60th birthday as a prisoner of the US army. The hole he had got himself into was more of a life-threatening hell-hole than the 'beastly hole' in which Mr Polly finds himself at the beginning of H.G. Wells's novel. Just as that novel traces Polly's life up to that point of crisis, this biographical outline traces Pound's life to the Pisan prison camp, trying to pick up along the way pointers to his arrival at such a place, before recounting the events of his later years. Whereas the aftermath of Mr Polly's crisis is one of comic struggle, triumph and peace, the denouement of Pound's life was to be much sadder, more salutary and elusive of any real peace before that of the grave.

A fictional parallel is appropriate here because any biographical account that goes, however briefly, beyond the most minimal facts involves the construction of a narrative that is both selective and interpretative. The amount of biographical material relating to Pound is vast, ranging from full biographies to letters, interviews, memoirs and personal anecdotes. In making a selection and interpretation of this material it is necessary to try to avoid reiterating unsupported speculations and opinions. Pound has, understandably perhaps, given his controversial and politically sensitive views and actions, attracted much partisan comment. For the most part I have been selective in favour of relating Pound's life to his work for two reasons. Firstly, although literary texts, like any other texts, take on a linguistic autonomy of their own that outlives their authors, I nevertheless take the view, as I noted in my introduction, that a knowledge of the interplay between biographical detail and artistic output enhances their understanding. Secondly, I am haunted by Pound's own dictum: 'You can spot the bad critic when he starts by discussing the poet and not the poem' (*ABC*, p. 84).

Pound was arrested by Italian partisans at his home in Sant'Ambrogio, near Rapallo, early in May 1945 and eventually handed over to the American authorities in Genoa: it was well known that he had been under an indictment for treason since 1943. There were already doubts about his sanity, suggested, for example, by his apparent lack of reality with regard to his dire situation: one American newspaper reported that, 'He is probably the only man ever to be interviewed while awaiting trial for treason who talked more of various interpretations of Oriental ideographs than he talked of his own impending trial' (Carpenter, 1990, p. 652).

By late May Pound had been transferred to the DTC at Pisa. The Centre was effectively a prison for American forces personnel who had committed crimes of various sorts while in occupied Italy. Within its concentration camp perimeter lesser offenders lived in one-person tents and were put through a gruelling regime to prepare them to return to their units. Major offenders, such as rapists and murderers, were kept in security cages, awaiting their execution or return to America for trial, though even they had small tents against the night and the weather and were allowed out for exercise. Pound was incarcerated in one of these cages for three weeks, at first without a tent, and always without being allowed out: he paced the narrow confines of his cage for exercise. He was also kept incommunicado under armed guard and at night his cage was floodlit. There is little doubt that this treatment would now be considered a form of torture.

After three weeks Pound's condition had so deteriorated in terms of weight loss, eyesight problems and incipient mental breakdown that he was moved to a tent in the Centre's medical section. Here, his living conditions improved and his physical health to some extent restored, he began to write, at first with paper and pencil. Later, with access to a borrowed typewriter, *The Pisan Cantos* began to emerge, remarkably, in more or less the form they are known today. More incredibly in some ways, when Pound had finished this section of his epic he went on to complete a translation of the Confucian text, using his own Italian version of an English translation as a crib. The result, *The Unwobbling Pivot*, was later published during Pound's subsequent years in St Elizabeth's Federal Hospital for the Insane.

As his detention at Pisa dragged on, without the preoccupation of composition and translation Pound's state grew worse. Rare visits by his wife, Dorothy, his partner, Olga, and their daughter, Mary, must have served to reinforce his sense of isolation. Access to English language newspapers and magazines with their versions of the war's events must at least have given him pause for thought and probably contributed to his depression. However, by November the American authorities judged that they had sufficient evidence for his prosecution and ordered Pound to be brought back to Washington.

Opinion as to what should be done with him was already polarized in the USA: there were those who wanted him summarily executed and others who wished him spared for his poetry's sake. On his arrival in America, even in his uncertain mental state, Pound began to realize that he was seen as a criminal and not the long-lost emissary he imagined himself to be. With the Nuremberg trials taking place and the horrific revelations of the concentration camps becoming more widely known, this was no time to be a traitor.

This, then, was the extreme situation in which the 60-year-old Pound found himself at the end of 1945. The most interesting question is whether his plight was the result of some aberration, some psychological defection, or whether it was a consequent development of earlier, deep-rooted values that are charted in Pound's poetry as well as his life.

'Born in a half savage country'

Ezra Pound was born in 1885 in Hailey, Idaho. Since Idaho Territory did not become a state until 1890 and Hailey was one of many mining towns in what might still be regarded as the 'wild west', there is an element of truth in Pound's ironic assertion at the beginning of *Hugh Selwyn Mauberley* that the country of his birth was indeed half savage. However, the reality behind that truth is rather different from any inferences Pound might wish us to make.

Far from being born into a poor mining family and raised in the Rockies, he was the only child of quite wealthy parents who were temporarily stationed in Idaho. His father, Homer, had gone to Hailey to check out the family silver mines as Register of the Hailey Land Office, a presidential appointment with a government salary. He bought the best newly-built house in the town for his wife-to-be, Isabel, also from a middle-class Anglo-Saxon background. Pound was still a baby when his parents decided to leave Hailey, Idaho, for good.

Itinerancy thus became an established feature of Pound's life from an early age: the next few years were spent lodging with relatives and staying in temporary homes, until his father secured a post at the US Mint in Philadelphia. The family lived at three further addresses before finally settling in the suburb of Wyncote in 1892. Looking back on his childhood in 1920, Pound stated, 'I was brought up in a city with which my forebears had no connection and I am therefore accustomed to being alien in one place or another' (Ackroyd, 1980, p. 6). Clearly, his cultivation of an exile mentality began at a young age.

At this time the cities of America were subject to massive influxes of mainly European immigrants. White middle-class Americans of Anglo-Saxon origin undoubtedly had a sense of being swamped. The move to the suburbs by Pound's family was partly motivated by a desire to be distanced from the urban melting-pot. Fears and prejudices were no doubt expressed in racial terms which Pound could not have been immune to. The numbers involved promoted the idea that a particularly American way of life was under threat, spawning a cultural defensiveness that could easily be applied to other contexts, and the notion that masses of people were dangerous, a potential for disorder.

Itinerancy had its positive aspects. There were trips to New York to stay with his grandmother, Mary Weston, and his wealthy Aunt 'Frank'. More significantly, shortly after he joined the military academy that provided his secondary education, this same Aunt Frank took Pound and his mother on what amounted to a 'grand tour' of Europe in the summer of 1898. Thus, at the onset of adolescence Pound had his first taste of the cities that would provide the setting for much of the rest of his life: London, Paris and the Venice to which he would return again and again and where he would eventually die. More importantly, he soaked up at this impressionable age something of the cultures that would dominate his way of thinking and inform his poetic development. At the age of thirteen he was a 'European'.

After a further three years of not particularly distinguished school experience Pound was pushed by his family into embarking on a precociously early university career. In a brief essay entitled 'How I Began', written in 1913, he claimed the following about those years: 'I knew at fifteen pretty much what I wanted to do. I believed that the "Impulse" is with the gods; that technique is a man's own responsibility . . . It is his own fault if he does not become a good artist . . . I resolved that at thirty I would know more about poetry than any man living . . .' (Schulman (ed.), 1974, pp. 24–5). To this end he enrolled at the University of Pennsylvania in 1901, though the first year curriculum was very broad, including maths and American colonial history as well as Latin, German and English Studies.

Pound was a student for the next six years: two years at Pennsylvania, then two years at Hamilton College, New York State, to complete his undergraduate studies (B Phil 1905), then back to Pennsylvania for a masters degree in Romance Languages (MA 1906). His final year as a student was the first of what would normally have been a two-year fellowship with the prospect of a PhD at the end of it, but the fellowship was discontinued after one year due to a combination of factors: his wilful approach to study, quarrels with professors, general disenchantment with the American academic establishment who found his eccentricities difficult to accommodate. This is one of the points where one can definitely say that the course of Pound's career and life could have been radically different: if he had been allowed to continue his fellowship and achieve fully acceptable academic status, despite his idiosyncrasies, he would have been able to fulfil his natural inclination to pedagogy in a university of quality and greater freedom. As it was, his attitude to academic life was soured, and he could only get a post at a narrowly conservative college where rejection was more or less inevitable. More importantly, his urge to instruct, introduce and explain new ideas, lead acolytes to enlightenment, had no legitimate academic outlet, something which rankled for the rest of his life.

Two aspects of these student years need further comment in relation to Pound's development: the studies which most influenced him and set his agenda as a poet and the relationships which meant most to him as both person and artist. With regard to his studies, some of which were no more than self-chosen reading programmes, three main areas may be highlighted.

1. The Classics: more specifically, the Homeric epics and the Latin poets Catullus, Ovid, Propertius, all of whose work was to pervade Pound's poetry as translation, paraphrase or quotation, were a major influence. Pound was of the opinion that he got into university at such an early age on the strength of his Latin. Ironically, his approach to translation was often too cavalier for 'real' Latin scholars and his knowledge of the language was mistakenly thought to be scant.

2. Romance Languages and Literature formed a large part of his later studies: the French of Villon and Flaubert, Dante and Cavalcanti in Italian, a grounding in Spanish which led to postgraduate study of the dramatist Lope de Vega, most of all his introduction to Provençal and the troubadours. Pound was a student at a time when medieval Italian and Provençal scholarship was at its peak. Furthermore, as Kenner makes clear, works of Dante and the troubadours were available in popular editions, as were biographies and fictional treatments of their lives (Kenner, 1972, pp. 76–8). In this climate Pound's fascination with 'the spirit of Romance' would not have seemed so esoteric as it may do today.

3. English Literature itself: this embraced the more formal study of Anglo-Saxon, whose rhythms and alliterations appear in Pound's own work, as well as avid reading of recent and contemporary literature, including Browning, Swinburne, the Nineties poets such as Arthur Symons and Ernest Dowson, and the early Yeats. Pound may have heard Yeats give a reading when he visited the University of Pennsylvania on a lecture tour in 1903. In any case, Yeats was Pound's favourite living poet. Pound's earliest poetry is written in the language of these English poets, with its archaisms, syntactic inversions and self-consciously poetic diction. Although he railed

Ezra Pound in a dressing gown, Kensington 1916.

against it in later years, both in his own and others' poetry, he never relinquished it entirely: indeed, some of his finest lines are written in a version of this archaic style.

Pound is generally reported to have been a fairly solitary student, protecting himself from the usual pranks of campus life with a mixture of arrogant flamboyance and studied aloofness. It hardly seems accidental that significant relationships were not with fellow humanities students. Three in particular require more detailed comment.

His first friend was William Brooke Smith, who was studying at
an art school in Philadelphia. Smith promoted the work of Wilde
and Beardsley and introduced Pound to English aestheticism and
the Nineties poets mentioned above. Pound spent a lot of time with
Smith in his first two years at Pennsylvania and remained in touch
with him until his death from consumption in 1908 at the age of
24. Three letters from Smith to Pound, quite recently uncovered
and discussed in Wilhelm's article of 1990, reveal something of the
relationship, and there are a number of other pointers to its im-
portance. Smith's letters are written in a style that reflects his art
school background and interest in late Victorian aestheticism: 'The
whole world of jade and sapphire is calling to me, and with God
in his heaven surely there is a song of joy and gladness. I can't
sing the song, so you must, because you are a part of me' (Wilhelm,
1990, p. 164). The allusion to Browning suggests that Smith may
have been the initial cause of Pound's interest in the poet who was
to be so influential on his later thinking about the structure of *The
Cantos*. The expressions of male bonding, tinged with melancholy,
might best be described as Tennysonian. In Smith's third letter
there are clear 'intimations of mortality'. He thanks Pound for
some 'beautiful verses', sends him the fare for a trip into town and
ends: 'My dear, I wish you were here to-night. I would put out
every light and I would not speak, but you would give me peace.
Peace and rest' (ibid., p. 168). Smith died in April 1908 when Pound
was already in Europe. One of Pound's early poems, entitled 'For
E. McC', written in the manner of a Provençal *planh* or lament,
is surely about Smith:

> Gone while your tastes were keen to you,
> Gone where the grey winds call to you,
>   By that high fencer, even Death....
> As old Toledos past their days of war
> Are kept mnemonic of the strokes they bore,
> So art thou with us, being good to keep
> In our heart's sword-rack, though thy sword-arm sleep.
>
>   (*CSP*, p. 19)

The fencing metaphor that is sustained throughout this moving
poem would have appealed to Eugene McCartney, a member of
the university fencing club with Pound. In that sense, it is for him,
as the title states, and McCartney was alive to read it. If the poem
is a response to Smith's death, then it would have been written
between the news of his death reaching Pound in Europe and the
publication of *A Lume Spento*, in which the poem appears. In fact,
when Pound had his first book of poems privately printed in
Venice in June of that year, he dedicated the volume to Smith's

memory, 'Painter, Dreamer of Dreams'. The title of the collection, *A Lume Spento* (With Tapers Quenched), a reference to a burial custom mentioned in Dante, was also chosen in homage to his friend.

With some degree of speculation, I also consider the poem 'Planh for the Young English King', published a year or so after Smith's death, to be Pound's further poetic response to the loss of his friend. The poem translates Bertrans de Born's Provençal lament on the death of Prince Henry, commonly known as the Young King, in 1183. Pound renders its spectacular display of mourning in his most archaic style, often a vehicle for intensity of emotion in his work:

> If all the grief and woe and bitterness,
> All dolour, ill and every evil chance
> That ever came upon this grieving world
> Were set together they would seem but light
> Against the death of the Young English King.
>
> (*CSP*, p. 36)

Here we have, in my view, Pound adopting the emotions of a given text, wearing a mask from the medieval past, in order to express his own feelings by a process of indirection. One criticism consistently levelled at Pound is the idea that he rarely expresses his own emotions, that his use of the persona renders his work second-hand. This poem, along with many others that involve translation or the adoption of a persona, suggests a quite different conclusion. The feeling is true not only because the poem captures the truth of the original but because Pound himself experienced it. The translation in persona affords him a less direct but possibly more dignified way of wearing his heart upon his sleeve.

Many years later Pound said in a letter that he could not understand how Smith came to know so much at such a young age in Philadelphia, adding, 'At any rate, thirteen years are gone; I haven't replaced him and shan't and no longer hope to' (*SL*, p. 165). It is significant that this letter was written after Pound had met most of those with whom he had major artistic and/or emotional relationships in the first half of his life and after the death of some of them in the trenches of the First World War. Because Smith died young without becoming artistically well-known like many of Pound's other friends, his importance is somewhat overlooked. In literary terms, he introduced Pound to, and impressed him with, a poetic mode which was to influence his own poetry for the rest of his life. Important too is the fact that Pound was passing on his fascination with Browning, Swinburne and the Nineties poets to the two most significant others in his student life: William Carlos Williams and Hilda Doolittle. Since all three became architects of poetic modernism in their various ways, their absorption of, and reaction to, Smith's aestheticism is worth noting. In psychological terms, Smith was Pound's first experience of that intense male friendship centred on shared artistic goals which was to be a significant aspect of his emotional life in the future. Along with so many significant others, Smith is recalled in the extremities of Pound's Pisan captivity:

> and Mt Taishan is faint as the wraith of my first friend
> who comes talking ceramics;
>
> (*CAN*, p. 479)

Sadly, that friendship allowed him to experience its loss in the face of senseless and irrational mortality: 'that grey fencer, even Death'. At least the fencer's chosen weapon was consumption, something not much could be done to combat. When later the fencer's weapon was a random shell in the trenches of a pointless war, grief would not be the only emotion in order. Pound would respond to such loss with a bitter and obsessive rage against those he reckoned to be responsible for the deaths of his friends.

The letter in which Pound expressed his feelings about Smith was addressed to William Carlos Williams, one of Pound's closest lifelong friends, whom he also met while a student at Pennsylvania. Williams was studying medicine and went on to be a doctor as well as one of America's finest poets. Pound was younger than Williams, but he was much more advanced in poetry, thanks to his literary studies and Smith's mentoring. Williams was already beginning to write poetry as a student and their friendship was founded on this mutual exchange of poems, criticism and literary ideas. According to Williams, meeting Pound was a revelation:

> Before meeting Ezra Pound is like B.C. and A.D. I had already started to write and was putting down my immortal thoughts daily. Little poems, pretty bad poems . . . The point is I had something to show when I met Ezra Pound. He was not impressed. He was impressed with his own poetry; but then, I was impressed with my own poetry, too, so we got along all right
>
> (Williams, 1967, p. 17)

Once Pound had left America on a more or less permanent basis in 1908, their friendship was mainly sustained by correspondence, though they did meet up when Williams visited London once and whenever Pound returned to America. Pound was instrumental in getting Williams's first commercially published volume of poems accepted by Elkin Matthews in London in 1913. He wrote an introductory note to the volume which begins characteristically: 'God forbid that I should introduce Mr Williams as a cosmic force.' He goes on to identify Williams as a specifically American poetic voice who has 'eschewed many of the current American vices' and 'not sold his soul to editors'. He recommends Williams to his English audience as a 'some one who has been through somewhat the same mill that I have been through; some one who has apparently a common aim with me' (ibid., pp. 23, 24). As well as the minutiae of literary business and the expressions of friendship, Pound's letters to Williams over subsequent years contain important discussion of modernist poetics and Pound's own poetry. Williams was equally supportive of Pound's poetry and status as a poet in his reviews of and comments upon Pound's work. In later years Williams expressed disenchantment with Pound's political involvements and disassociated himself from them. However, his loyalty as a friend remained. He visited Pound in St Elizabeth's and campaigned for his release, as did many of Pound's other friends, at the risk of compromising his own reputation. In an interview in 1950, Williams stated, 'We don't always get along together, and I don't approve of his attitude in many things, but basically his has been one of the most outstanding friendships that I've ever enjoyed' (Wagner, 1976, p. 9).

Williams and Pound were both friends with Hilda Doolittle. As Williams puts it, 'Ezra was the official lover, but Hilda was very coy and invited us both to come and see her' (Williams, 1967, p. 19). However, the relationship between Pound and Doolittle was ultimately more important for their poetic development and the direction modernist poetry was to take. They first met by chance in 1901 when Pound was in his first year at university and Doolittle was still at school, but it was not until Pound's return from Hamilton College in 1905 that their romantic involvement became fully fledged. Primary sources, such as Williams's autobiographical notes, Doolittle's letters and memoir *End To Torment* and certain letters of Pound, make clear that the pair were caught up in a highly romanticized relationship underpinned by shared readings of William Morris, Swinburne and the Pre-Raphaelites. In her memoir Doolittle recalls that they 'climbed up into the big maple tree in our garden, outside Philadelphia. There was a crow's nest that my younger brother had built – bench boards and a sort of platform. The house is hidden by the great branches' (Pearson and King (eds), 1980, p. 12). Here she was his 'Dryad' on their tree-house trysts. Their semi-official engagement had the approval of Pound's parents. However, Doolittle's father, a professor of astronomy at the university, felt Pound was so unsuitable that he effectively quashed any possibility of an approved marriage. When Pound was forced to look for work in 1907, their period of passionate intensity was over. How seriously Pound was affected by all this is difficult to determine.

21

His drift into other romances and at least one further 'engagement' seem natural responses to a genuine sense of rejection.

The immediate poetic legacy of their relationship was *Hilda's Book*, a collection of 25 poems Pound wrote for Doolittle and bound in vellum. As Tytell notes, 'Filled with the burden of an inexpressible and thwarted love, the twenty five poems to Hilda are flushed with tentative and youthful passions set in the context of a medieval heroic heraldry showing the influences of William Morris and Dante Gabriel Rossetti' (1987, p. 26). However, the poems contain elements which were to remain part of Pound's poetic output to the point of being structural principles: pagan mysticism, the psychological reality of myth, the power of metamorphosis. These elements figure in 'The Tree', which was to survive as a poem in Pound's later, public, collections:

> I stood still and was a tree amid the wood,
> Knowing the truth of things unseen before;
> Of Daphne and the laurel bow
> And that god-feasting couple old
> That grew elm-oak amid the wold.
> ...I have been a tree amid the wood
> And many a new thing understood
> That was rank folly to my head before.
>
> (*CSP*, p. 3)

However, a much more important poetic outcome than these immature poems was to emerge from the relationship of Doolittle and Pound a few years later with the 'invention' of imagism.

In the autumn of 1907 Pound took up his one and only teaching post in his native land at Wabash College, Crawfordsville, Indiana. There is some evidence that he was lured there on false pretences by the President at interview, since he was offered the post of head of a department in which there were no other staff. However, Pound must take some responsibility for accepting a post which, for all his youthful naivety, he must have known would be totally unsuitable for him. The college was small, run on Presbyterian lines with daily compulsory chapel, and set in a midwestern town of conservative tastes and customs. From the outset the college stimulated Pound's natural iconoclasm. He was not a habitual smoker but, because smoking was banned, he took to the very public consumption of 'cigarillos'. He had very little interest in alcohol, yet he began to carry a hip flask of rum. College dress was formal, so Pound indulged his preference for colourful, if not outrageous, clothes. Within a few months Pound was dismissed from his post following a well-documented incident in which he gave shelter for the night to a stranded actress. There is little reason to doubt that this was as innocent as Pound claimed and the college authorities eventually acknowledged. However, the incident provided the college with an opportunity to get rid of Pound which they were reluctant to let slip. In his turn, Pound was quite glad to get away and may even have contrived the incident, knowing its likely repercussions. At any rate, he was to receive his salary for the rest of the academic year and this allowed him to embark on his lifelong European adventure.

Back home, Pound was 'tacitly cold-shouldered by a distinguished section of a narrow slice of the American continent, in Philadelphia, because of a scandal, not very near, in Indiana, a very minor scandal, if a scandal at all' (Pearson and King (eds), 1980, p. 43). Pound asked Hilda Doolittle to accompany him to Europe and went so far as to make a formal request for her hand in marriage to her father. Predictably, this was rejected and, although Doolittle was by this time twenty-two, she was unwilling to go against parental wishes and elope with Pound. Pound left America in March 1908. Although he made several return visits and there was to be his lengthy incarceration in St Elizabeth's, in one sense he left it for good to become, in his own much later formulation, 'the last American living the tragedy of Europe' (Dick (ed.), 1972, p. 113).

'This damn'd profession of writing'

Pound's London years, 1908 to 1920, were hectic, but productively so. He wrote many fine individual poems and a number of important collections or cycles of poetry. With regard to the development of modernism he was at the centre of various critical and theoretical 'movements', influencing a range of major literary figures and helping to set the modernist agenda. His unstinting promotion of other writers was at its height during this period. Almost incidentally he produced a large body of criticism and reviews, not just of literature but also of music and the visual arts, and wrote thousands of letters.

Pound arrived in London in August after a few months in Venice where he had used some of his meagre resources to pay for the publication of his first volume of poems, *A Lume Spento*. London seemed the obvious place to promote his book and make a quick literary reputation: above all, he was desperate to meet and associate with Yeats whom he considered to be the greatest living poet. Pound had to work quite hard to transform himself from a completely unknown outsider into someone who was accepted in the best literary circles and salons of Edwardian London and on more or less equal terms with the most highly regarded writers of the day. A focal point for his efforts was Elkin Mathews's bookshop.

Mathews published a number of well-known poets, including Yeats, and literary people were frequently to be seen there. Pound paid for the first printing of a second slim volume of his own poetry, *A Quinzaine for this Yule*, and spent a lot of time at the bookshop. There were two consequences: when his books sold in reasonable numbers, Mathews agreed to finance the publication of a third volume, to be called *Personae*; at the same time Pound was introduced to a widening circle of literary practitioners and patrons. The most significant was Olivia Shakespear, novelist and wealthy socialite, who eventually introduced him to Yeats and was also the mother of his future wife, Dorothy. Other important early acquaintances were Selwyn Image and Laurence Binyon, Nineties poets (the latter was to introduce him to Wyndham Lewis), and May Sinclair, the novelist, who was one of the first in London to extol Pound's qualities as a poet. She introduced him to Ford Madox Hueffer (who later changed his name to Ford), an important catalyst in Pound's poetic development. In less than a year Pound was a regular attender of several literary groups and salons, including Yeats's coveted Monday evenings, and had a well-reviewed volume of poems to his name.

Ford Madox Ford was the editor of the most prestigious literary journal in London, the *English Review*, and one of Pound's early successes came when Ford published his poem 'Sestina: Altaforte'. This is a dramatic monologue in the manner of Browning, but presented in the highly intricate verse form of the sestina in which a series of six-line stanzas maintain a shifting pattern of the same six line-end words. The poem's persona is Bertran de Born, the warlike troubadour:

> Damn it all! all this our South stinks peace.
> You whoreson dog, Papiols, come! Let's to music!
> I have no life save when the swords clash.
>
> (*CSP*, p. 28)

The poem sustains the warmongering rage and aggression of this opening through to its very last line: 'Hell blot black for always the thought "Peace"!' As well as its success in the magazine, the poem became one of Pound's favourite party pieces, delivered at literary clubs and salons with histrionic ferocity. This was one of the poems Pound recorded in May 1939 for Harvard University's Poetry Room (*PV*). His dramatic delivery to the accompaniment of a drum gives a taste of what his early recital might have sounded like. In his *How I Began* essay Pound gives an account of the composition of the poem and concludes, 'Technically it is one of my best, though a poem on such a theme could never be very important' (Schulman (ed.), 1974, p. 26). This suggests that his personal antipathy for military conflict predates the psychological damage of the First World War. However, bearing in mind Pound's theory of the persona as a means of exploring aspects of one's own personality through the mask of another, it is reasonable to suggest that he wrote the poem out of the belligerent side of his nature, perhaps using war as a metaphor for the battle of literary London, as he saw it.

Pound consolidated his position as the modern voice of Provençal poetry with a further volume, *Exultations*, which contained at least one excellent new poem, 'Piere Vidal Old'. He was also establishing himself as something of an expert on Romance literature by giving a series of lectures on the subject at the London Polytechnic and using this material as the basis of his first major prose work, *The Spirit of Romance*. With these projects complete, he returned to America in the summer of 1910: he had certainly made his mark on the London literary scene, though there was much more to come.

The next two years were particularly nomadic ones. After a fairly lengthy stay in America Pound returned to London, only to spend much of his time crossing and recrossing the Channel for stays in Paris, other parts of France, Italy and Germany. Two continental experiences are especially worthy of note.

On a visit to Ford Madox Ford in Germany Pound showed the older writer his latest book of poems, *Canzoni*. Pound later recalled that Ford rolled around on the floor in agony by way of ridiculing the flowery, outmoded style of the language. The incident had a road-to-Damascus quality for Pound: it finally brought home to him that he had to find a way of using contemporary language as a vehicle for his poetry. This did not happen overnight, however. In his next volume of poetry, *Ripostes*, the diction, phraseology and much of the metrical patterning are still backward-looking, though many of the poems are fine achievements in their own right, including Pound's version of the Anglo-Saxon poem 'The Seafarer'. Nevertheless, there are some indications that Pound was breaking new ground with the manic chant of 'The Alchemist' and the rhythmically startling 'The Return', a poem Yeats later called 'the most beautiful poem that has been written in the free form' (Longenbach, 1988, p. 97). An extract from another less conventional poem, 'The Plunge', shows how effectively Pound was able to depart from the metrically exact line and the lineation of the well-formed verse:

> And you,
> Love, you the much, the more desired!
> Do I not loathe all walls, streets, stones,
> All mire, mist, all fog,

> All ways of traffic?
> You, I would have flow over me like water,
> Oh, but far out of this!
> Grass, and low fields, and hills,
> And sun,
> Oh, sun enough!
>
> > (*CSP*, p. 70)

Another continental experience of these years was motivated by Pound's continuing interest in the world of Provençal poetry. He undertook a walking tour of southern France in the summer of 1912 with the express purpose of visiting significant places in the lives and poetry of his favourite troubadours and absorbing the feel of the landscape. Ford was also of the opinion that poets should go out into their environment more consciously and use travel as a way of invigorating their work. Pound may have taken this to heart, though he was already an inveterate wanderer. A fairly strenuous programme of daily walking allowed him to visit de Born's castle, Poitiers, Perigueux (the Perigord of his poems), Rodez and many other haunts. His poem 'Provincia Deserta' gives an account of this tour: its images are vivid with the relish of lived experience. The poem concludes, 'I have walked over these roads; I have thought of them living' (ibid., p. 123), and it is clear that the personages who have meant so much on the basis of words both by and about them have achieved an actuality for Pound through the landscape they inhabited.

One of the literary groups Pound regularly attended in this period was chaired by T.E. Hulme, the philosopher. Other members of the group were A.R. Orage, the editor of the radical magazine *The New Age*, and the poet F.S. Flint. Orage not only published Pound's poetry but also gave him a regular income from prose articles of various kinds. At a later date these were to include art criticism written as B.H. Dias and music reviews as William Atheling, only two of the dozens of pseudonyms used by Pound in the course of his writing. Pound's music criticism as Atheling is particularly interesting: it is collected in Shafer's *Ezra Pound and Music* (1978). Hulme provided sustenance of a different kind, both literary and philosophical. His literary stance was against Romanticism, disparaging the rhetoric he associated with its poetry, and very much for the orderly and precise in language. Together with Ford's strictures, these ideas began to help Pound towards his own formulations. Hulme's literary views may be seen as a more specialist application of his general philosophy, which assumed that order was good in itself and that the only way to achieve it was by the authoritarian rule of those fit for the purpose. How far Pound absorbed these views and their political implications is uncertain. Essentially anti-democratic and elitist views of this kind were common, and many of Pound's most influential associates held similar ones, so they would not have appeared unusual and may have appealed to him, given his childhood experience of family unease about 'the masses'.

Innovation across the arts was creating an exciting climate in which a new 'ism' seemed to be born every day in the visual arts, music and dance. For Pound there was not only a need to reform his personal poetic philosophy, but also to identify, if not instigate, some new movement for poetry in general. Hulme had given a series of talks on the philosophy of Henri Bergson, including a commentary on Bergson's theory of the image, which Pound attended. The notion of the image as an organizing principle of poetic composition was no doubt planted in his mind, but he was not able to take it any further until he had some examples of poetry written on the basis of the image as it was being outlined by Hulme. To the astonishment of the Hulme group, Hulme himself, who was no poet as far as they knew, provided a set of five short poems, which Pound went on to publish at the end of *Ripostes* as 'The Complete Poetical Works of T.E. Hulme'. Pound wrote a preface to these poems, suggesting they represented the poetry of the 'School of Images' and asserting that, 'As for the future, Les Imagistes, the descendants of the forgotten school of 1909, have that in their keeping' (*CSP*, p. 251). Pound was now in the position of needing some more poems by 'Imagistes' to fulfil his prophesy.

Hilda Doolittle was in London by this time, having at last been persuaded by Pound to go against her parents' wishes. Pound's letters to her were destroyed by her father, so there is no way of knowing whether Pound raised false expectations of a renewed relationship. That Doolittle had such expectations is clear from her memoir. Pound was by this time engaged to Dorothy Shakespear and Doolittle was devastated by this news. Nevertheless, she decided to stay in London. Despite the obvious tensions there must have been between them, Doolittle and Pound remained friends and he introduced her to his literary acquaintances, including Richard Aldington, her future husband.

In 1912 Pound obtained the first of his highly influential editorships. He was invited by Harriet Monroe, the editor of the Chicago magazine *Poetry*, to contribute some poems, but wrote back offering to be her 'foreign correspondent' and general gatherer of the best poetry on the London scene. The subsequent association allowed Pound to promote in America a wide range of English and American poets who were otherwise being neglected. However, the immediate problem was to establish 'Les Imagistes'. Pound first chose Aldington's poetry, which was billed as the work of 'one of

27

the "Imagistes", a group of ardent Hellenists who are pursuing interesting experiments in vers libre . . .' (Carpenter, 1990, p. 187). Aldington was a Greek scholar and his poetry was written in unrhymed irregular lines, so there was some truth in this, though there was no group. The only other conceivable member of such a group was Doolittle.

The story of Doolittle's transformation into 'H.D. Imagiste' is well known. Doolittle showed some of her latest work to Pound in the tearoom of the British Museum. Pound recognized their excellence with what was to become his legendary eye for talent. He also saw in them the very kind of poetry he needed, but made some editorial cuts and changes on the spot to reinforce the qualities he wanted. Having done so, he signed them 'H.D. Imagiste' and sent them off to Monroe for the January 1913 issue of *Poetry*. His accompanying letter contains an early formulation of what would later be incorporated into the imagist doctrine: 'Objective – no slither; direct – no excessive use of adjectives, no metaphors that won't permit examination' (*SL*, p. 11). Pound's adjustments to Doolittle's poetry were probably quite minor. She had been in London a year and was involved in some of the debates about the directions poetic language might be taking: in this context her own distinctive poetic voice was emerging. Even so, Pound's treatment, while launching Doolittle's career, was felt as a painful appropriation.

Compounding this was the fact that at least one of the poems, 'Hermes of the Ways', was a cryptic reflection on their relationship and for Doolittle a kind of therapeutic strategy for coping with her sense of romantic betrayal. Robinson, H.D.'s biographer, claims that Pound's insensitive approach was traumatic for Doolittle and left her psychologically scarred in ways that were important for the quality of her poetry for the rest of her life (Robinson, 1982, p. 36). Doolittle's memoir suggests that she was never emotionally free of Pound. While this contributed to her eventual need to undergo psychoanalysis with Freud, her poetry flourished because of it. Had they continued in a close relationship, 'Ezra would have destroyed me and the center they call "Air and Crystal" of my poetry' (Pearson and King (eds), 1980, p. 35). What is certain is that H.D. was a founding practitioner of imagism who was able to maintain that practice with sureness and control to become one of the most consistently fine modernist poets.

With imagism named and launched as a movement, Pound saw the need for some kind of public manifesto and an anthology of imagist poems. He recruited F.S. Flint to produce an article entitled 'Imagisme', to which he added his own 'A Few Don'ts by an Imagist', and began to assemble a collection of poems by such widely different poets as H.D., William Carlos Williams and Ford Madox

Ford which was published in 1914 as *Des Imagistes*. Pound's own poetry during this period shows marked changes. The poems in *Des Imagistes* and another group published as 'Contemporania' reveal among other things two important innovations. Firstly, poems about the contemporary social and literary scene which are written in a colloquial style without the usual archaisms: their tone is essentially satiric. Secondly, poems which seem conscious in their attempt to apply imagist principles as Pound was beginning to develop them, including the famous 'In a station of the Metro', the archetypal imagist poem. These latter poems also include a group influenced by Pound's reading of Chinese literature in translation, the first sign of an interest that would soon lead to important developments in his thinking about the language of poetry.

The poems of 'Contemporania' were read by Mary Fenollosa, widow and literary executor of Ernest Fenollosa, an American who had been an academic at Tokyo University and later the curator of Oriental Art at Boston Museum. Fenollosa had died in London in 1908 and left a substantial collection of manuscripts, including draft translations of some 50 Japanese Noh plays and a wealth of Chinese poetry, the latter filtered through the interpretations of his Japanese colleagues. Mary Fenollosa recognized an affinity between some of Pound's imagist poems and her husband's notes on the translations of Chinese poetry. After meeting Pound in late 1913 she gave him the remainder of the manuscript collection because he seemed to be the only person who could make use of it in accordance with her husband's method of approach. The manuscripts also contained the draft of an essay which Pound was to revise and publish as 'The Chinese Written Character as a Medium for Poetry'. His excitement at what he saw to be the links between image and ideogram prompted another phase of creative endeavour that resulted in, among other things, the great cycle of poems known as *Cathay*.

Pound spent three consecutive winters in a cottage in rural Sussex with Yeats. Officially Pound was employed as Yeats's secretary to allow the senior poet more time to write. However, Yeats had already experienced Pound's 'corrections' to his work, with initial indignation, but later with some sense that Pound was pushing him in the direction of more tightly organized, less flowery language and that this was where he wished to go. Years later Yeats would concede that Pound had been his most helpful critic. In any case, there was some expectation that Pound would be more useful than someone who merely handled the mail. In reality the winters at Stone Cottage became a kind of retreat where intense periods of creative activity took place for both poets and where ideas, theories and influences were exchanged. Longenbach's comprehensive study of the Stone Cottage collaboration (1988) makes it possible to review the content of these winter retreats together in order to gauge their importance as a whole.

Winter 1913/14: Pound worked on Fenollosa's manuscripts and in particular the Japanese Noh plays. The end result of this work was *'Noh' or Accomplishment*, published in 1916 and credited to Fenollosa and Pound. The translations of the plays are accompanied by Pound's introductions and notes together with an essay by Fenollosa on the Noh drama. In his introduction Pound notes: 'The art of allusion, or this love of allusion, is at the root of the Noh. These plays, or eclogues, were made only for the few; for the nobles; for those trained to catch the allusion' (*TEP*, p. 214). This reads very much like a potential rationale for the methods of *The Cantos*, which were embryonic during Pound's stays at Stone Cottage. The translations themselves alternate and mix poetry and prose, the formal and the colloquial, in an essentially musical way that is attractive to read on the page. Their quality as play scripts is rather harder to judge without seeing them realized on stage. There are also interesting affinities between the language of these works and that of *Cathay*. For example, the following prose catalogue of events bears striking structural resemblances to the narratives of 'The River Merchant's Wife' and 'The Exile's Letter':

> I was made esquire at twelve, with the hat. The soothsayers unrolled my glories. I was called Hikaru Genji. I was chujo in Hahakigi province. I was chujo in the land of maple-feasting. At twenty-five I came to Suma, knowing all sorrow of seafare, having none to attend my dreams, no one to hear the old stories.
> (*TEP*, p. 233)

Most important was the influence this work had on Yeats, whose own stage works derive some of their elements from Pound's versions of the Noh drama. Yeats was working on Irish folklore, the occult and mystical texts: these ideas refreshed Pound's interest in mysticism which he had held since making a link between the ancient Greek Eleusinian mysteries and the courtly love of the troubadours. Yeats also encouraged a harder-edged stance in favour of the aristocratic notion of the artist, reinforcing whatever anti-democratic sentiments Pound had at this time. Pound was still compiling the imagist anthology during this first winter and Yeats introduced him to a poem by James Joyce: 'I Hear an Army'. Pound managed to trace the unknown writer to Trieste and wrote to him for the first time from Stone Cottage.

Winter 1914/15: Pound had at last married Dorothy Shakespear and this winter and the next she accompanied her husband on the retreats to Sussex with Yeats. Pound's work on the Fenollosa manuscripts had moved on to the Chinese poems and the *Cathay* volume was finished here. This winter was the first of the First World War and both Pound and Yeats were seeking ways to respond to the war in their poetry. Some of the poems in *Cathay* are in effect anti-war statements in the personae of soldiers from a civilization remote in time and place. There were also shared readings of Confucius and Icelandic sagas. The former was to become a central presence in *The Cantos*. Yeats was preoccupied with his memoirs of the 1890s and gave Pound information about the poets of The Rhymer's Club. Pound remembered the details and they figure in parts of *Hugh Selwyn Mauberley*.

Winter 1915/16: Yeats was increasingly concerned with the paranormal, clairvoyance, visions. Pound was formulating and beginning to write the first drafts of his 'big long endless poem' (Longenbach, 1988, p. 230) and was attracted by some of Yeats's obsessions as potential elements of an epic poem. Certainly visions, the voices of the dead and the power of memory all play important roles in *The Cantos*. Pound did further work on Noh dramas and even tried his hand at more contemporary one-act plays. However, it was Yeats who succeeded in bringing his dramatic work to theatrical fruition with the first performance of his Noh-influenced play *At the Hawk's Well* in 1916. Pound's ultimate achievement of the winter was the completion of his first three cantos, which were published in 1917. Even though they did not become part of *The Cantos* in their final form, they allowed Pound to find out what he no longer wanted and experiment with ways of achieving what he did.

Yeats and Pound never worked together so closely again. However, the three winters had cemented a friendship that was confirmed by the way Yeats supported Pound in his attempt to get his next collection, *Lustra*, published in uncensored form. The squibs in imitation of Catullus and the contemporary satiric pieces were judged too daring in tone and vocabulary by Pound's publisher. Eventually, there were two editions, a complete 'private' limited edition and a public expurgated one with some poems suppressed and others bowdlerized. One of the poems censored, for its use of the word 'whores', was 'The Lake Isle', a witty parody of Yeats's poem 'The Lake Isle of Innisfree'. The poem concludes:

> O God, O Venus, O Mercury, patron of thieves,
> Lend me a little tobacco-shop,
>   or install me in any profession
> Save this damn'd profession of writing,
>   where one needs one's brains all the time.
>   (*CSP*, p. 117)

31

Yeats liked the parody. That Pound could write it with the expectation that Yeats would share the mockery of one of his most famous poems suggests that there was between them not only friendship but a sense of professional equality. Pound's intimate working practices with Yeats at Stone Cottage may not have been as sensational as his association with Lewis, as spectacularly fruitful as his collaboration with Eliot or as entrepreneurial as his support of Joyce. However, the mutual influence ran very deep, more obviously in the way Pound affected Yeats's poetic language and style, but no less importantly in the way Yeats implanted and/or nourished certain attitudes and approaches which pervade both Pound's work and life.

Yeats is probably the greatest object of Pound's nostalgia in *The Cantos*, possibly because he was one of the few people to whom Pound felt disciple as well as critic and also because Pound felt some regret at the way their association soured in the years before Yeats's death in 1939. During Pound's Rapallo years Yeats and his wife were frequent visitors, renting a flat there. Out of this association Yeats wrote *A Packet for Ezra Pound*, published in 1929. This includes an engaging sketch of Pound the cat lover and hater of oppressors, 'a man with whom I should quarrel more than anyone else if we were not united by affection' (Yeats, 1969, p. 3). That affection was strained by Pound's querulous mentality in subsequent years: his judgement that one of Yeats's plays was 'putrid' caused some strain in their relationship. Nevertheless, Pound met Yeats for the last time in London in 1938 a few months before his death. Nearly 30 years later, following Eliot's funeral in London, he flew on the spur of the moment to Dublin to visit Yeats's widow. In the last drafts and fragments of *The Cantos*, with their glimpses of paradise, the memory of Yeats in Rapallo is there, rekindling the friendship:

> Sea, blue under cliffs, or
> William murmuring: "Sligo in heaven" when the mist came
> to Tigullio. And that the truth is in kindness.
> (*CAN*, p. 807)

The months between Pound's winter retreats were filled with social and literary activities, the two sometimes indistinguishable when it came to his promotional work. His marriage to Dorothy Shakespear in April 1914 had given him some financial security, since she had a reasonable allowance from her family. Nevertheless, his frantic round of reviews, articles and editorships was partly motivated by a need to earn his own money. More importantly, Pound wanted to be in positions of influence and power where he could carry out his mission to promote the best in contemporary writing. Over these years he was responsible for the publication of work by Robert Frost, D.H. Lawrence, William Carlos Williams, Wyndham Lewis, James Joyce, T.S. Eliot, H.D., Marianne Moore and many others. In particular, Pound's association with Lewis, Eliot and Joyce, the so-called 'men of 1914', was crucial to the development and lasting impact of what is sometimes now referred to as classic or canonical modernism.

In his first letter to Joyce, Pound had said, 'I am bonae voluntatis – don't in the least know that I can be of any use to you – or you to me' (Carpenter, 1990, p. 224). In fact, Pound was to be of enormous practical use to Joyce over a period of about ten years. In return, the example of Joyce's writing and *Ulysses* in particular was to teach Pound something about the organizing power of myth which gave him fresh perspectives on how to approach *The Cantos*. Joyce replied at length to Pound, describing his ten years of effort to get *Dubliners* published without censorship and enclosing the first chapter of *A Portrait of the Artist as a Young Man*. Pound claimed to have little discrimination where prose was concerned, but this is belied by his immediate enthusiasm for Joyce's work which he saw as the prose embodiment of his imagist principles: hard, clear, direct.

Pound was literary editor of *The Egoist*, a magazine which had begun life as *The Freewoman* in 1911, a humanist journal with feminist sympathies. *The Freewoman* had been rescued from financial collapse by Harriet Shaw Weaver, a former social worker of independent means, and renamed *The New Freewoman*. The assistant editor, Rebecca West, recruited Pound to expand the literary content of the magazine. By December 1913 the magazine was renamed *The Egoist* to prevent it being thought of as an exclusively feminist journal. A number of commentators assert that Pound demanded the name change for his own ends, but this is not borne out by Weaver's biographers (Lidderdale and Nicholson, 1970, p. 75). In fact, the title change reflected Weaver's own independence of spirit. When she took over the editorship of the magazine herself, she definitely became one of the 'women of 1914'.

Pound had Joyce's letter on the misfortunes of *Dubliners* published in the magazine and also wrote a review of the collection of short stories. He also persuaded Weaver to run *Portrait* as a serial. Within a few months all this exposure had persuaded one of Joyce's recalcitrant publishers to bring out *Dubliners*. Joyce continued to send chapters of *Portrait* to Pound for its serialization. Weaver herself read Joyce's work with admiration and steered *Portrait* through various censorship problems. After serialization she financed its publication in book form under the aegis of The Egoist Press. In effect, she became Joyce's patron, sending him regular sums of money to supplement what funds Pound could raise so that he would be free to work on his next major literary project. Pound's efforts on behalf of Joyce were truly amazing. Over these years he managed to extract one-off payments or regular sums from the Royal Literary Fund, the Society of Authors, various wealthy individuals and even Parliament in the form of a Civil List grant. Joyce wrote to Yeats, thanking him 'for having brought me into relation with your friend Ezra Pound who is indeed a miracle worker' (Carpenter, 1990, p. 227). To Pound himself he wrote, 'I owe you and Miss Weaver very much for your prompt kindness. But for you I should have been derelict' (Stock, 1970, p. 210). It is worth remembering that Pound did all this for someone he had never met and, because of the war and other contingencies, would not meet until 1920.

During this period in London Pound was also involved with avant-garde developments in the visual arts, largely through his friendship with Henri Gaudier-Brzeska and Wyndham Lewis and acquaintance with the sculpture of Jacob Epstein. This involvement influenced Pound both at the personal level, because of the intense emotions and ideas aroused by the friendships, and in artistic terms, in that their painting and sculpture seemed to be a visual realization of what Pound was trying to do in poetic form.

Gaudier-Brzeska was a young French artist living in conditions of some poverty in London with his partner Sophie Brzeska, a Polish woman twenty years his senior, whose name he had incorporated into his own. There was clearly a mother–son element to their relationship in which she was rather possessive and jealous of his artistic acquaintances. Gaudier-Brzeska held anarchistic views about life and art and was influenced by the avant-garde movements of cubism and futurism as well as the forms of African tribal art. Pound first saw Gaudier-Brzeska's work and met the artist at an exhibition in 1913. He was fascinated, if slightly nonplussed, by the formal configurations of the sculpture, but he recognized its genius and, typically, bought pieces with his own meagre funds. Pound also felt an immediate emotional rapport with Gaudier-Brzeska himself, who may have reminded him of William Brooke Smith and his artistic milieu in Philadelphia.

Once their friendship was fully established, Pound and Gaudier-Brzeska shared each other's work and exchanged ideas on the value of art and its role in what was clearly a pre-war society. Their deliberations, along with the contributions of Wyndham Lewis and his associates, led to the short-lived avant-garde movement known, and named by Pound, as 'vorticism'. In his usual generous, if sometimes misguided, way Pound promoted Gaudier-Brzeska's work by buying it, persuading others, most notably the American patron of the arts John Quinn, to buy it and by writing about it in his various magazines. In addition, Pound 'commissioned' a bust of himself by purchasing a massive marble block for Gaudier-Brzeska to work. The resulting sculpture, known as the 'Hieratic Head of Ezra Pound', was a monumental synthesis of primitive totemic styles forged by Gaudier-Brzeska's uniquely modernist hand: it is still a sight to behold.

Shortly after Pound's arrival in London he made his first acquaintance with Wyndham Lewis. In this case there was no immediate rapport and it was several years before they became friends, then collaborators in the vorticist movement and the publication of *Blast*. Lewis had been expelled from Rugby School, attended the Slade School of Art and lived for seven years on the continent before returning to London, both as writer of fiction and painter. Lewis experimented with quasi-abstract designs derived from cubism and became increasingly dissatisfied with the 'arts and crafts movement' ethos that dominated the London artistic scene. With a number of like-minded artists, including Gaudier-Brzeska, he founded a 'Rebel Art Centre' for the promotion of new art. The Centre had a very short life, but it was here that the concept of the vortex was developed and vorticism born.

Throughout this period the Italian futurist movement's leader Marinetti spoke regularly in London, extolling mechanical speed and aggressive action as a means to create a new artistic order and destroy an outworn tradition. Much of this appealed to the aggressive, iconoclastic aspect of Pound's temperament, though the actual artistic products of futurism did not impress him. Furthermore, certain traditions (e.g. troubadour life and art, Homeric epic, Latin lyric poetry) were vitally important to Pound and he was very selective when deciding which traditions were outworn (e.g. Romantic poetry, Victorian 'Tennysonianism'), so a total repudiation of the past could have little real attraction for him. However, the style in which vorticism promoted itself, most obviously in *Blast*, was influenced by the frenetic tone of the futurist manifesto, though one of the express purposes of *Blast* was to differentiate the new movement from futurism as such.

The first issue of *Blast* magazine was published in June 1914 with the subtitle 'A review of the Great English Vortex'. Its outsize pages, pink covers and bold lettering set the tone. The contents ranged from fiction by Ford and Rebecca West, poems by Pound, a play by Lewis, to paintings, drawings and illustrations by Lewis, Gaudier-Brzeska, Epstein and others. In addition, there were position statements about vorticism, a vorticist manifesto and lists of the blasted and the blessed, an idea borrowed from a futurist magazine.

As the voice of a new artistic movement, the magazine had little coherence, but it did succeed in upsetting some members of the literary and artistic establishment. Pound was effectively blacklisted by some publications because of his association with *Blast*. However, apart from those who were offended by *Blast*, considered opinion at the time recognized the magazine as little more than a kind of adolescent 'let's do something shocking' prank. Richard Aldington particularly saw Lewis's influence in the tone of Pound's language and suggested that Pound's 'enormous arrogance and petulance and fierceness are a pose' (Tytell, 1987, p. 110). This raises the issue of how influential Lewis was at this time on Pound's thinking, personal, artistic and political.

Even reasonably measured biographers of Lewis have difficulty in avoiding the implication that he was a rather unpleasant character, self-obsessed and driven by a seemingly inextinguishable inner rage. A deep-seated anti-humanitarian attitude manifested itself most flagrantly in his treatment of women. His biographer comments, 'Lewis enjoyed manly intellectual camaraderie as an antidote to what he felt were degrading yet necessary relations with women, whom he considered less intelligent than men and resented for their power to awaken and exploit his passions' (Meyers, 1980, p. 70). Pound is unlikely to have been impressed by Lewis's capacity for taking up with, then abandoning, women with whom he had fathered children. His own attitudes towards women were certainly not free of the male chauvinism that was the norm in those times, but he was never a callous user of women or indeed people in general. His ideas on courtly love, the troubadour ethos and the role of sex in artistic creativity leant themselves to what might be called 'traditional sexism', but he was far from being a misogynist. However, 'manly intellectual camaraderie' was very important to him, and Lewis may have reinforced Pound's sense of male intellectual superiority. Lewis's views on the role and place of the artist were undoubtedly elitist and would have underpinned the kind of ideas that Pound was developing in association with Yeats, Hulme and others regarding serious artists as the potential imposers of order on the chaos of mass culture. Politically, these views were anti-democratic in nature and open to a totalitarian perspective. What Pound possibly learned from Lewis in the *Blast* era was how to express these kinds of views in a reckless and railing manner. Pound later said of Lewis that 'A man with his kind of intelligence is bound to be always crashing and opposing and breaking. You cannot be as intelligent, in that sort of way, without being prey to the furies' (ibid., p. 33). Perhaps Pound, consciously or not, was also referring to himself here, justifying an aspect of his own make-up under the guise of defending Lewis.

Cover of the second issue of Blast *(*Before Antwerp, *Wyndham Lewis).*

The excited iconoclasm embodied in the first issue of *Blast* was ironically dissipated by the advent of world war. Lewis, Hulme, Gaudier-Brzeska and a group of painters associated with the vorticist movement all went to the trenches. Pound attempted to enlist in the British army but was unsuccessful: later he was harassed for being an alien. He spent much of his time promoting the work of his absent friends: a vorticist exhibition, the serialization of Lewis's novel *Tarr* in *The Egoist*. The war issue of *Blast*, its second and

37

only other edition, was published in July 1915. It contained poems by Pound and T.S. Eliot and a manifesto labelled 'Vortex Gaudier-Brzeska (Written from the Trenches)', followed by a brief note headed 'Mort pour la patrie' in which Pound announced Gaudier-Brzeska's death at the front in June.

The short-lived, but clearly very special, friendship between Pound and Gaudier-Brzeska had been maintained by correspondence while the Frenchman was in the trenches. Gaudier-Brzeska carried on his exchange of theoretical and aesthetic ideas with Pound as well as describing some of the horrors of the war. Details of the latter probably influenced Pound's wording in some of the *Cathay* poems which he then sent to Gaudier-Brzeska for comment. Gaudier-Brzeska's death was to haunt Pound for the rest of his life. Just how significant this death was in triggering off Pound's later obsessions has been debated by many of his critics and biographers. Within a year of Gaudier-Brzeska's death, Pound had written a memoir of the man which incorporated his artistic theories, samples of his work and an assessment of his stature. *Gaudier-Brzeska: A Memoir* was not only a personal testimony but also instrumental in promoting Gaudier-Brzeska's work and ensuring its later influence on sculptors such as Henry Moore. Pound's immediate comments, and those from subsequent years gathered together in later editions of this book, suggest that he was particularly affronted by the waste of a great artist, but that this was underpinned by a deep sense of personal loss: 'A great spirit has been among us, and a great artist is gone'; 'He was certainly the best company in the world, and some of my best days, the happiest and most interesting, were spent in his uncomfortable mud-floored studio when he was doing my bust'; 'For eighteen years the death of Henri Gaudier has been unremedied . . . There is no reason to pardon this either to the central powers or to the allies or to ourselves' (*GB*, pp. 17, 47, 140). There may have been a sense of personal guilt in this, since Pound had financed the sculptor's return to France to join up. When Pound was in St Elizabeth's Hospital, one of his regular visitors, the American postmodernist poet Charles Olson, reports that Pound was still obsessive about Gaudier-Brzeska and suggests that his hatred of the Allies and democracy 'and all his turn since has been revenge for the boy's death': Olson's editor notes that this view was confirmed by Dr Kavka, one of Pound's psychiatrists at St Elizabeth's (Seelye (ed.), 1975, pp. 45, 123n).

What is certain is that Gaudier-Brzeska was Pound's prime example of the waste of human excellence perpetrated by war. His obsession with the prevention of such waste by means of economic reform, the elimination of the financiers of the arms race and strong authoritarian rule was at least partly triggered by the loss of Gaudier-Brzeska. Clearly, aspects of Pound's temperament, aesthetic stance and developing political ideas provided the right psychological climate in which such a triggering could take place. It was in some ways unfortunate that, in this particularly receptive state of mind, Pound was introduced to the theories of Major C.H. Douglas through his connection with the magazine *The New Age*. Douglas's ideas on economic reform were particularly attractive to Pound because he interpreted them as an attack on usury and the profits of capitalism which he believed, not unreasonably, contributed to the outbreak of war. They also gave consideration to the economic status of the artist in society. In themselves, Douglas's monetary theories were at least worthy of debate. It was the vehemently obsessive way in which he later adopted and promoted Douglas's ideas that proved damaging to Pound both as poet and human being.

There was little chance that vorticism could survive the war years. Even without the dispersal of its main protagonists the movement had the feel of something which was of the moment, though Pound seemed to think the great artistic vortex of London would revive once the war was over. That it did not, at least not on his terms and not with him as a central force, added to the bitterness of his final departure in 1920. With the death of Hulme at the front in 1917 vorticism lost probably the only associate of the movement who could have given it real intellectual coherence and the possibility of sustaining itself as a postwar artistic movement.

Vorticism as a movement fizzled out, then, but vorticist notions were to underpin Pound's approach to poetic composition for the rest of his career as a poet. The notion of the poem as a vortex of ideas, multiple perspectives, paratactically situated details, develops quite rapidly in this period. Alongside the squibs of *Lustra* and the polemics of *Blast*, there are examples of poems which attempt to apply vorticist principles within the context of a sustained narrative, the most successful being 'Near Perigord', one of Pound's finest single poems before the full onset of *The Cantos*. Long before the human vortex that was the First World War had ended, Pound had embarked on what was to be the ultimate vorticist poem with the draft of 'Three Cantos' forged at Stone Cottage. As he told Joyce in a letter at the time, the poem was to be 'endless . . . of no known category' (Read (ed.), 1969, p. 102).

The fourth man of 1914, T.S. Eliot, arrived in London in September 1914 from Germany to pursue his studies at Oxford. In the previous three years or so Eliot had written a string of poems, including 'The Love Song of J. Alfred Prufrock' and 'Portrait of a Lady', which had failed to find a publisher, one editor finding their Laforgue-influenced sensibility 'absolutely insane'. Pound's instant recognition of Eliot's talent is perhaps the most remarkable example of his literary perceptiveness. Within a week of meeting Eliot and reading his work, Pound had embarked on another of his promotional campaigns with the editors of *Poetry* and other magazines, as his letters show: 'I was jolly well right about Eliot. He has sent in the best poem I have yet had or seen from an American . . . He has actually trained himself *and* modernized himself *on his own* . . . I enclose a poem by the last intelligent man I've found . . . Here is the Eliot poem. The most interesting contribution I've had from an American' (*SL*, pp. 40–1). After some resistance from the editor of *Poetry*, 'Prufrock' was eventually published in June 1915.

The promotion continued. Eliot's 'Preludes' appeared in the second issue of *Blast*. The so-called *Catholic Anthology*, which Pound edited in November 1915, was more or less a showcase for Eliot's poetry to date. Pound also introduced Eliot into the literary and artistic circles to which he had access, this process being made easier once Eliot was living in London, first as a teacher, then as an employee of Lloyds Bank. By 1917 Pound had secured for Eliot the literary editorship of *The Egoist* and persuaded Harriet Shaw Weaver to publish Eliot's first collection, *Prufrock and Other Observations*, for which he and Dorothy provided the finance. This volume, in retrospect the first entirely modernist collection by a single poet, met with hostile reviews and Pound immediately countered these with positive reviews in both *The Egoist* and *Poetry*: 'The Egoist has published the best prose writer of my generation. It follows its publication of Joyce by the publication of a "new" poet who is at least unsurpassed by any of his contemporaries'; 'Mr Eliot is one of the very few who have brought in a personal rhythm, an identifiable quality of sound as well as of style . . . Confound it, the fellow can write – we may as well sit up and take notice' (Grant (ed.), 1982, pp. 72, 80).

The support was not all one way. When Pound's *Lustra* was published in an American edition in 1917, Eliot wrote an accompanying essay entitled *Ezra Pound: His Metric and Poetry*, which provided an overview of Pound's work. Its tone was much more measured than Pound's, though its intent was still promotional. Eliot perceives that an important element of Pound's technique is his way of 'scorning the limitations of form and metre, breaking out into any sort of expression which suits itself to his mood', while acknowledging that 'Pound's *vers libre* is such as is only possible for a poet who has worked tirelessly with rigid forms and different systems of metric' (Eliot, 1965, pp. 165, 168). These comments particularly reflect the technical practitioner interchange that was a fruitful aspect of the collaboration between the two poets. In his

Poetry review Pound had quoted Eliot's dictum, 'No *vers* is *libre* for the man who wants to do a good job' (Grant (ed.), 1982, p. 78), and they were to carry on this debate about the status of free verse and its relationship to metrically regular forms not only in theoretical terms but also as a basis for future approaches to poetic composition. In particular, their 'return' to metrically more formal verse in Pound's *Hugh Selwyn Mauberley* and Eliot's *Poems 1920* was a practical outcome of this debate.

During this period Pound began another major association with a literary magazine, *The Little Review*, founded and edited by Margaret Anderson, originally in Chicago, but by the time of Pound's involvement centred in New York. His express need was for a regular outlet for the work of himself and his friends. He was able to negotiate such an arrangement with Anderson through the financial help of his patron, John Quinn, as always a generous supporter of Pound's ventures. Anderson was a remarkable editor, with a passion for the modern and the excellent in literature, who preferred to leave pages of her magazine blank rather than publish what she considered to be inferior material. Significantly, she was also willing to print work that was likely to invite censorship. Pound's arrangement was to fill and pay for a quota of pages in each issue: the result was a stream of poetry and prose of major importance by himself, Eliot, Lewis, Yeats and others. The crowning achievement was the publication in instalments over two years from March 1918 of a substantial portion of Joyce's *Ulysses*, until, after a series of harassments and confiscations, publication was halted by a successful obscenity trial in 1921. Early in his association with *The Little Review*, Pound wrote to Anderson that 'We want all the available energy poured into our vortex' (Scott *et al.* (eds), 1988, p. 124). Certainly, he himself poured enormous amounts of personal effort into promoting the work of those he saw as central to that vortex and many others who were on the edges of that whirlpool of creativity.

It is hardly surprising, then, that Pound's own poetic output suffered during his last few London years. What is more remarkable is the fact that he managed to produce two major works during that time. The first of these, *Homage to Sextus Propertius*, was conceived during 1917 but not published in its entirety until 1919 in the collection *Quia Pauper Amavi*. This sequence of poems, based on the works of the Latin elegiac poet, caused great controversy from the moment a few of its sections appeared in *Poetry*, since it seemed to be a translation of sorts which, according to Latin professors of the day, was riddled with inaccuracies. Pound's defensiveness, though understandable given the vehemence of some of the criticism, led him into self-contradiction. He attempted to justify the translation of so-called mistakes, while at the same time strongly claiming that the work was not really a translation at all. The fact that the criticism came from an academic establishment which had effectively rejected him in the past did not help matters. Entrenched arguments were never resolved and the status of the sequence as translation still distracts from its main achievements, for here Pound uncovered a major persona through which he was able to explore not only contemporary issues relating to the war, but also his own intimations of mortality and sexuality. Moreover, he was able to do so in a vortex of linguistic exuberance and pathos that is still a delight to read.

Hugh Selwyn Mauberley, Pound's other major cycle of poems from this period, was published in June 1920. As noted above, its tightly structured and densely allusive style was partly arrived at in collaboration with Eliot as a corrective to what they saw as the lack of poetic skill exemplified by most attempts at free verse. Pound's use of the persona is at its most ambiguous and rendered more complex by the autobiographical elements in the poem. By the time of its composition Pound was beginning to consider leaving London for good and saw the poem as a way of summing up the London phase of his career, conducting a retrospective on the state of poetry in the context of the English literary establishment and exploring aspects of his own psychological impulse to poetry into the bargain, an ambitious programme for what appears to be a cycle of short lyric verses. Furthermore, the crafted perfection of many passages only serves to underline the bitter anger that pervades the poem as a whole.

The end of world war had made European travel possible once more and Pound spent several months in Italy and France during 1920. The long-looked-forward-to meeting between the 'shell of cantankerous Irishman' and the 'miracle of ebulliency, gusto, and help' finally took place in June at Sirmione. Pound persuaded Joyce that Paris was the optimum place for the writer to live and work and went ahead to pave the way for his arrival. Before returning to London, Pound introduced Joyce to Parisian literary society. One contact effected in this way was with Sylvia Beach, who within two years was to publish the first complete edition of *Ulysses*.

Pound was finding it increasingly difficult to live and work in London. Because of his involvement with vorticism and *Blast*, he was both unwelcome in some literary circles and unable to get published in certain magazines. His vociferously negative comments on the British imperial enterprise did nothing to endear him to the conservative establishment. Disparaging views and remarks about the reading public did further damage to his reputation. His work was under attack for being either obscurely learned or of shaky scholarship and sometimes of both at once. His income from reviewing was seriously depleted by the demise of the art critic 'B.H. Dias' and his sacking from the post of drama critic of the *Athenaeum* magazine for a particularly scathing review of an influential actress.

If *Mauberley* had summed up a poetic and intellectual phase of Pound's life at the same time as being a fairly conscious goodbye to London, then *Indiscretions*, an autobiographical sketch serialized in *The New Age* in the summer of 1920, was a hedged account of his life from the perspective of exile at the age of 35. Though the option was considered, Pound made a conscious decision not to return to America. In many ways this was a more momentous choice than his initial decision to leave it, and one can only speculate on the course of his life and poetry had he returned to a New York that was far from the barren literary wilderness he sometimes made it out to be. As it was, he chose to continue beating out his exile, first in France and then in Italy, with the consequences already foreshadowed. In December 1920 Pound and his wife left London, effectively emigrating to mainland Europe.

'Drinking the tone of things'

Pound's relatively brief stay in Paris encompassed the year in which two of the major texts of literary modernism, Joyce's *Ulysses* and Eliot's *The Waste Land*, were published and a third, Pound's own *A Draft of XVI Cantos*, was completed. Postwar Paris was the centre for many avant-garde artistic movements, such as Dadaism and surrealism, and the scene of much experiment in the visual arts and music as well as literature. The city was both a stimulating and relatively cheap place to live and attracted large numbers of talented expatriates including many now famous American writers. Pound was an important, if fairly temporary, figure in this milieu, recalled with affection in Hemingway's memoir, *A Moveable Feast*. In addition to literary activity, Pound extended his interest in other art forms and also enjoyed himself socially, so that the Paris years have the feel of a holiday after the dismal exit from London.

As always, a large amount of Pound's energy was taken up with helping others, financially, practically or artistically. Hemingway records that 'Ezra was the most generous writer I have ever known and the most disinterested. He helped poets, painters, sculptors and prose writers that he believed in and he would help anyone whether he believed in them or not if they were in trouble' (Hemingway, 1977, p. 76). In this way a string of young, aspiring writers were advised and supported by Pound in his Paris years: most notably, Hemingway himself and e.e. cummings acknowledge the influence of Pound on their very different writing styles. However, it is Pound's part in making sure that 1922 was 'after all a grrrreat litttttterary period' (*SL*, p. 170) that gives credibility to the idea that he was the midwife of modernist literature.

The first task was to secure the publication of *Ulysses* in its entirety, now that its serial publication in America had been curtailed by the censor. Sylvia Beach, an American who ran the bookshop Shakespeare and Company, offered to publish the book under the shop's imprint and Pound was involved in the subscription drive to raise money to finance the project: in this way the greatest single work of modernist literature was published in February 1922. Throughout his stay in Paris Pound had an arrangement with yet another American magazine, *The Dial*, published in New York, to supply a regular account of the artistic and literary activity of the city. He used the May edition of his 'Paris Letter' for what now reads as propaganda for *Ulysses*, if that word can be used for such obviously sincere praise of the work. Pound extols Joyce for completing the job Flaubert began, sees him as a rival to Rabelais and beyond the scope of Proust and Henry James. He is also of the opinion that, while *Ulysses* is too idiosyncratic to provide a model for the novel of the future, 'it does add definitely to the international store of literary technique' (*LE*, p. 405), a view largely borne out by the subsequent history of the novel in this century.

With this essay Pound's nurturing of Joyce's career was more or less at an end. Once Pound had left Paris for good, physical distance reinforced whatever differences that may have developed regarding their literary, aesthetic and political agendas. Pound's view that *Ulysses* was unrepeatable was correct and Joyce was not one to repeat himself anyway, so the 'work in progress' that was to become *Finnegans Wake* was bound to be radically different and either astonish and delight or nonplus and disappoint. Nevertheless, Joyce must have been dismayed when Pound, of all people, confirmed the generally negative responses to his work in progress: in a letter from Rapallo in 1926 he acknowledges the receipt of Joyce's manuscript, wishes him well, then says, 'I will have another go at it, but up to present I make nothing of it whatever' (*SL*, p. 202). However, there is no reason to suggest that this view of the embryonic *Finnegans Wake* stemmed from jealousy or resentment of Joyce's success on Pound's part. Joyce's new and difficult work was coming into being at a time when Pound's political and economic obsessions were not only affecting his own work but also clouding his judgement about the work of others. Increasingly, any new writing that did not contain an economic perspective seemed to him unworthy of championing and his promotional energies were now directed towards his own economic and political goals.

Despite the fact that Pound made some injudicious remarks about Joyce's work in subsequent years and Joyce, like most of Pound's friends and literary colleagues, felt he had no choice but to disassociate himself from some of Pound's more extreme views, the two writers were in no way estranged. Though they met rarely after Pound left Paris, and for the last time in 1934, their correspondence lasted to the end of Joyce's life. His last written communication, a postcard to his brother Stanislaus in Italian, dated January 1941, names Pound as someone 'who might, I think, help you' (Ellmann, (ed.), 1975, p. 409). In the physical and emotional extremity of Pisa, Pound recalls with affection their very first meeting at Sirmione:

> at the haunt of Catullus
> with Jim's veneration of thunder and the
> Gardasee in magnificence
>
> (*CAN*, p. 470)

Years later, in the freedom of the post-St Elizabeth's years, Pound visited Joyce's grave in Zürich in 1967, a final act of homage to the writer who had, in Pound's own words, produced in *Ulysses* 'a triumph in form, in balance, a main schema, with continuous inweaving and arabesque' (*LE*, p. 406).

Pound's role in the production of the most famous and archetypal modernist poem, Eliot's *The Waste Land*, is better known and now more fully acknowledged than it was in Eliot's lifetime since the publication of the original drafts with Pound's annotations (Valerie Eliot (ed.), 1971). In the second half of 1921, when he was already working on a projected long poem, Eliot was suffering from non-specific nervous exhaustion. Late in the year he spent a month in Margate, working on the poem, then went to Switzerland for treatment for his 'psychological troubles'. Eliot stopped over in Paris on his way to and from Switzerland, on both occasions seeing Pound and showing him the manuscript of his poem. As the original drafts show, Pound performed radical surgery on the poem, advising drastic cuts, the reordering of whole sections and even changes in the wording of individual lines. This process was carried on by letter after Eliot's return to London. Although Eliot was responsible for the final draft, he accepted most of Pound's recommendations. It is clear that the structure of the poem as we now have it, a structure whose five sections foreshadow and may well have prompted Eliot towards the five-movement pattern of his *Four Quartets*, was largely Pound's conception. Furthermore, the overall tone of the poem as well as the tenor of some individual lines and sections must now be seen as Pound's achievement as well as, or even rather than, Eliot's. Any comparable deployment of textual skill would now certainly be counted as editorship. The view that Pound should be considered the co-author of *The Waste Land* is at least defensible.

In his letters to Eliot about the poem Pound shows a serious concern to get it 'right', to do justice to material that he obviously admires: 'One test is whether anything would be lacking if the last three were omitted. I don't think it would . . . The thing now runs from "April" to "shantih" without a break . . . I do advise keeping Phlebas. In fact I more'n advise. Phlebas is an integral part of the poem . . .' Alongside this there is a squib about his own role in the poem's birth, ending with the line, 'Ezra performed the caesarean Operation' (*SL*, pp. 169, 170). At least one critic has suggested that the production of the poem encapsulates the relative strengths and weaknesses of the two poets in as much as 'Pound could not have produced the raw material; Eliot could not tell the difference between good and bad passages' (Harwood, 1993, p. 195). The first part of this assertion is questionable, and I would argue that Pound could and did produce comparable 'raw material' throughout *The Cantos*. That his skill at telling the good from the bad and performing the necessary editorial revision was much less acute in respect of his own work is also contestable and ignores the possibility that Pound ultimately wanted his work to be the way it is. Nevertheless, the mock expressions of congratulation and jealousy in the above letters reflect Pound's awareness of such issues: he was genuinely in awe of the quality of Eliot's material and also conscious that his own poetic endeavour was floundering. However, far from giving up writing in the face of Eliot's achievement, as he jokingly suggested all poets might as well do, within weeks he was attacking the problems of his first batch of cantos with renewed urgency. This first section of *The Cantos* was completed in 1924, but it was not published until 1925, in a lavish limited edition.

Throughout modernism's great year Pound was also trying to help Eliot financially with a scheme known as 'Bel Esprit', whereby he attempted to collect sufficient funds from subscribers to allow Eliot to give up his work at Lloyds Bank. Hemingway, Williams, Aldington and other friends and literary acquaintances were enlisted as subscribers. Pound's manifesto for this venture outlines Eliot's situation as follows: 'Too tired to write, broke down; during convalescence in Switzerland did *Waste Land*, a masterpiece; one of most important 19 pages in English. Returned to bank, and is again gone to pieces, physically' (*SL*, p. 173). Pound strenuously denied that his scheme was charity, arguing that those who want good quality writing should be willing to support those who are capable of producing it. This line of thinking fitted in with Douglasite economic doctrine regarding the relation between purchasing power and means of production, or at least Pound's version of it. However, the venture proved an embarrassment to Eliot and ultimately unworkable. Hemingway recalls, 'I cannot remember how Bel Esprit finally cracked up but I think it had something to do with the publication of *The Waste Land* which won the Major [Eliot] the *Dial* award, and not long after a lady of title backed a review for Eliot called *The Criterion* and Ezra and I did not have to worry about him any more' (Hemingway, 1977, p. 77). This version of events is reasonably accurate, though Eliot's editorship of *The Criterion* did not immediately free him from the bank. However, it did help him to be perceived as a member of the English literary establishment and within two years he had joined the publishing house of Faber, though not before Pound had given him whatever money the Bel Esprit scheme had raised.

The Waste Land was published almost simultaneously in *The Dial* and *The Criterion*, then in book form with the infamous notes concocted by Eliot to pad out the volume. The poem eventually carried the dedication 'For Ezra Pound, il miglior fabbro', a conscious reference on Eliot's part to Pound's book *The Spirit of Romance*, in which the chapter on the troubadour Arnaut Daniel is called 'Il Miglior Fabbro'. Pound quotes this phrase, meaning 'the better craftsman', as part of Dante's praise for the skills of the Provençal poet (*SR*, p. 23). One inference of its use by Eliot could be the comparison: Eliot is to Pound as Dante is to Daniel, i.e. Pound is the better craftsman but Eliot is the greater poet, though it is uncertain that Eliot himself intended this interpretation. However, he did not make his debt to Pound explicit and the dedication may be seen as his only public acknowledgement of Pound's role at the time of publication.

The manuscripts of *The Waste Land* were sold to John Quinn, Pound's American patron and generous supporter of writers and artists recommended by him. They were subsequently lost and the evidence of Pound's contribution became unavailable. Eliot remained publicly ambiguous about Pound's role: he clearly felt unable to spell out in detail the extent to which Pound had influenced the poem which had brought him so much fame and secured his place in English letters, while at the same time wanting to acknowledge the fact that Pound played some part in its production. In 1938, for example, Eliot said that he chose the dedication 'il miglior fabbro' because he wanted to honour Pound's 'technical mastery and critical ability ... which had also done so much to turn *The Waste Land* from a jumble of good and bad passages into a poem' (Carpenter, 1990, p. 416). In 1946 he wrote, 'I placed

47

before him in Paris the manuscript of a sprawling chaotic poem called *The Waste Land* which left his hands, reduced to about half its size, in the form in which it appears in print' (Norman, 1969, p. 250). In his *Paris Review* interview in 1959 Eliot again mentions Pound's role in cutting *The Waste Land* down to its present size. When asked if the cuts change the intellectual structure of the poem, he replies, 'No. I think it was just as structureless, only in a more futile way, in the longer version' (Dick, (ed.), 1972, p. 119). Eliot's suggestion that the poem in its published form lacks structure is tongue in cheek. The poem's intellectual and emotional coherence in Pound's revision was clear to Eliot from the outset and by 1959 had been analysed and commented upon at great length by a wide range of critics. Eliot's ironic remark may be no more than diffidence at yet another discussion of his most famous poem, but it may also reflect his continuing unease about Pound's less than fully recognized role in its provenance.

Pound seems never to have minded that his part in *The Waste Land* was largely unrecognized and made no attempt to claim a portion of its success except as part of a movement in which he had played a leading role. Even in his brief and gracious preface to the newly discovered and published original drafts of the poem he simply states, 'The more we know of Eliot, the better. I am thankful that the lost leaves have been unearthed' (Valerie Eliot (ed.), 1971, p. vii). The relationship between Eliot and Pound remained one of loyalty and friendship for the rest of their lives throughout the relative stability of the one and the chaotic ordeal of the other, though the period of intense collaboration was over. It was Pound who named Eliot 'Possum', a name that Eliot not only took to privately but also adopted for one aspect of his public persona: without Pound we might still have had a book of practical cats, but they would not have been Old Possum's. For whatever reasons of indebtedness and respect for his poetic abilities, Eliot used his position at Faber to ensure that Pound's work was published: cantos, retrospective collections of poems, prose works. Despite the sometimes scathing remarks Pound made about Eliot's position in the English establishment and the strain that his political and economic views placed on their friendship, Eliot remained loyal. His status as Nobel Prize winner lent weight to the campaign to have Pound released from St Elizabeth's in which he played a major part. When Eliot died in 1965, Pound attended the memorial service in Westminster Abbey and later wrote a moving note to Eliot's memory: 'His was the true Dantescan voice – not honoured enough, and deserving more than I ever gave him ... Am I to write "about" the poet Thomas Stearns Eliot? or my friend "the Possum"? Let him rest in peace. I can only repeat, but

Manuscript page from Pound's opera Le Testament de Villon, *1921, with such idiosyncratic marks as 'Trombones, as rowdily and boozily as possible'.*

with the urgency of 50 years ago: READ HIM' (Heyman, 1976, p. 277).

During his Paris years Pound's involvement with music went be-yond his London activities as a professional music critic. He became both a composer and a promoter of other composers' music and ventured more systematically into setting down his theories of music. His musical activities also provided the context for a relationship that would last the rest of his life. Although Pound had previously dabbled in setting troubadour songs, he now embarked on the rather more ambitious project of writing an opera based on the poetry of the fifteenth-century French poet François Villon. Since Pound had no training in music or composition, the process of writing the opera was one of trial and error. A number of professional musicians gave advice or worked through Pound's draft score and the piece was eventually edited by George Antheil. The result was *Le Testament*, a one-act opera set in and around a Villonesque brothel. Villon and various other characters, including the brothel keeper and an ancient prostitute, take part in a series of tableaux with very little dramatic action which end with a scene in which Villon's epitaph is sung from the gallows by nine corpses. The musical texture of the work is relatively thin and chamber-like, with an idiosyncratic sound that is 'neoclassical' rather than anything else. This reflects not only Pound's inexperience as a composer but also his desire to experiment with a new form of counterpoint based on verbal rhythms. This linear structure also counteracts what he considered to be the overblown orchestral textures of late Romantic music, especially opera, for which he expressed general distaste. The work was not given any kind of performance till 1926, when a truncated version was performed in Paris. This led to a production by BBC radio in 1931, after which the music was unheard until a further BBC broadcast in 1962. There have been subsequent productions, including the premier English staging at the Cambridge Poetry Festival in 1985. The work is well worth hearing as a piece of experimental music of its time as well as for what it can tell us about Pound's involvement in the avant-garde musical scene in Paris. Imaginatively staged, it can also provide an entertaining theatrical experience.

Pound's compositional efforts were reinforced by his association with the young American composer and pianist George Antheil, who arrived in Paris with a reputation for outrageous musical compositions involving loud, mechanistic assaults on the keyboard and provoking riotous behaviour at his recitals. Pound saw his work as the musical equivalent of vorticism of the *Blast* vintage and began to help Antheil financially. There followed a year or two of concerts and recitals promoting Antheil's music in which Pound was also sometimes involved as both composer and performer, usually on drum or tambourine. Pound also commissioned Antheil to write sonatas for the violinist Olga Rudge, and these were also featured in recitals in Paris and London to suitably offended audiences. In his usual well-meaning but appropriative way, Pound wrote a propagandist appreciation of Antheil which included such claims as the following: 'Antheil has not only given his attention to rhythmic precision, and noted his rhythms with an exactitude, which we may as well call genius, but he has invented new mechanisms . . . Antheil has purged the piano, he has made it into a respectable musical instrument, recognizing its percussive nature' (Shafer (ed.), 1978, p. 259). The Antheil piece was incorporated into a book called *Antheil and the Treatise on Harmony*, published in Paris in 1924. The important section of this book was Pound's theoretical discussion of harmony, which was subsequently published separately. Its editor places Pound's treatise alongside discussions of harmony by such composers as Schenker and Schoenberg as a 'beautifully succinct and individualistic conception of the purpose and function of harmony' (ibid., p. 293) and goes on to point out that his conclusions about musical harmony are founded on his preoccupation with poetic rhythm and melody.

Pound continued to support Antheil's career throughout the 1920s, particularly while he was still giving concerts with Olga Rudge, and travelled to Frankfurt in 1930 for the first production of Antheil's opera, *Transatlantic*. While there, Pound also made contact with Leo Frobenius, the German anthropologist, whose recently discovered work proved influential and found its way into both his critical writings and *The Cantos*. Antheil eventually returned to America where he composed film music in Hollywood and more conventional, though still interestingly contemporary, classical music. Pound retained an interest in Antheil's career and even in the extremity of his impending trial for treason in 1945 mentions in a letter to his mother the publication of Antheil's autobiography, called, incidentally, *Bad Boy of Music*.

Pound had first seen Olga Rudge when she gave a recital in London in 1920 for which he wrote a review. However, it was not until 1923, when she was fully involved in the Paris musical scene, that their relationship began to develop from a mutual interest in promoting and performing music, especially new or newly 'rediscovered' music, into a lifelong partnership. Although born in America, Rudge had been brought up and educated in London and Paris and was less of an exile and more of a European citizen than Pound. By all accounts she was a fine violinist with a repertoire ranging from early and baroque music to avant-garde pieces such as Antheil's. Her general musicianship also contributed much to the flourishing musical scene which Pound promoted in Rapallo, especially in respect of the revival of Vivaldi's music.

Pound's short stay in Paris ended rather abruptly in the autumn of 1924. Several reasons probably came together to precipitate the move. Firstly, he was dissatisfied with artistic and literary Paris as a venue for both his own work and his growing economic and political preoccupations, which he did not feel were being taken seriously. Secondly, Paris provided too many distractions from this work and he wanted a quieter environment to pursue his poetic and economic endeavours, which were becoming conflated in his projected developments for *The Cantos*. His quaint attempts at sculpture, inspired by Brancusi, and even his musical composition dissipated his energy for poetry and he seems never to have enjoyed socializing for its own sake without some artistic purpose to give it point. Thirdly, he had suffered various health problems in Paris, possibly related to his other reasons for wanting to leave, and the Italian Riviera was an attractive place to convalesce. Finally, and perhaps most importantly, it was clear that his relationship with Olga Rudge was going to be of a permanent nature. For whatever reasons, including, presumably, the wishes of the other parties involved, he was unable or unwilling to resolve the situation by separating from his wife, by making a choice. Therefore, it was necessary to set up some domestic arrangement that would be at least tolerable to Dorothy, Olga and himself away from the very public Parisian milieu. This need was even more pressing when Olga became pregnant with Pound's child.

The Pounds had already made several trips to Italy from Paris and Pound had expressed his delight in Rapallo, a small town east of Genoa. It was here that the couple eventually set up house in February 1925 in a sixth-floor apartment that was to be one of Pound's homes. He committed himself to a quasi-double life where the true nature of the situation was obscured for friends and family alike in vagueness and uncertainty. Dorothy and Olga cooperated in their different ways with the arrangements. Dorothy regularly absented herself from Rapallo, and once she had a child of her own domiciled in England, there was every reason for her to spend lengthy periods away from Pound. Olga and Pound also arranged to have their child reared by foster parents so as to allow Olga to pursue her musical career and be close to Pound whenever it was convenient, while living with the fact that she had no legal status in relation to Pound and could never be publicly acknowledged as his partner. Nevertheless, a way of living, however unconventional and no doubt painful at times, was arrived at and stuck to for much of the next twenty years.

On the surface, then, the move to Rapallo allowed Pound to leave behind the hectic social and artistic climate of Paris for the peace and quiet of a small Italian seaside town. Here he could pursue his literary, musical and economic interests in relative tranquillity in the country which he increasingly felt was his cultural and political home. He could also rely on the attentions of two women whose very different personalities and talents he valued and needed. If the price of this was some personal guilt and social unease, then he would have to pay it.

'Full impetus of vehement will'

Pound's Rapallo years, culminating in the Pisan prison camp, were marked by both an enormous productivity and an obsessive frame of mind that might loosely be characterized by such terms as paranoia and megalomania. Pound's mental state and his productivity were not unrelated, of course. Much of his output, including some of the sections of *The Cantos* he wrote in this period, was the result of an obsessive drive to cajole, persuade and convert whoever he assumed was reading him, and some of it is couched in increasingly bitter, belligerent and fanatical terms. The period also chronicles Pound's growing isolation from the literary and artistic world he had known, reinforced by the physical removal from artistic centres and the cultural parochialism of the place he had chosen for his home.

At first, domestic and family concerns were his main preoccupation. Olga Rudge gave birth to their daughter, Mary, in the summer of 1925 in the Tyrol, a German-speaking region of northern Italy. Mary was brought up by foster parents on a farm in the area, visited by her real parents from time to time and spending holidays in Venice where Olga had her own home. Little more than a year later Dorothy Pound also had a child, Omar, born in Paris in September 1926. Pound was very reticent about the birth and his secrecy caused understandable anxiety among family and friends. Omar was taken to England to be brought up by Olivia Shakespear, who arranged for him to be looked after by a nursery and later at boarding schools. Pound saw him when he was four and again when he was twelve at the time of Olivia's death. Dorothy was with her son for extended summer visits each year until the war prevented any further travel, but Omar did not see Pound again until the St Elizabeth's years. On the other hand, Pound saw Mary regularly in the Tyrol and at Olga's house in Venice. When Pound's parents decided to live in Rapallo after his father Homer's retirement, Mary acquired a grandfather who adored her. Pound's domestic arrangements became less easy to conceal from 1929 onwards when Olga took an apartment in Sant'Ambrogio, a village high above Rapallo about two miles from the Pounds' home. From this time on Pound spent his weeks and days divided between the two women in his life. Much later, as war approached, Mary also visited her mother in Sant'Ambrogio, and eventually lived there, completing her convent education under Pound's supervision and beginning her work on translating *The Cantos* into Italian. Even so, she was unaware of the existence of Dorothy and Omar until 1943 when Pound, caught up in Italy's dire wartime political and military situation, made his hazardous trip to the Tyrol to see her and clarify things. It is clear from her own moving and beautifully written account of her life as Pound's daughter, *Discretions*, published in 1971, that Mary accepted his revelations unflinchingly and gave him her devoted support for the rest of his life.

Against the backdrop of these ongoing domestic and family arrangements Pound acted out the furious tragicomedy of his life in the Rapallo years, recognized and labelled from the start by the local Italian community as the eccentric 'il poeta'. His major preoccupations were literary and political, though there was more overlap in these aspects of his work than there had ever been before, but he also contributed much to the cultural, particularly musical, life of his adopted home. Pound's literary activities may be divided into such categories as involvement in little magazines, promoting new writers, the selection and collection of his previous work, translations, new batches of cantos and critical writings. These literary activities intersected with and were to some extent motivated by his political and economic interests, which were realized in a spate of letters, pamphlets, magazine articles and several books as well meetings with political figures and the broadcasts on Rome Radio during the Second World War.

While still continuing to contribute to literary magazines like *The Dial* and Eliot's *The Criterion*, Pound also finally achieved one of his long-held ambitions: to publish a magazine which was editorially under his control and mainly financed by his own money. It was called, almost eponymously, *The Exile*, and only managed to survive for four issues in 1927–28. Unfortunately, its content was not very impressive, being a mixture of new work by inferior writers and Pound's own mainly political offerings on the state of the world, especially the USA, and culminating in issue four in a lengthy article extolling, among other things, the virtues of Lenin. However, issue three contained the first publication of one of Yeats's finest late poems, 'Sailing to Byzantium', and the work of Louis Zukofsky, a young American poet with a Russian Jewish background. In Zukofsky, Pound felt he had discovered a poet who might be at the centre of a Poundian school. Certainly Zukofsky admired and was influenced by Pound's vorticist style and his own poetry became notable for its obscurity and incomprehensibility. Zukofsky labelled a group of poets, including Basil Bunting and William Carlos Williams, the Objectivists, but there was no real unity of approach in their work and the movement came to nothing. In later years Zukofsky stayed with Pound in Rapallo and met him on other occasions. He gave his name to various defences of Pound in the postwar years and was of the opinion that his best work would outlive the fact of his anti-Semitism.

Basil Bunting, Pound's main disciple in his early Rapallo years, was from the north-east of England and came from a Quaker background. His pacifism had led to his imprisonment during the First World War. Bunting's restless lifestyle, supported by casual manual jobs, led him to Paris where, full of admiration for *Homage to Sextus Propertius*, he first met up with Pound and followed him to Rapallo. Bunting was one of the first students at what became known as the 'Ezuversity', informal tutorial sessions where Pound held court. Bunting's work was undoubtedly influenced by Pound, particularly the early work's range of reference, allusiveness, imagism and use of persona. The principle of presentation over description or explication, Pound's 'direct treatment of the thing', is always present in Bunting's work and his masterpiece *Briggflats* represents a consummate synthesis of imagist and vorticist technique. Bunting's political stance was very different from Pound's: he had no time for anti-Semitic posturings and his anti-fascism led him to abandon his pacifism during the Second World War when he was a squadron leader in the Royal Air Force. However, Bunting remained loyal to Pound as a person and a mentor, lending his support during the years of Pound's incarceration, despite his conviction that Pound's support for the Fascist cause was wholly wrong. In the preface to his *Collected Poems* Bunting lists those who influenced him from the past and adds, 'but two living men also taught me much: Ezra Pound and in his sterner, stonier way, Louis Zukofsky' (Bunting, 1978, unpaginated). With this acknowledgement Bunting places himself in the modernist line of poetic endeavour fostered by Pound and perpetuated by Bunting himself through his own influence on later practitioners of modernist poetry.

One further literary association that began in Pound's Rapallo years is worth noting here, namely that with James Laughlin, the founder of the famous avant-garde publishing company New Directions. This association began in the early 1930s when Laughlin, a young Harvard student, visited Rapallo's 'Ezuversity'. Pound thought little of Laughlin's literary talents and told him, 'No Jas, it's hopeless. You're never gonna make a writer . . . do something useful . . . Go back and be a publisher' (Gordon (ed.), 1994, p. x). To his credit Laughlin rode the criticism and followed Pound's advice, becoming literary editor, with Pound's help, of the magazine *New Democracy*. Laughlin was from a wealthy background and used family finance to set up the publishing house which took its name from his literary page in the magazine. The modernist content of the first *New Directions in Prose and Poetry* of 1936 was a foretaste of the pioneering spirit with which Laughlin was to continue promoting new and experimental work into the postwar years. From 1940 onwards, with the publication of the American edition of *Cantos LII–LXXI*, New Directions became the major publisher of all Pound's work in America. A substantial body of correspondence chronicles this endeavour, other literary matters and the friendship that built up between poet/mentor and publisher/disciple.

In 1926 Pound prepared his collected poems for publication. The first edition, called *Personae: The Collected Poems of Ezra Pound*, was in fact a selection of poems representing what he wished to preserve from his earlier collections from *A Lume Spento* to *Lustra*, plus complete versions of *Cathay*, *Propertius* and *Mauberley*. This book went through various editions and enlargements to become his *Collected Shorter Poems* in 1968. Although *The Cantos* were well under way by the time this collection was made, Pound excluded them, so that both chronologically and conceptually the collection represents everything that comes before them. *The Cantos*, however uncertain their design and coherence, are unmistakably one long poem and the division in Pound's work between them and the *Collected Shorter Poems* appears quite marked, since he wrote virtually no new poetry but cantos from that time onwards. Indeed, he more or less vowed that there would be nothing but cantos from then on and was very dismissive of pleas by friends to write poetry in his previous styles, telling them to write it themselves.

Translation, however, never lost its appeal for Pound. To some extent, the subject matter of the original gave him the freedom not to write about the obsessive ideas he felt otherwise compelled to expound. On the other hand, Pound was able to see or impose some connection between the material of his translations and his wider concerns. For example, his reading of Confucius helped to underpin whatever rationale, if that is the right word, he had for supporting fascism. In his Rapallo years Pound worked on translations of both Confucius and Cavalcanti. The former's *Ta Hio* or *The Great Learning* was translated with the help of a French version and published in 1928. It was from this work that one of Pound's most famous catchphrases, 'Make it new', ultimately derived. In translating the words that were supposed to have been written on the bathtub of an ancient Chinese king, Pound used the term 'Renovate'. However, a few years later he chose to call a collection of his literary essays *Make It New*, clearly a reference to the Confucian tenet. When he came to refer to this material in his sequence of Chinese cantos, published in 1940, the principle was writ large:

> Tching prayed on the mountain and
> wrote MAKE IT NEW

on his bath tub
            Day by day make it new
                                    (*CAN*, p. 264)

Pound's work on the Italian poet and philosopher Guido Caval-
canti was an extension and revision of much earlier translations
from his London years. The project escalated into a kind of crit-
ical edition of Cavalcanti's work with translations and commentaries
by Pound. He spent an enormous amount of time and eventually
money on something he took seriously enough to consider submit-
ting it as a doctoral thesis to the University of Pennsylvania. This
idea came to nothing, but it is an interesting indicator that even
at this stage Pound still had academic ambitions which, had they
been fulfilled by a sympathetic American university system, might
have occasioned his return to America before his situation became
wholly irretrievable. As it was, Pound's *Guido Cavalcanti Rime* was
published in a limited edition at his own expense in 1932.

For Pound, Cavalcanti's most important poem was 'Donna mi
priegha', a complex discussion of the nature of love. The text of
this poem, Pound's first translation of it, critical commentary and
attempted explication were brought together in an essay entitled
'Cavalcanti' for the collection *Make It New* of 1934. Pound con-
cedes that the original poem is obscure in places, but claims that
this is because we no longer know the precise meaning of some of
Cavalcanti's terminology and because 'the philosophy of the time
has been completely scrapped' (*LE*, p. 162). Pound's discussion and
commentary are slightly obscure themselves, but he makes clear
that he values the poem because he believes it subverted the reli-
gious orthodoxies of Cavalcanti's day and attempted to expound a
philosophy of love that was natural, i.e. both aesthetic and sexual.
These ideas fitted in with Pound's own views on sexuality and its
relationship to creativity which, rightly or wrongly, he believed the
troubadours and medieval Italian poets exemplified, providing a
link back to pagan celebrations of sexuality, such as the Eleusinian
mysteries, which Christianity had undermined and eradicated. Pound
wrote a second complete translation of 'Donna mi priegha' as a
substantial part of Canto 36. Both translations are written in his
archaic mode, though the second achieves greater fluidity and lit-
erality of expression through, among other things, changes in word
order and shifts from nouns to verbs as centres of meaning. The
following examples juxtapose the same passage in the original and
both translations by way of comparison:

                In quella parte dove sta memoria
                Prende suo stato si formato chome
                Diafan dal lume d'una schuritade

57

> In memory's locus taketh he his state
> Formed there in manner as a mist of light
> (original and first translation from Cavalcanti essay
> in *LE*, pp. 164 and 155 respectively)

> Where memory liveth,
>   it takes its state
> Formed like a diafan from light and shade
> (from Canto 36 in *CAN*, p. 177)

In its form in *The Cantos* 'Donna mi priegha' is a masterpiece of melopoeia, Pound's term for the melodic and rhythmic aspects of poetic structure. Like great instrumental music, the poem gives the impression of semanticity without recourse to transparent meaning. Attempts to paraphrase it for logical argument are always more or less unsuccessful and tend to detract from its melopoeic effect.

Pound's translations and the critical work associated with them fed into the cantos of this period as his mammoth poetic effort progressed alongside his other activities. *A Draft of XXX Cantos*, which incorporated the previous sixteen, was published in Paris in a limited edition by Nancy Cunard's Hours Press. Pound had first met Cunard during his London years, had helped her to get established as a writer and befriended her black lover, Henry Crowder, in Paris. In a moving letter to Pound in St Elizabeth's written in 1946 she recalls this with affection, even though the overall point of her letter is to condemn Pound for his fascist sympathies. Cunard supported the Republican cause in the Spanish Civil War, recording in her survey of other artists' views that Pound was neutral rather than pro-Franco. However, her disenchantment with Pound could not survive his radio broadcasts, some of which she heard and found abhorrent. Her letter makes clear that she is not willing to accept the excuse of madness and eloquently expresses what many admirers of Pound's poetry have thought over the years: 'I cannot understand how the integrity that was so much you in your writing can have chosen the enemy of all integrity' (Scott (ed.), 1990, p. 82).

Over the next ten years or so Pound produced three further batches of cantos, comprising 41 in all. The first of these was *Eleven New Cantos XXXI–XLI*, published in 1934. Canto 41 records Pound's audience with Mussolini which took place in 1933. For about a year Pound had been trying to meet Italy's fascist leader with the main purpose of impressing him with the virtues of Major Douglas's economic theories, but also to show him the first volume of *The Cantos*. The Boss, as Pound subsequently referred to him, expressed the view that the book was 'amusing'. It is unlikely that Mussolini had actually taken in or even read any of Pound's work, but Pound interpreted the remark in a very positive way. Mussolini had been in power all the years that Pound had lived in Italy, eventually establishing a dictatorship and abandoning parliamentary demo-cracy. This in itself did not bother Pound who was very sceptical of democracy and inclined to notions of order through strong lead-ership. In 1927 Olga Rudge had met Mussolini specifically to dis-cuss the musical life of the country and to try to promote Antheil's music, so Pound had a good personal reason to think favourably of him. Over the next few years Pound absorbed a good deal of fascist literature, but this was only part of a broader interest in political systems which prompted him to read books by and com-municate with, among others, communist political thinkers: his main obsession was to promote Social Credit economics and he would have been willing to talk to any leader or regime on the topic. How-ever, his audience with Mussolini seems to have created in Pound an unquestioning idealization of the leader and probably marks the beginning of his real commitment to the fascist cause, even if he was never a member of the Fascist Party as such. The incident also tells us something about the state of Pound's mind, even at this relatively early stage on his road to St Elizabeth's. The fact that he thought he had influence over someone in Mussolini's position, his utter belief that his interpretation of Douglasite economics could solve everyone's problems and save the world, suggest that Pound was already so out of touch with himself and the real political sit-uation that the futile trip to America in 1939 and his subsequent radio broadcasts were almost inevitable.

The immediate outcome of this intense sense of mission felt by Pound immediately after his audience with Mussolini was the production of two books of political/economic content. *ABC of Economics*, published in 1933, was a 'brochure' of Social Credit theory, structured in short sections and aphoristic lists of points. One section, entitled 'Dictatorship as a Sign of Intelligence' con-tains overt support for Mussolini. Clearly, the pamphlet is driven by an inner compulsion to promote Douglasite economic theory. As Pound notes, 'I shall have no peace until I get the subject off my chest.' However, there are, as is usual with Pound, persuasive argu-ments, such as that for a shorter working day on the grounds that, among other things, 'Leisure is not gained by simply being out of work. Leisure is spare time *free from anxiety*' (*SP*, pp. 231, 203, 213). *Jefferson and/or Mussolini* was written about the same time, but had trouble finding a publisher and was not published until 1935. The basic premise of the book is that Jefferson and Mussolini have much in common and that the philosophy of the founding fathers of the United States is somehow being realized in fascist Italy. The notion of Mussolini as artist is used and the appeal to order is made to excuse the facts of dictatorship. But Pound falls short of advocating a fascist revolution in America, merely asserting that Jeffersonian ideals need to be revived by right-thinking and energetic Americans. Pound sent copies of both books to Mussolini and also wrote him frequent letters. During this period he also wrote letters to President Roosevelt and various American senators and governors, and contributed dozens of letters and articles to magazines: the tone of many of these was irascible or even hysterical. Friends and literary associates were dismayed or alarmed at the direction Pound's career was taking, but he was convinced that economic issues were more important than poetry. Those who cared about him began to question his mental stability, and even the Italians who processed his letters to Mussolini were of the view that 'One thing that is clear is that the author is mentally unbalanced' (Tytell, 1987, p. 239).

Parallel in some ways to these 'textbooks' on economic and political theory was the *ABC of Reading*, published in 1934. This book had its origins in a series of articles called 'How to Read', published in 1927, in which Pound characteristically tilts at the stultifying nature of formal education, narrow syllabuses and reliance on critical commentary, but also revisits and synthesizes important elements of his poetic philosophy and makes pertinent, if sometimes quirky, pronouncements about a wide range of literature. A number of his more famous one-liners appeared in the articles and are repeated in the book, for example, 'Great literature is simply language charged with meaning to the utmost possible degree' and 'Literature is news that STAYS news' (*ABC*, pp. 28, 29). There is also the classification, or perhaps declension is a better term, of those who create literature: inventors, masters, diluters, good writers without salient qualities, writers of *belles-lettres*, starters of crazes (ibid., pp. 39, 40). The second part of the book is largely a very personalized selection of 'exhibits', samples of poetry, with snippets of commentary that provide an acute poet's-eye view of mainly English literature. And there is Pound's ironically wry solution to the over-production of bad literature: 'The chief cause of false writing is economic. Many writers need or want money. These writers could be cured by an application of banknotes' (ibid., p. 193). The *ABC of Reading* has retained its freshness and is still well worth reading, not only for its iconoclasm but also for the insights it gives on the nature of poetry for reader and writer alike.

In the midst of all the sound and fury of political and literary polemic, music provided a mental and emotional distraction. It hardly seems credible now that Pound found time to organize concerts in Rapallo, but with Olga's help and contribution as a player from 1933 to the outbreak of war there was a season of concerts each year held in the Town Hall, the local cinema and private houses. These concerts also exemplified Pound's monetary philosophy by being small-scale, focusing on chamber music and employing, whenever possible, local musicians. In an article entitled 'Money versus Music', published in 1936, Pound expresses the need for concerts which allow for the proper evaluation of different kinds of music performed under uniform conditions, and he goes on to say that 'A small town can provide a laboratory and can specialize in work not being done in the heavily monied "centres" up to the quality and number of its local performers' (Shafer (ed.), 1978, p. 323). The range of music performed was indeed wide and rich, with concerts juxtaposing, like the sections of one of his cantos, such diverse composers as Bach and Bartók, Scarlatti and Ravel, fulfilling Pound's notion of the ideogramic method. Pound wrote reviews of many of the concerts, mostly in a local newspaper and in Italian. These are collected in English translations in Shafer's book and reveal Pound's fine musical sensibility and genuine care for the quality of both composition and performance. Pound's contribution to the wider musical culture of Italy is related to the Vivaldi revival. In 1936, by which time Vivaldi had become a major focus of the Rapallo concerts, Pound encouraged Olga to catalogue the Vivaldi archive of the National Library of Turin: she eventually published this catalogue in Siena. Pound himself obtained microfilm of Vivaldi works held in Dresden and copied them by hand. Both Pound and Olga wrote articles on Vivaldi and organized workshops for the study and performance of his music. Ultimately, Pound's contribution to this enterprise was far outstripped by Olga's because of her superior musicianship and the amount of time she could give to it in the postwar years.

Alongside all this activity Pound still managed to write the next section of his poem, published in 1937 as *The Fifth Decad of Cantos*. Complementary in many ways to this batch of cantos is the *Guide to Kulchur*, written very quickly in 1937, but delayed in publication till 1938 because of potential libel problems. Pound replied to his publisher on this issue as follows: 'Waal Whale: I dun finished reading my bukk, and there is a few phrases which mebbe iz libelous ... I hereby give permish to omit names of bloody lice like ___r or ___n, when they occur in indiscrete circs. Yuh git me?' (*SL*, p. 294). *Guide to Kulchur*, Pound's attempt at a guided tour of human learning and civilization, is a prose vortex of his own likes and dislikes. There is no doubting its desultory wisdom: one reviewer acknowledges about 100 statements of genuine insight scattered through the book, but concludes that it is 'just pure bosh in an excited tone of voice'. Another laments: 'And no one has more *'pai deuma'*

to give an audience. But timidity, or self-consciousness, or some-
thing, gets in the way. Then we have the sneers about the profs,
the linguistic rough stuff, the bad boy strutting and shocking.' The
most anguished review came from Pound's long-standing friend,
William Carlos Williams: 'And his conclusion from all this is
totalitarianism! The failure of the book is that by its tests Mus-
solini is a great man; and the failure of Pound, that he thinks him
so. The book should be read for its style, its wide view of learning,
its enlightenment as to the causes of our present ills. The rest can
be forgiven as the misfortune of a brave man who took the risk
of making a bloody fool of himself and – lost' (Homberger (ed.)
1972, pp. 334, 336, 337).

One figure who occurs regularly throughout the book is Leo
Frobenius, the German anthropologist whose work Pound had dis-
covered some ten years earlier. Frobenius's main area of expertise
was African culture and mythology, upon which he had written
at great length. In *Guide to Kulchur* Pound reports consulting him
about the economic system of certain African tribes and expresses
interest in his theories of racial characteristics in relation to which
he remarks, 'Race prejudice is red herring. The tool of the man
defeated intellectually, and of the cheap politician' (*GK*, pp. 61,
242). What is both puzzling and disheartening about this remark
is the apparently total lack of awareness that others might think it
applied to Pound himself. He was particularly impressed by what
he saw as Frobenius's approach to the 'New Learning' associated
with cultural anthropology. He identifies Frobenius's term 'paideuma'
as characteristic of this and glosses it as follows: 'When I said I
wanted a new civilization, I think I cd. have used Frobenius' term
. . . for my own use and for the duration of this treatise I shall use
Paideuma for the gristly roots of ideas that are in action' (ibid.,
p. 58). Arbitrary or not, this use of the term 'paideuma' as short-
hand for 'embedded patterns of culture' permeates Pound's writing.
When a journal entirely given over to the study of Pound's life
and work was founded in 1972, it was, almost inevitably, called
Paideuma.

Williams's review of *Guide to Kulchur* was published in June 1939
when Pound was actually in America and the two poets had re-
cently met. In a letter written shortly afterwards, Williams wrote,
'The man is sunk, in my opinion, unless he can shake the fog of
fascism out of his brain during the next few years, which I ser-
iously doubt he can do. The logicality of fascist rationalization is
soon going to kill him' (Tytell, 1987, p. 253). Although Williams's
final prophecy here did not turn out to be literally true, his mis-
givings about his friend's state of mind were entirely justified.
Pound had arrived in America in April with a sense of mission.

His feelings towards his native country were an ambiguous, if not confused, mixture of hatred for current political, academic and artistic institutions, upon which he poured vitriolic scorn at every oppotunity, and a conviction that there had been a golden age during the time of Adams and Jefferson to which he could help America to return by promoting Social Credit economics and fascist thinking. To this end he intended to meet as many senators and other officials as possible and, most of all, have an audience with the President. Not everyone was unsympathetic to his views. In particular, there was a strong lobby to keep America out of any future European war: as this was one of Pound's foremost platforms, some senators were willing to listen. However, the trip as a whole was a mixture of the pathetic and the farcical. Given his public pronouncements about Roosevelt, there was never any chance of him seeing the President. That Pound could even entertain the idea betrayed his unreal sense of his own status as far as politics were concerned. Those meetings he did manage to arrange were marred by his hectoring talk of economics and his fascist apologetics. In addition, his anti-Semitic remarks were increasingly overt and unpleasant in tone. By this time the oppressive treatment of Jews in Germany was being widely reported, even if the full extent of Nazi policy was still unknown, and Pound cannot have been totally unaware of it. Although anti-Semitism was still widespread in America, it is unlikely that Pound's remarks would have impressed the people he most wished to influence with his economic theories. While in America, Pound was at last honoured by the academic establishment he had come to despise when Hamilton College conferred on him an honorary doctorate. Even here, his fascist sympathies intruded and farce broke out at the post-ceremony lunch when he took part in a slanging match with another honoured guest who made anti-fascist remarks in his speech. Perhaps the only worthwhile thing to come out of Pound's trip to America was the recording he made of some of his poems for Harvard University (*PV*). These include 'The Seafarer', accompanied by atmospheric drumbeats, and 'Sestina: Altaforte', its fiercely delivered advocation of war disturbingly appropriate to the times.

Pound returned to Italy only a matter of weeks before the outbreak of the Second World War, though in the early stages Italy was not involved in hostilities. He continued to write anti-Semitic and pro-fascist articles in Italian journals and newspapers, but was also preoccupied with the imminent publication of his next group of cantos, which were published in England in early 1940 as *Cantos LII–LXXI* and in America towards the end of the year. During the war years Pound was preoccupied with mainly non-artistic activities as well as an increasingly difficult domestic situation in which the compartments of his life, which he had for so long managed to keep as separate as possible, were at last forced to coincide. For the whole of 1940 Pound conducted his keep-America-out-of-the-war campaign by letter and newspaper article. His main targets were President Roosevelt and Jewish financial institutions whom he believed were part of a conspiracy to get America to join the Allies for their own profit and political gain. Having realized the immense potential of radio during this time, he applied to the Italian authorities for permission to broadcast on short wave programmes aimed at the United States and Britain and was eventually allowed to do so. The broadcasts began in early 1941. Pound visited Rome every few weeks to record batches of his talks which were each broadcast several times. There was at least one fairly serious attempt to return to America with his wife, but the American consular authorities made it clear that he would not be allowed to return to Italy again and Pound abandoned the idea with some acrimony. As long as America was not at war, Pound's broadcasts were more of an irritant than a treasonable offence. However, Japan's attack on Pearl Harbor in December 1941 altered circumstances radically. Nevertheless, Pound decided to carry on broadcasting, prefacing his talks with an announcement that he was exercising his right to free speech on the understanding that he would not be asked 'to say anything whatsoever that goes against his conscience, or anything incompatible with his duties as a citizen of the United States' (Norman, 1969, p. 385). Despite this disclaimer, from this time onward Pound's words were monitored and transcribed by US federal investigators.

The contents of Pound's broadcasts on Rome Radio have been available more or less in their entirety for some time now (Doob, 1978). Doob's qualitative and quantitative analyses of themes and referents show a much wider range of topics than is often revealed by critics wanting to give an entirely negative impression: apart from matters relating to the Second World War, its causes, effects and likely outcomes, there are substantial amounts of Poundian economic theory, particularly against usury and international capitalism, comments on government of a general and abstract nature and frequent remarks about cultural and literary matters. The United States, Britain, their political leaders and policies are the most frequent referents, along with Jews and generalized enemies, but also many literary figures and philosophers. The speeches are also highly self-referential with Pound frequently invoking his own experience and opinions: there is virtually nothing to suggest he was speaking on behalf of any other agency.

It is difficult, probably impossible, to gauge the impact or effectiveness of these broadcasts from this distance in time, in a very different world and from transcripts: I have only occasionally heard very brief samples of the speeches themselves. However, my own reading of the transcripts leads me to conclude that Pound's main arguments were mostly accessible through sheer repetition and linguistic force, but that the detail of his many unglossed references and personal anecdote would have been lost on a mass listening audience. Specific references to the war aside, much of what he says is a recapitulation of beliefs and explanations that he had been promulgating for the previous twenty years. To the extent that *The Cantos* embody these beliefs and explanations, it is possible to see the broadcasts as a spoken prose version of the poem as it stood in 1943, lacking the lyric, mythic and narrative elements that are so often the source of its poetic power. Even though his political and economic arguments are clearly biased towards the Axis cause, they might still have been taken as legitimate and radical views about global finance, the power of what are now called 'multinationals', and the role of the 'military–industrial complex' in the promotion of war, if they had been presented in a sane and sober fashion. However, at a relatively trivial level the schoolboy name-calling and general petulance are a distracting irritant. More seriously, the speeches are marked by Pound's brand of anti-Semitism at a time when the totalitarian system he supported was perpetrating genocide. An isolated example from the radio broadcasts will always run the risk of being misleading. However, the following extract is, I think, representative of one common line of argument that Pound reiterated many times:

> '. . . every sane act you commit is committed in homage to Mussolini and Hitler. Every reform, every lurch towards the just price, toward the control of a market, is an act of homage to Mussolini and Hitler. They are your leaders, however much you are conducted by Roosevelt or sold up by Churchill'
>
> (Doob, 1978, p. 150)

Presumably Pound's intention here was to highlight certain economic reforms which he mistakenly believed the Axis powers to be implementing, but, addressed to an audience at war with those powers, the effect is at least propagandist and may well have been judged treasonable in a court of law. The tone and manner in which these talks were delivered can only have served to exacerbate the content. Pound's daughter, Mary, who witnessed him rehearsing the broadcasts, notes that his voice was 'angry, sardonic, sometimes shrill and violent for the radio speeches . . .' She later laments, 'He was losing ground, I now see, losing grip on what

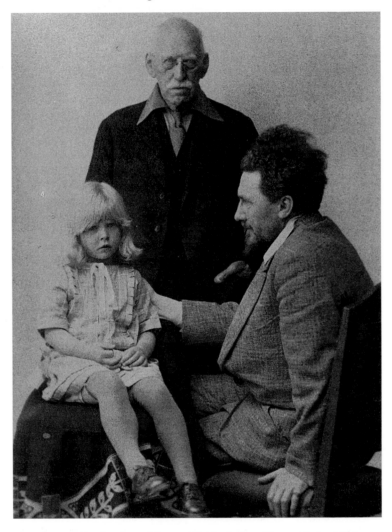

Pound with his daughter, Mary, and his father, Homer, Italy 1929.

most specifically he should have been able to control, his own *words*'
(de Rachewiltz, 1971, pp. 150, 173).

In these stringent times Olga, Mary and even Dorothy were
much more obviously his dependents. Early in 1942 Pound's father
died, leaving his widowed mother alone in Rapallo, another domestic
commitment. The fees he received for his broadcasts were therefore

a vital part of his income. However, there is no evidence that Pound was given any privileges, and life in wartime Rapallo was fairly spartan. There was some literary activity during this period. In particular, Pound was involved in helping Mary, who was now living with Olga at Sant'Ambrogio, to translate his cantos into Italian. He was also working on his own Italian translations of Confucius. The war began to turn against the Axis forces and once Italy became subject to Allied bombing, Mussolini was arrested and a new peace-seeking government installed in July 1943. Almost simultaneously, Pound was being indicted for treason by a grand jury in Washington for adhering to the enemies of the United States and giving them aid and comfort. Pound was actually surprised when he heard of his indictment for treason, since he genuinely believed the preface to his broadcasts exonerated him from the charge. Pound was in Rome when Italy officially surrendered to the Allies and he may have thought he would be summarily executed if captured by Allied forces. Whatever the case, he decided to make his way to the Tyrol to see Mary who had retreated to her childhood home. The journey of nearly 500 miles through mainly German-occupied territory was made on foot and by train, Pound driven on by a desire to see his daughter and share the truth of his domestic situation with her.

By September 1943 Mussolini had been rescued by the Germans and set up as head of a puppet state, the so-called Salo Republic, in northern Italy. It was only at this stage that Italy became involved in the implementation of the Holocaust: Italian Jews were systematically arrested, deported and ultimately slaughtered in the death camps. Since the Republic involved Mussolini, Pound was zealously loyal in its cause and contributed to its propaganda broadcasts from Milan both as speaker and scriptwriter. It was during this period that Pound wrote Cantos 72 and 73 in Italian. They were published in a journal of the Salo Republic in 1944. German military activity in Rapallo intensified as the Allies advanced through Italy and in May 1944 Pound and his wife were evicted from their apartment. They could have gone to live with his mother, who still lived on her own in the town, but Pound wanted to be with Olga and Dorothy went with him. For almost a year until his arrest and incarceration, Pound finally experienced the uneasy proximity of the two women with whom he had spent the last twenty years. In April 1945 Mussolini was captured and killed by Italian partisans and the Germans surrendered Italy to the Allies. Within days Pound was taken from his home by two Italian partisans and handed over to the American authorities. The ordeal of Pisa and the ignominious return to America were under way.

'Abstract yatter'

Following his repatriation to America from the detention centre at Pisa, Pound was temporarily incarcerated in a district prison. After a stay in the psychiatric ward of a public hospital he was then transferred to St Elizabeth's Hospital, the federal asylum in Washington, in December 1945. He was to remain there for nearly thirteen years. In the few weeks he had been in the United States, Pound had been assigned a lawyer and examined by a team of psychiatrists. The lawyer, Julien Cornell, decided more or less immediately that Pound should lodge a plea of insanity, possibly as a means of getting bail or even, ultimately, an unconditional release. However, it is worth bearing in mind that this decision was also made in the context of a vociferous public debate as to whether Pound should be summarily executed. The team of psychiatrists, led by Dr Winfred Overholser, concluded their initial diagnosis with the view that Pound's 'personality, for many years abnormal, has undergone further distortion to the extent that he is now suffering from a paranoid state which renders him mentally unfit to advise properly with counsel or to participate intelligently and reasonably in his own defence' (Torrey, 1984, p. 196). Controversy continues to surround this diagnosis. Those who think Pound ought to have stood trial and been punished, possibly with the death penalty, assert that the diagnosis was, if not entirely false, deliberately misleading. It would appear that Overholser took an immediate liking to Pound and influenced the rest of the psychiatric team to subscribe to his view of Pound's mental state. However, this does not in itself prove that the diagnosis was a false one. Indeed, the behavioural characteristics Pound increasingly manifested in his Rapallo years, together with the mental stress of his Pisan ordeal, suggest that 'suffering from a paranoid state', in so far as that term is well defined, may have been a reasonable conclusion. On the other hand, the assertion that this paranoid state rendered him mentally unfit for trial may have been made with the likely consequences of his trial and conviction in mind. The general assumption, not only by lawyers and doctors but also by Pound's friends and admirers of his poetry, seems to have been that, if he stood trial, his conviction for treason was a foregone conclusion, though Archibald MacLeish did hold the view that 'no jury on earth could think this kind of drivel would influence anybody ... Treason is a little too serious and a little too dignified a crime for a man who has made such an incredible ass of himself ...' (Carpenter, 1990, p. 699). However, a guilty verdict was by no means certain. While there is no doubt that Pound's 'drivel' did contain invective against American policy and politicians as

well as offensive racial prejudice, its treasonable status was con-
testable. Pound could have defended himself on the grounds that
there is 'no treason without a treasonable intention'. He believed
and went on maintaining that his broadcasts were designed, among
other things, to prevent American soldiers dying in a senseless
conflict and even to uphold the American constitution, views which
some, of course, cited as further evidence of his insanity. One could
equally argue that such motives were hardly ignoble, even if naively
realized. While a successful plea of insanity would undoubtedly spare
him the possibility of execution, it also prevented him from argu-
ing his case. There were also legal technicalities concerning witnesses
which might have prevented a guilty verdict.

Nevertheless, in February 1946, after his lawyer's defence plea had
been accepted, Pound was declared 'of unsound mind' and there-
fore unfit to stand trial for treason. The logic of this verdict was
both simple and terrible. As long as Pound was considered insane,
far from being released, he could be held indefinitely. Should he
ever be considered to have recovered his sanity, however, he could
be brought to trial and sentenced accordingly, if proved guilty.
With hindsight, the defence strategy may be judged to have been
erroneous. Although Pound was psychologically troubled and had
been for many years in a way that is possibly captured by the term
'paranoid state', it is unlikely that he would have been unable to
take part in his own defence. If MacLeish's estimate was an accur-
ate one, he may have been acquitted. If convicted, he would most
likely have served a fixed-term custodial sentence. As it was, he
remained incarcerated for much longer than many convicted war
criminals. In the unlikely event of a death sentence, Pound was
no coward and would have faced such an outcome in the spiritual
company of his model poet, François Villon, whose verse was real,
Pound once said, because he lived it. On the other hand, given
that it was the risk of such an outcome which probably motivated
the defence plea, Cornell and the doctors are vindicated by the
body of work Pound managed to accomplish in his St Elizabeth's
years.

For more than a year Pound was kept in a cell in Howard
Hall, the prison for the criminally insane within the grounds of
St Elizabeth's Hospital. This was a world of Judas-holes and strait-
jackets, lunatic noise and suppressed violence, which Pound re-
ferred to as the hell-hole. In this situation he was claustrophobic,
unable to concentrate, jumpy, but still as talkative as ever and in
need of visitors for audience. One of his earliest regular visitors
was Charles Olson, an aspiring writer already influenced by Pound
who was to go on to become one of the foremost postmodernist
poets of American literature. Olson was politically antipathetic to

Pound, but attracted to him by the admiration he felt for his poetry. Over a period of more than two years Olson gave Pound his company. Sometimes the meetings were painful to Olson, who was angered by Pound's smouldering anti-Semitism and fascist remarks. Olson kept a journal of his visits which were edited and published after his death. His notes reveal his ambivalent feelings towards Pound. At one moment he wonders 'how such a man came to the position he reached when he allowed himself to become the voice of Fascism', and later concludes that 'Hate blinds. It makes a man of exquisite sense a false instrument', but he never loses sight of Pound's charm: 'It is his charm which has betrayed him for he assumes it can manage people. In itself, it is lovely, young, his maintaining of youth a rare thing' (Seelye (ed.), 1975, pp. 19, 56, 87). For his part, Pound was fully aware how important Olson's visits were in those early days at St Elizabeth's and expressed the view that Olson had saved his life. In the end Olson could no longer take Pound's expressions of prejudice and drifted away, by which time Pound's circumstances were much improved and the St Elizabeth's version of the 'Ezuversity' was under way.

Pound's abrupt departure from Italy had left the domestic complications of his life unresolved, and they were to remain so throughout the St Elizabeth's years. His wife, Dorothy, followed Pound to America and lived in Washington for the duration of his stay. She became a kind of personal assistant to Pound, handling his correspondence and performing other chores on her daily visits. More importantly, she became the legal guardian of his finances. Ironically, Pound had begun to make reasonable amounts of money from his work for the first time in his life, but, being classified as insane, he was not allowed to have any control of it. Officially, his money was impounded by the courts and administered by Dorothy, who also had control of his published work. Olga Rudge lived and worked at her musical career in Siena, but had every intention of visiting Pound as soon as she was able. In the meantime she organized a petition in Rapallo protesting Pound's innocence and collated transcripts of some of his broadcasts into a publication designed to show that he was not a traitor. Mary married in 1946. Her husband, an Italian with a Russian aristocratic background, acceded to the title Prince Boris de Rachewiltz, though this had no estate or wealth attached to it. As if to compensate for the domestic uncertainties of her childhood, Mary's idea of a home was literally a castle and the couple lived in two. While at the first, Mary took in Pound's mother Isabel, who was very old and frail and still living on her own in Rapallo. Pound wrote a steady stream of letters to his mother from St Elizabeth's and expressed his appreciation at Mary's gesture. It was symptomatic of her desire to create an extended family centred on her home, an extension that would eventually not only include Pound and Dorothy but also accommodate his visitors, disciples and assorted hangers-on. Isabel herself died at this first castle without having managed to make her planned return to America to see her son. The second castle, the ruined Schloss Brunnenburg in the Italian Tyrol, was to be the young couple's permanent home and they gradually renovated it while taking in lodgers to supplement their income. They had their own children in the early years of their marriage and Pound was delighted to be a grandfather: the homespun 'Old Ez' persona that Pound liked to adopt now had some focus in reality. The care, courage and sense of purpose with which Mary accomplished all this shine through in her fine autobiographical account, *Discretions*.

Pound's circumstances at St Elizabeth's were vastly improved when he was moved out of the prison section of the hospital. He was eventually transferred to Chestnut Ward where he was privileged to have a small room of his own that was to be his home for the next ten years. Here, visiting hours were more relaxed and he began to entertain a wider range of callers. He was eventually given permission to spend his visiting hours on fine days in the grounds of the hospital, officially under Dorothy's supervision, and this gave him further scope for holding court to an ever larger stream of friends, interested celebrities, budding poets and academics. A visit to Pound became a kind of pilgrimage. Since many accounts focus entirely on the time Pound spent with his visitors during the one or two hours of freedom he had each day, it is worth remembering that he was for most of the time still incarcerated in a noisy, communal environment populated by highly disturbed and unstable individuals. Nevertheless, Pound's cistern began to overflow again and as well as hundreds of letters he wrote more or less the rest of his output as poet and translator in his St Elizabeth's years.

The Pisan Cantos were finally published in July 1948 and were immediately a cause for controversy, some critics being of the opinion that they should not have been published at all: during this period the publishers of at least one anthology considered removing Pound's poems from a new edition. However, a much greater storm arose when a newly constituted literary award, the Bollingen Prize, was given to Pound for *The Pisan Cantos* in 1949. The prize was decided upon by a panel of so-called Fellows of American Literature which included such prestigious poets as W.H. Auden, T.S. Eliot and Louise Bogan. Although there were some dissenters, Pound was voted for by a substantial majority of the panel. The award caused outrage in some quarters: the left-wing *Partisan*

Review attacked the judges, and the question concerning the relation between art and politics that has always been provoked by Pound's work was keenly debated. Another panel member, Karl Shapiro, who voted against Pound, stated that his politics did vitiate the poetry and lower its standards, while Allen Tate, the overall organizer of the prize, was of the opinion that the award was a victory for intellectual integrity. Public opinion, in so far as it was reflected in newspaper comment and correspondence, was fairly evenly divided and ultimately in favour of Pound's work being judged on literary merit. Another admirer of Pound's work, John Berryman, collected signatures for a letter in defence of the prize and by the time this was published in late 1949, the controversy was more or less over.

Robert Lowell was also a member of the Bollingen Prize panel. He had been fascinated by Pound for many years and had wanted to make contact with him before the war. Lowell was a conscientious objector who was eventually imprisoned for his refusal to do military service. Since Pound's political outpourings included a forceful anti-war argument, this may have been his initial attraction for Lowell. He began visiting Pound in St Elizabeth's in 1947, while he was poetry consultant at the Library of Congress in Washington. In his view *The Pisan Cantos* were Pound's 'most human and nuttiest work . . . those magnificent reveries of recollection . . . Pound let the heart break through his glass ribs' (Axelrod, 1978, p. 123). Lowell continued to see and correspond with Pound throughout the St Elizabeth's years, despite his own periodic bouts of mental illness, and also gave lectures on Pound and his madness. Lowell's own poetry shows the influence of Pound, in that the basis of so-called confessional poetry is one of recollection and nostalgia, letting the heart break through glass ribs, but also in the inclusion of politics and history in his poetic enterprise. Lowell took part in a memorial tribute to Pound in 1973 and recalled their last meeting in Rapallo when Pound, in the mental set of misgiving that marked his last years, told him, 'I started with a swelled head and end with swelled feet.' Lowell concluded, 'I can't see him as a bad man, except in ways we all are. I do see him as a generous man to other artists, and this in a way none of us will touch' (Hamilton, 1982, p. 438).

Lowell was only one of many genuine friends and admirers who visited Pound: Eliot, Williams, MacLeish and many others gave their support, keeping him company, defending him and trying to find some way of getting him released. But these supporters were eventually far outnumbered and practically displaced by the stream of acolytes and hangers-on who sat about the lawns of St Elizabeth's where Pound held court. Not all of these visitors were harmless, if rather parasitic, disciples. Some were fascist activists, anti-Semites and anti-communists who wished to elicit Pound's support for their views and activities. That he made such people welcome, and responded to their calls, is particularly disheartening: despite all that he had been through, he was not yet able or willing to see aspects of his beliefs for the bigotry they were. Both Olga Rudge and Mary de Rachewiltz managed to make visits to see Pound in the early 1950s. Mary's account reveals someone both bewildered and saddened by her father's behaviour, but also desperate to understand it: 'Why did he allow this farce to go on in his presence? Why didn't he teach these young people manners! And then I saw the caged panther, the boredom, the weariness of the man hit by history full blast . . .' (de Rachewiltz, 1971, p. 295).

Pound was now well into his sixties. Although his living conditions were more relaxed and he was able to entertain people in his own room outside of formal visiting hours, he was still confined for what at this stage seemed like the rest of his life. Being surrounded on the one hand by disturbed inmates and on the other by sycophants cannot have been either healthy or conducive to creative work, but in this situation Pound once more became characteristically and, as it turned out, terminally prolific. The first major work to be completed was the translation of the Confucian odes. This vast collection of Chinese songs, hymns and lyrics, reputedly selected by Confucius and set to music by him, was translated in 1949, though not published until 1954 under the title *The Classic Anthology as Defined by Confucius*. It is one of Pound's most accessible works, confirming his consummate ability to convey the sensibility of a culture distant in time and custom in a fresh and delightful way. His language is a synthesis of the colloquial and the poetically arch and archaic that has the flexibility to capture the varied mood of each ode's 'voice'. Take, for example, the slangy tone of this extract from a song of Cheng:

> Hep-Cat Chung, don't jump my wall
> nor strip my mulberry boughs,
> The boughs don't matter
> But my brothers' clatter!
> > Have a heart, Chung,
> > > it's awful.
> > > > (*CON*, p. 38)

This stands in contrast to the more formally rendered lyricism of:

> White the marsh flower that white grass bindeth,
> my love's afar,
> > I am alone . . .

> The overflow seeps north from the pool,
> rice hath its good therefrom;
> singing I sigh
> for a tall man far from home.
>
> (*CON*, p. 142)

The Chinese scholar Achilles Fang, who frequented St Elizabeth's at the time Pound was working on the odes, wrote an introduction to the published collection in which he claims that Pound chose a ballad metre for the translations. As can be seen even from the brief extracts above, this hardly captures the rhythmic and linear variety and flexible use of rhyme and half-rhyme that Pound brings to his language, which a strict use of ballad metre would exclude, though it does reflect the lyric intent of translations of what were essentially songs.

Pound himself would have been well aware of the great linguistic variety his translations had achieved over the years, since he had revisited all his previous translations for a collected edition published in 1953 while *The Classic Anthology* awaited publication. This perusal of his translations prompted his next major work, as he recalls in his *Paris Review* interview: 'The Trachiniae came from reading the Fenollosa Noh plays for the new edition, and from wanting to see what would happen to a Greek play, given that same medium ... The sight of Cathay in Greek, looking like poetry, stimulated cross-currents' (Dick (ed.), 1972, p. 94). Pound's version of Sophocles' tragedy was first published, as *The Women of Trachis*, in 1954 and given a BBC radio production the same year. As with his other major translations, there was debate about the accuracy and appropriateness of his language. If the formal properties of the Noh plays are reviewed in this translation, its language is more obviously influenced by Pound's work on the Confucius anthology, particularly in its colloquial quality, as in the following extract:

> Messenger: That fellow was lying, one time or the other, one
> heck of a messenger!
> Daysair: Put it on the line, what do you know?
> Get it out clearly.
> Messenger: All started when he had a letch for the girl ...
>
> (*WT*, p. 36)

This kind of language did not find favour with some Greek scholars and academics or more conservative reviewers: it was seen as inappropriate for a tragedy in which the wronged wife of a great hero causes his agonizing death unwittingly and kills herself. Counter-arguments to this view focus on the way in which Pound's translation is much more accessible and of its time than more stiltedly literal versions. More important to Pound's own work was his translation of what he called the key phrase of the play. When Herakles comes to understand the patterns of fate that have led to his impending death, he says to his son: 'Come at it that way, my boy, what SPLENDOUR, IT ALL COHERES' (ibid., p. 66). Splendour and coherence, their absence, the struggle for their achievement, are major concerns not only of the cantos to come, but also of Pound's increasingly troubled thoughts about his epic poem's overall struc- ture and value.

Within a year Pound had completed another batch of cantos, first published in Italy in 1955, entitled *Section: Rock-Drill de los cantares*, marking the ten years or so that Pound had now been institution- alized. Throughout that period there had been a more or less regular lobby for his release. Influential friends, like Eliot and Williams, as well as his daughter Mary and various visitors, disciples and asso- ciates, made overtures to both hospital and government authorities. This desire to see Pound released became both more focused and more widespread the longer he was in the asylum. It was generally agreed that he could not be allowed to stand trial and therefore the indictment would have to be quashed. The campaign to persuade the US government to do this met with sympathy from national and international newspapers. However, the process was to take another three years. Archibald MacLeish was the most active campaigner after the shock of his first visit to Pound brought home to him the reality of the poet's situation. MacLeish's record of persistent activ- ity on Pound's behalf is impressive, particularly his determined ef- forts to persuade the Attorney General to drop the treason charge. MacLeish also enlisted the help of Robert Frost, who would be more influential with a Republican administration: ultimately the decision to waive the charges against Pound was first signalled at a meeting between Frost and the Attorney General. In April 1958, at a hearing of the District Court of Washington, Pound had his indictment for treason dismissed, thirteen years after his first im- prisonment in Pisa, and he was officially handed over into the custody of his wife.

Pound had two months of freedom in America before his return to Italy. During that time he visited the studios of the Caedmon publishing and recording company to do some readings. He re- corded a complete *Hugh Selwyn Mauberley* plus several cantos, 'The Exile's Letter' from *Cathay* and miscellaneous shorter poems. The influence of Yeats noticed by Dorothy so many years previously in London is still very much in evidence in these recordings. Pound also visited his childhood home in Wyncote, Pennsylvania, and actually spent a night in the house at the invitation of the current occupants. Following a brief visit to see William Carlos Williams, his oldest living American friend, Pound left the United States to become an exile again.

'A blown husk that is finished'

Pound was in his early seventies when he arrived in Italy and had another fourteen years to live. If there was any expectation by his family, friends, acolytes or even Pound himself that his life after St Elizabeth's would see the glorious completion of his work or possibly some late flourish of new achievement, it was not to be fulfilled. After a life of frantic activity, enormous output and apparently self-confident assertiveness, Pound's final years were more or less barren and characterized by what may be best described as chronic misgiving. Clearly, anyone re-entering the outside world after thirteen years of incarceration is faced with enormous problems of adjustment, and the social and cultural distance between 1945 and 1958 was quite vast, but Pound's combination of restlessness and apathy, followed by an almost permanently silent state reflecting severe depression, seems to have confounded everyone close to him.

The depression that was to overtake Pound was not immediately apparent. At first there was the euphoria of release, the joy in freedom of movement and travel, the return to Italy. There was also the companionship of Marcella Spann, a woman some 40 years Pound's junior who had been a visitor to St Elizabeth's and become a more exclusive companion, secretary and literary collaborator in the editing of the poetry anthology *Confucius to Cummings*. Spann had accompanied Pound and his wife in America after his release and travelled with them to Italy. She was to live wherever Pound was for about a year and her presence seems to have given him inspiration and the strength to work on the last drafts and fragments of *The Cantos*: details of her physicality and his perception of it appear in the poems. However, her presence, as might be imagined, must also have created emotional tensions that would eventually need to be resolved.

Initially, Pound lived at Brunnenburg Castle with his daughter Mary and her family. Mary had prepared for this eventuality for years and even before her father arrived, the place had become a stopping-off point for Pound disciples in Europe. After Rapallo and St Elizabeth's it now became the third campus of the Ezuversity with a constant stream of visitors. Pound alternated days of hyperactivity with others of exhaustion. Despite Brunnenburg's status as a shrine, however, he was unable to settle there and moved to Rapallo with Dorothy and Marcella in March 1959. This unrealistic ménage did not last very long. Pound's daughter Mary is under-

standably elliptical on the matter, merely saying, 'But by the follow-
ing October he wrote: "I want to come back to Brunnenburg, to
die"' (de Rachewiltz, 1971, p. 306). In any case, Marcella Spann
returned to America. Whatever the exact truth, Pound's spirit seems
to have been decidedly broken at this stage. He refers to himself
in a range of communications as collapsed, tired and incapacit-
ated. In his memoir of Pound, Daniel Cory speculates, 'A source
of stimulation had been taken from him ... It was obvious that
some profound emotional ebb-tide was leaving him stranded and
incapable of sustained concentration' (Cory, 1968, p. 35). Pound
wrote virtually nothing in the remaining years of his life.

During this first year after his release Pound finalized the last
complete section of cantos: *Thrones de los cantares XCVI–CIX* was
published in late 1959. These had been composed in St Elizabeth's.
New work was more or less impossible due to a period of severe
depression, weight loss and illness requiring surgery. This resulted
in the domestic arrangement that was to provide Pound with
stability and comfort in his old age. In 1962 he moved back to
Sant'Ambrogio to live with Olga Rudge and spent his last years
with her both there and in Venice. With her support he was able
to travel quite extensively, make appearances at public occasions
and receive, albeit in nearly total silence, his many visitors. Nev-
ertheless, these final years were characterized not by stereotypical
serenity but by the depression and unease of which his elective
mutism was the most obvious symptom. The progression of Pound's
sense of his own failure both as a poet and, to some extent, as a
person is logged in a series of recorded and/or recollected inter-
views and encounters throughout the post-St Elizabeth's period
with such people as Donald Hall (in 1960), Grazia Livi (1963),
Daniel Cory (1966), Noel Stock and Allen Ginsberg (1967). In the
Hall interview, although there are indications of despair and dis-
appointment, Pound is still harbouring intentions of further work
on *The Cantos*:

> Interviewer: Are you more or less stuck?
> Pound: Okay, I am stuck. The question is, am I dead, as
> Messrs A.B.C. might wish? In case I conk out, this is provision-
> ally what I have to do: I must clarify obscurities; I must make
> clearer definite ideas or dissociations. I must find a verbal
> formula to combat the rise of brutality ...
> (Dick (ed.), 1972, p. 110)

Three years later Pound is much more overtly self-critical of his
words and his life in his interview with Livi. Particularly sad is
the sense of despair at realizations come too late: '... all my life I
believed I knew something. But then one strange day came when

I realized that I knew nothing . . . My intentions were good, but my means of realizing them were misguided . . . Knowledge came too late. Too late I arrived at the certainty that I know nothing' (Livi, 1979, pp. 245, 246). Cory's account of his association with Pound from the early 1930s culminates in the poet's much quoted pronouncements on the overall quality and structure of *The Cantos* as 'a botch . . . I picked out this and that thing that interested me, and then jumbled them into a bag. But that's not the way to make . . . a work of art' (Cory, 1968, p. 38). Stock, Pound's first comprehensive biographer, recalls that the very last words Pound spoke to him early in 1967 were, 'I have done enough evil' (Stock, 1989, p. 55). Later that year the leading Beat poet Allen Ginsberg elicited a number of disparaging remarks from Pound about his own work: 'my poems don't make sense . . . a lot of double talk . . . My writing. Stupid and ignorant all the way through'. When Ginsberg, himself a Jew, counters this with praise for Pound's poetry and sympathy for his economics, he responds: 'Any good I've done has been spoiled by bad intentions – the preoccupation with irrelevant and stupid things . . . But the worst mistake I made was that stupid, suburban prejudice of anti-Semitism' (Reck, 1968, p. 29). Some have seen this last remark as a trivialization of his vehement pronouncements on Rome Radio and elsewhere. However, it does accurately locate the roots of Pound's racism in his childhood experience of suburban paranoia about immigration, though it is hardly a penetrating self-analysis. Pound was at this stage probably incapable of such an analysis and his remarks from this period have the feel of escaped inner speech rather than calculated apologia or self-justification. With regard to the negative self-assessment of his contribution to poetry and his stature as a poet, it is fair to conclude that depression marred his celebrated ability to judge artistic achievement and that such remarks do not constitute a reasoned evaluation of his own work.

In 1969 the first edition of the final section of cantos was published as *Drafts and Fragments of Cantos CX–CXVII*. Subsequent editions have added various fragments, creating an appropriate uncertainty about where the poem actually finishes. The latest edition, quoted from in this book, now ends with a fragment dated August 1966 which asserts its place in the ultimate canto and is effectively a dedication of the whole work to Olga Rudge:

> That her acts
> Olga's acts
> of beauty
> be remembered.

(*CAN*, p. 818)

And it was with Olga, true partner and protector of his final years, that Pound made a last visit to America in 1969. There he was welcomed as a guest of honour at Hamilton College in very different circumstances from his previous visit and also went to see the rediscovered manuscript of Eliot's *The Waste Land* in New York. A projected trip to his birthplace in Hailey, Idaho, went unaccomplished, however: the distance involved, the energy required, prevented him from fulfilling his wish to 'see again' his 'half savage country'.

Pound died in Venice on 1 November 1972, the day after his 87th birthday. He was buried in the city's island cemetery of San Michele.

2   *Literary, cultural and political background*

Pound lived most of his life in the twentieth century: his involvement in the miraculous decades of early modernism, his reaction to the First World War, his identification of economics as the key to both the causes and solutions of global conflicts, his support for fascism and the consequences of that support in the aftermath of the Second World War, all confirm that he was very much a person of his time. Yet, like most major contributors to what might be called archetypal or even, somewhat paradoxically, 'canonical' modernism, Pound was born and spent his formative years in the nineteenth century, and more significantly in that era whose special historical position gave it its name: the *fin de siècle*. This 'mere fact' of birth meant that Pound was brought up in a moral and cultural context in which those factors contributing to the development of modernism already pertained. Furthermore, these factors were likely to be 'more intensely experienced, more emotionally fraught, more weighted with symbolic and historical meaning, because we invest them with the metaphors of death and rebirth that we project onto the final decades of a century' (Showalter, 1991, p. 2). With hindsight, we can see that much of Pound's life and work were preoccupied with responding to such factors and finding radical solutions to their critical interpretation. In addition, the 'endism' he grew up in can now be seen in transitional terms, possibly helping to explain why, like many early modernists, he was also concerned to perceive, preserve and disseminate valued traditions.

The philosophical, social, economic, political and artistic factors pertaining to the advent of modernism were both complex and interdependent. Here, I select only a few for comment as they relate to Pound's own developing sense of the modern. First, the notion of a religious, and specifically Christian, world view had been undermined by Darwin's theories of evolution. This not only provided a context for humanist and secular explanations, but also led to a resurgence in alternative belief systems such as occultism and theosophy. Pound's detestation of conventional religion is modern in its rejection, while his equally sincere pantheism is an example of his own brand of modernism's interest in lost but live traditions. Another factor in the development of a modernist consciousness is the growth in size and importance of cities. The mass movement of people from the countryside into urban centres resulting from the industrial revolution had created a working underclass that both shamed and threatened middle-class sensibility. The representation of this dislocation had, of course, been a major theme of great nineteenth-century realist fiction, but with modernism the dissonance of urban and industrial life becomes, as it were, the medium of representation as well as its subject. At the same time, though, the city in art represents a reaction to the purely pastoral in nature with its shallow celebrations. This aspect of Victorian and Georgian verse, probably exaggerated by Pound, was a target of his modernist agenda. Against this, the city is a centre of cultural vibrancy and exciting ideas where it is possible to 'make it new'. A third significant factor was Freud's discovery of the unconscious and the development of psychoanalysis as an alternative means of explaining human behaviour. The central role of sex in psychoanalytic theory reinforced the already lively debate about sexuality and gender going on in the late nineteenth century. The development of a more active feminist movement had begun to challenge the norms of patriarchy. To the extent that these norms applied in art and literature, modernism was a reaction to and an attempt to implement this challenge. Pound had a range of interests related to this area, such as the nature of the subjective, the psychology of creativity, the role of sex in art and the exploration of the self through literary masks.

Many aspects of Pound's life, lifestyle and political and moral choices constitute attempts to respond to these and other factors in the pre-modernist context. He also concerned himself with these issues directly in terms of his theoretical, critical and other prose writings as well as addressing them in the content of his poetry. Furthermore, the formal, technical and conceptual development of his poetry traces his attempts to shape a response in literature. The following sections provide an outline of some of the main literary, cultural and political theories and ideas which concerned Pound and the contexts in which he explored them as part of the modernist enterprise.

Wearing masks ["Masks"]

In an article of 1914, later reprinted as part of his tribute to Gaudier-Brzeska, Pound recalled his early search for a poetic identity and authentic self-expression: 'I began this search for the real in a book called *Personae*, casting off, as it were, complete masks of the self in each poem. I continued in a long series of translations, which were but more elaborate masks' (*GB*, p. 85). This much-quoted

81

statement needs careful scrutiny since its implications are theoretically complex. It also provides a useful starting point for discussion of the early influences on Pound's poetry.

The concept of the literary persona derives ultimately from the fact that in the Classical period Roman actors wore clay masks. The Latin word for such a mask, 'persona', was itself derived from a verb meaning 'to sound through', since the masks had very large mouth holes through which the actor's voice could resound. Even in Classical times the word also came to mean 'character' and eventually 'person' in the modern English sense. Pound cleverly plays on both meanings: a series of personae, masks, need to be tried on and discarded in the search for the 'real' person, in the attempt to let the authentic self sound through. His statement is one of some personal psychological insight, but can also be seen as representative of a modernist reaction to the self-assuredness of a prior age which some of the factors outlined above had undermined: there is no confidence that the search for the 'real' poetic self is finite. Furthermore, the wearing of masks, regardless of the psychologically complex motive for doing so, has the effect of depersonalizing the poet: the persona hides the person, though, as Pound implies, it may reveal aspects of the unmasked self. Again, this can be seen as a contribution to a larger poetics of impersonality that is quintessentially modernist.

The wearing of masks, the adoption of a persona, results in a poetic first person whose relationship to the poet needs to be explored in the context of more general theory concerning the relationship between author and textual 'I'. Relatively straightforward syntactic theory as well as more sophisticated theories of discourse caution us against a simplistic equation between textual 'I' and an assumed writer. For example, in the sentence 'I went to the bank yesterday', the 'I' is a pronominal marker signalling a subject relation within a larger grammatical construct. The fact that the writer of this sentence, namely myself, did not go to the bank yesterday does not invalidate it as a textual entity. On the other hand, given certain mundane facts about my life, the sentence could have, probably has been, and most likely will be used to report a factual event pertaining to me. In the sentence 'Zeus impregnated me with Helen of Troy', the 'me' is a pronominal marker signalling the object relation within a larger grammatical construct. Again, the fact that the writer of this sentence, namely myself, is not Leda does not invalidate it as a textual entity. However, it is clear that the sentence has never and could never pertain to me.

In many ways poems involving sentences of the second kind, where referential impossibilities make obvious the adoption of a persona, are much easier to handle. Take, for example, the opening lines of Browning's poem 'My Last Duchess':

> That's my last Duchess painted on the wall,
> Looking as if she were alive. I call
> That piece a wonder, now: Fra Pandolf's hands
> Worked busily a day, and there she stands.

Contextual factors such as time, place and setting, even without simply checked facts about Browning's life, all confirm that the poet is dramatizing the voice of another character. The only problem for the reader might be with 'local' detail such as 'Fra Pandolf' or other obscure references. Another poem of Browning's, 'Two in Campagna', illustrates the kind of first person text where the adoption of a persona is, to say the least, much less likely:

> I wonder do you feel today
>   As I have felt, since, hand in hand,
> We sat down on the grass, to stray
>   In spirit better through the land,
> This morn of Rome and May?

We might even be tempted, after checking a few biographical details, to say that this is Browning speaking to his wife Elizabeth Barrett after their retreat to Italy where they spent their married life. This would be too simplistic. It may be that factual events between Browning and his wife triggered off the poem, but it is also highly unlikely that it was written at the scene of those events or that its final polished form is in any way a transcript of first thoughts, feelings or speech events. Nevertheless, it would be perfectly reasonable to read such a poem as an autobiographically situated text. On the other hand, we may choose to read it as a text like my sentence 'I went to the bank yesterday', a linguistic construct with no basis in actual events at the time of writing which is rendered ambiguous by the referential possibilities that exist between author and textual 'I'. To pursue the theatrical analogy, this is the half-mask, the mask that reveals part, usually the lower half, of the actor's face. In practical terms, poems where the textual 'I' is neither an identified persona nor readily attributable to an implied other usually allow for, if not invite, an autobiographically situated reading, though this may be rejected in favour of purely intratextual interpretation.

Trying to relate the above theory to Pound's statement, we can suggest that his 'complete masks' are those personae which, like Browning's Duke of Ferrara, are remote in time and setting and allow for a dramatic presentation of a voice that is not his own. Specifically, we can cite the monologues derived from the medieval world of the troubadours. To what extent these are 'masks of the self' and how that concept is given form in such poems will be addressed in the detailed reading of one of these poems in the critical survey below. At the time of Pound's statement the great cycles of translation were yet to come and he was referring to a range of poems from the Provençal, Italian and Latin, as well as the Anglo-Saxon 'The Seafarer'. These 'more elaborate masks' prefigure the great cycles *Cathay* and *Propertius* which in their more or less systematic paralleling of contemporary issues may be seen as masks of history through which the present resounds. The poetic equivalent of the half-mask, where referential equivalences between poet and textual 'I' are plausible, may be discerned in some of the early poems, but it is in *Hugh Selwyn Mauberley* that the ambiguity between poet and persona reaches its single most complex realization. In the early work too there are also poems which more or less invite an autobiographically situated reading. With *The Cantos* we enter the domain of multiple personae, where the masks and half-masks of self and history parade with the poet across a temporal stage whose dimensions are both millennial and contemporaneous.

The adoption of a persona results in a poetic first person that speaks in situated monologue. To the extent that such monologues project a character in the immediacy of a particular situation's actions and events, they are dramatic. Such dramatic monologues are by definition commonplace in plays, archetypally in Shakespeare from the drunken porter's speech in *Macbeth* to Hamlet's soliloquies. However, it was Browning's use of self-contained dramatic monologues, as in 'My Last Duchess' above, that was the major influence on Pound's appropriation of the device. Pound was clearly impressed by Browning's virtuosity in language and form, but he also admired the psychological depth Browning achieved in presenting insights about human nature. In an early poetic tribute written in 'Browningese' Pound calls Browning 'ye old mesmerizer', 'Old Hippety-Hop o' the accents', 'crafty dissector' and 'clear sight's elector' (*CSP*, p. 13) in obvious reference to these qualities. Apart from the use of a persona in a specific setting, there are no other absolute requirements for a dramatic monologue, though Browning often implies another, silent, character who is the actual recipient of the speech. Pound also uses this device, most obviously in 'Sestina: Altaforte' where the addressee is Bertran de Born's minstrel, Papiols. However, Pound more often allows the voice of his personae to speak, as it were, directly to the reader. Nor is the element of irony so often found in Browning's poems, whereby the speaker's self-regard or self-deceit are revealed, a major feature of Pound's monologues. These factors, together with the choice of personae, contribute to the general sense that Pound's monologues are more lyrical and mood-sensitive than dramatic in quality and reflect the realization of his concept of 'masks of the self'.

The search for the self, for the real beneath the mask, was also a search for 'sincere self-expression', a bid to find the right language. In retrospect, it may seem incongruous that Pound should have adopted the language he did to speak through the masks of troubadours, Villon and the rest. As well as showing the influence of Browning's dramatic monologues, Pound's language is a fusion of Rossetti, Swinburne, the early Yeats and the poets of *fin de siècle* aestheticism, a language first forged in his own *Hilda's Book*. However, in an introductory essay to his earliest translations of Cavalcanti, written in 1910, he makes a statement which not only provides a rationale for the language of those translations but may also be applied to the language of his early poems: '. . . the poetry of a far-off time or place requires a translation not only of word and of spirit, but of "accompaniment", that is, that the modern audience must in some measure be made aware of the mental content of the older audience, and of what these others drew from certain fashions of thought and speech' (*TEP*, p. 17). So much of his early work is either a translation of cultures far off in time or place or a projection of the sensibilities of such cultures onto his own experience that the presence of 'accompaniment', in the form of artificially archaic and distancing language, is understandable. Years later, looking back on the language of those early translations and by implication on the language of his early work in general, Pound was disparaging about both its quality and its origins: 'I was obfuscated by the Victorian language . . . the crust of dead English, the sediment present in my own available vocabulary . . . I hadn't in 1910 made a language . . .' (*LE*, pp. 193, 194). As with other pronouncements about his own work, these remarks need not be taken as definitive. Insofar as he was referring to such characteristics as artificial syntactic inversions, archaic vocabulary and the over-use of the obsolete second person singular form, Pound was right to discern that his poetic language needed a modernizing overhaul in favour of 'the living tongue' and the greater clarity and precision that imagism would promote. However, it is also clear that, despite the protestations and embarrassed disclaimers, in 1910 Pound had begun to make a language in which the above features would retain a place because his acute poetic ear had discerned that in his hands such a language could be used to stunning effect. If poetry is the art of making strange, then the use of the archaic in the middle of the twentieth century has a defamiliarizing power. At the same time such usage invokes a tradition and

ates the authority associated with that tradition to its own
.

Making it new: the 'isms' of modernism

The period of early modernism was one of innovation across the
whole spectrum of the arts. The sense that everything new in art,
music and literature happened or started to happen within the
first two decades of this century may be strictly inaccurate, but
serves as an index of the revolutionary nature of that period. Nor
was the buzz of innovation confined to the arts: scientific, tech-
nological and political revolutions provided the contexts and in
some cases the means for artistic invention. The interplay, if not
the interdependence, of these various strands of innovation is an
important aspect of modernism and, as we have seen in the bio-
graphical outline, Pound was both inclined and well situated to
exploit this interplay. His interest in and knowledge of music as
reviewer, composer and theoretician undoubtedly influenced both
the theory and practice of his poetry. Though he was not a prac-
titioner of the visual arts, despite his Brancusi-inspired attempts
at sculpture, his work as an art critic and his involvement with
avant-garde painters and sculptors again informed his thinking
about poetic composition.

Before looking in more detail at the specific 'isms' associated with
Pound and their relation to the modernist enterprise as a whole,
it is worth trying to characterize in more general terms the nature
of early modernism. Most commentators, including Lunn (1985)
and Butler (1994) whose discussions inform the following outline,
start from the premise that modernism is a reaction to realism or
the mimetic quality in art. Lunn comments: 'modernists escape from
the timeworn attempt, given new scientific pretensions in natural-
ist aesthetics, to make of art a transparent mere "reflection" or
"representation" of what is alleged to be "outer" reality' (p. 35).
This is perhaps most obvious in the visual arts. For example, the
techniques of artists exhibited under the collective title of Post-
Impressionists in the London exhibitions of 1910 and 1912, such
as pointillism, fauvism, primitivism and cubism, are not only anti-
mimetic but demonstrate ways of dissecting and distorting 'reality'
to create new perspectives and multiple viewpoints within a two-
dimensional framework. Parallels in music can be made. If we
accept that mainstream western classical music's harmonic system
and concepts of well-formed melodic line were seen as the 'natural'
form of musical expression, then various challenges to its version
of musical reality may be discerned in the early modernist period.
The most extreme rejection of this reality was Schoenberg's atonal

system of composition. The two main features of this theoretically and musicologically complex system are its abandonment of tonality, i.e. the use of the conventional keys of western diatonic music, and the rejection of melodic repetition as a compositional device. The effect of these features is to create a music that seems to be in a constant state of change, this musical disorientation reflecting a wider aesthetic and psychological abstraction that has affinities with the work of painters like Kandinsky who entitled some of his major canvases 'Compositions'. There were as many routes to modernism in music as there were in the visual arts and I mention only two more here. Firstly, there was the rediscovery, aided by the new technologies, of nationalist folk musics. For example, the great Hungarian composer Bartók collected hundreds of samples of Hungarian, Romanian, Bulgarian and Moroccan folk music on piano rolls in a pioneering feat of musical anthropology. Elements of these 'primitive' musics, such as polytonality (the use of different keys at the same time) and rhythmic instability, were incorporated into his compositions as a way of challenging conventional musical reality. Parallels may be drawn here with the influence of African art on the paintings of Matisse and Picasso and the sculpture of Gaudier-Brzeska. Secondly, another source of musical innovation became apparent with the emergence from America of ragtime and jazz. The harmonic, rhythmic and melodic difference of these new musics was not lost on so-called classical composers, such as Debussy and Ravel, who incorporated rag and jazz elements into their work. This is probably best seen as a form of intertextuality, an allusion, if not to specific compositions, to alternative modes of music-making.

The reaction to prevalent realism, then, however that was seen to manifest itself in different art forms, together with the contexts and conditions outlined earlier in this section, gave rise to the range of avant-garde activities and practices underpinned by theoretical stances and manifestos which constituted early modernism. Although particular art forms developed techniques and theories appropriate to the demands of their own media, theory was subject to integration and practice was replicated across the arts. Furthermore, these phenomena may be seen as part of a syndrome of attitudes and sensibilities with a much wider philosophical, social and psychological provenance. Modernism was also developmental in two fundamental senses. Firstly, across all the arts innovation was provisional and ongoing, with some of its manifestations being very short-lived and others subject to refinement or radical change. Secondly, many modernist innovations were refinements or adaptations of previous practice and many early modernist innovators were keen to invoke one or more traditions within which they saw themselves as working. Schoenberg himself saw his atonal method of composition as an evolution from late Romantic harmonic and melodic freedoms rather than the revolution it appeared to others. However, this is not to underplay the startling quality that so much early modernist art achieved, nor to deny the excitement of revisiting the period through its products and contemporary accounts of their making.

Having looked, however sketchily, at the provenance of modernism with examples from music and the visual arts, it is now possible to attempt a synthesis of its characteristic features with specific reference to literature. I do this in the form of a list, with the proviso that such lists can never be exhaustive or capture the entire complexity involved.

1. Anti-mimetic: loss of interest in providing a textually complete and accountable version of some external reality. This does not automatically imply inconsistency of detail or 'factual' inaccuracy, but rather that any presentation will be more or less dependent on perspectives and possible distortions integral to the text.

2. Textual relativity: a blanket term for the effects of multiple perspectives or personae, the paradoxes of narrator unreliability, the ambiguities of a poetic voice that is hedged by uncertainty.

3. Simultaneity: attempts in what is essentially a linear medium 'to exemplify the Bergsonian view of the present as composed of all the past that is present to consciousness . . .' (Butler, 1994, p. 158). The illusion of simultaneity in literary texts is achieved by various means such as: verbal collage by analogy with visual art, linguistic montage following the example of cinema, thematic juxtaposition approximating to the fugue in music.

4. Fragmentation: following from the above, the potential for a sense of dislocation or discontinuity is high. The unit of fragmentation is a key factor here in textual quality: fragmentation at the level of syntactic units, which are relatively small, gives a quite different texture and makes different demands on the reader from fragmentation by larger units of discourse, narrative voices or personae.

5. Subjectivity: fragmentation of perspective and loss of individual identity result in what is more or less an obsession with the subjective. Paradoxically, this subjectivity is explored according to a poetics of impersonality and authorial invisibility.

6. Exposure of psychological and/or cognitive processes: the subjective point of view, focalized perceptions or self-attention of character and persona are presented directly, using techniques of interior monologue or stream of consciousness.

7. Urban context: the city, both as historical entity and site of large-scale human cohabitation, provides the favoured setting for

the representation of individual anomie. But that setting is full of tension, since it not only offers examples of human squalor, but juxtaposes them with the cultural splendour and liveliness of the city scene.

8. Textual self-consciousness: the artificial nature of the literary enterprise is exposed to the reader either by overt discussion or by display of artistic contrivance, something which may be seen as a necessary consequence of the dismissal of realism. The teasing or playful preoccupation with the formal properties of the text underlines the view that literature is 'only' a linguistic construct.

While the above list provides an albeit partial summary of the concerns and characteristics of modernist literature, there is no suggestion that all the features listed are necessary or even sufficient 'ingredients' for all modernist texts. Emphases of concern, technique and approach will vary across genres, from one writer to another and, within one writer's work, from text to text according to the developmental factors noted above. However, it is a fair claim to say that the culminating classic texts of early modernism, Joyce's *Ulysses* and Eliot's *The Waste Land*, exemplify the above characteristics in full. As someone intimately involved in the evolution of those two works, Pound was well placed to appreciate their status as the quintessence of modernist literature to date. That he did so at the time, without hindsight and with some of his most unreserved literary praise, is an acknowledged tribute to his critical judgement. It also reflects his own preoccupation with how to create a new form of epic poem written on modernist principles. This is not to suggest that the items on my list were articulated as the agenda of any one early modernist, not even Pound himself: they are definitely the product of hindsight. On the other hand, Pound addresses most of those concerns one way or another in his theoretical and other prose writings and exemplifies their realization developmentally in his earlier poetry and at large in *The Cantos*. The process by which he did so was also evolutionary rather than revolutionary.

Pound's contribution to the 'isms' of modernism is primarily associated with imagism and vorticism. In the biographical section above I briefly outlined the context in which these ideologies emerged before and during the First World War in London, 'a city without much avant-garde tradition and inhibited by a conservative opposition with a proven reputation for outrage' (Butler, 1994, p. 209). Here I want to trace the development of those ideologies in a more detailed interpretative and evaluative way.

From the outset, imagism was articulated more or less exclusively in relation to poetry, and it is evidence of some narrowness of interest or vision that its potential within a larger framework of what might now be termed 'literary stylistics' is ignored. For example, the qualities of excellent prose are regularly evoked as a kind of gold standard for the language of poetry, but what might constitute a fictional imagism is not explored. The language in which imagism is described remains fairly impressionistic and rarely provides real analytical insight into the language of the image itself. These theoretical shortcomings may have been due to the fact that the appropriate tools of modern linguistic analysis were not yet developed. More likely they stemmed from an apparent lack of clarity about the status of imagist pronouncements by those who wrote them, especially Pound himself. Philosophical definition and technical advice are mixed in a fairly undifferentiated way, although Pound's later, better defined and more clearly elaborated terminology does achieve greater explanatory adequacy as literary theory.

First published in 1913, F.S. Flint's 'tenets of the Imagiste faith', as Pound later referred to them, are the mandatory starting point for any discussion of imagism, repeated as they were with commandment-like regularity and authority. Their programmatic impulse is offset by irritatingly vague expression, though this may be appropriate to their status as doctrine rather than theory.

The first tenet, 'Direct treatment of the "thing", whether subjective or objective' (*GB*, p. 83), is the most problematical: all its major terms require definition and elaboration. It is unclear what 'direct treatment' actually means and how it might manifest itself poetically. Perhaps the most helpful interpretation is one that assumes reference to the linguistic realizations of direct and indirect discourse. 'Direct treatment' would then imply a preference for statements as the main clause type, realized mainly in 'simple' tense forms lacking the periphrasis of indirect speech. Further, patterns of direct discourse, if used in their free form, i.e. without superordinate clauses of saying and thinking, result in an elliptical, paratactic syntax that is characteristic of, among other things, realizations of interior monologue. Under this interpretation, 'direct treatment' is a rather vague label for linguistic processes that are more likely to produce the harder, clearer poetic line that Pound extolled, the antidote to 'Georgian verbiage', and also reflect mental processes of a more dynamic, less ruminative kind. Things, then, which, as the quotation marks suggest, are not simply concrete items, are to be textually realized directly, i.e. in the manner elaborated above, but this textual realization may be either subjective or objective, a distinction which itself needs further debate.

In a paper published two years later, in 1915, Pound himself attempted an elaboration of the imagist doctrine which included a discussion of subjective and objective images. The paper shows him labouring to say something coherent and intelligible about imagism

and not entirely succeeding. The passage on subjective and object-
ive images is typical in this respect:

> The Image can be of two sorts. It can arise within the mind.
> It is then 'subjective'. External causes play upon the mind, per-
> haps; if so, they are drawn into the mind, fused, transmitted, and
> emerge in an Image unlike themselves. Secondly, the Image can
> be objective. Emotion seizing up some external scene or action
> carries it intact to the mind; and that vortex purges it of all save
> the essential or dominant or dramatic qualities, and it emerges
> like the external original.
>
> (*SP*, p. 344)

This elaboration is unsatisfactory because, having made the claim
for two distinctive kinds of image, it fails to differentiate convinc-
ingly between them. The claim that subjective images have some
psychologically self-contained origin is immediately countered by
the idea that they are the results of processing external stimuli.
Despite his use of vorticist terminology, Pound's account of the
origin of objective images is more or less the same: the processing
of external stimuli. The actual difference claimed is that subjective
images transform external stimuli while objective images somehow,
despite radical purging, preserve their semblance. Without his appeal
to 'external causes' subjective images could have been generally
labelled 'inner' and related to dreams, visions, involuntary memor-
ies and associations, all of which may involve distortions or trans-
formations. The dichotomous notion of objective images might
just then have been preserved under the label 'external'. This might
have made more coherent a formulation which, in my view, is
more fundamentally unsatisfactory.

It is rather surprising that Pound felt the need to invoke the
concept of objective images at all, since the philosophical basis for
imagism and its parallels in the visual arts was one of subjectivity
and intuitiveness. Furthermore, in 1914 he had identified imagism
as the 'sort of poetry where painting or sculpture seems as if it
were "just coming over into speech"' (*GB*, p. 82). The impact of
the Post-Impressionist exhibitions, his first encounters with cubist
and abstract art, the sculpture of Gaudier-Brzeska and Epstein,
the geometric forms of Wyndham Lewis, all raised his awareness
of the importance of colour, line, form and composition in art in
contrast to its more representational functions. In particular, the
theories of the abstract expressionist painter Kandinsky seem to
have made an important contribution to his thinking: 'The image
is the poet's pigment; with that in mind you can go ahead and
apply Kandinsky, you can transpose his chapter on the language of
form and colour and apply it to the writing of verse' (*GB*, p. 86).

'Heiratic Head of Ezra Pound' by Henri Gaudier-Brzeska, 1914.

The chapter in question was the seventh of the treatise *Concerning the Spiritual in Art*, first published in German in 1910. In this Kandinsky discusses the relation between form and colour in artistic composition, often using metaphors from music, such as the idea that 'Colour itself offers contrapuntal possibilities' (Kandinsky, 1947, p. 51). In his thinking about objective images Pound may have been particularly influenced by Kandinsky's statement:

> The effects we receive, which often appear chaotic, consist of three elements: the action of the colour of the object, of its form, and of the object *per se*, independent of either colour or form. At this point the individuality of the artist asserts itself and makes use of these three elements.'
>
> (Kandinsky, 1947, p. 50)

The poet's image, like the artist's pigment, captures the essential in an object by means of its verbal colour and form.

The idea of poetry as verbal painting or textual sculpture was a powerful one that Pound promoted as an antidote to the 'stale creampuffs' that he adjudged much of his early work to be. That representational forms can be processed with varying degrees of abstraction, idealization, distortion or formal reconstitution clearly influenced his formulation of subjective images which parallels the subjectivity and intuitive nature of abstract painting and its counterpart in Schoenberg's music. Objective images, as we have seen in relation to Kandinsky's statement above, cannot be taken as the poetic equivalent of a purely representational art. Although they relate to an external object, they present its essential aspects in verbal colour and form. This suggests that the dichotomy between subjective and objective images is far from clear-cut and that all images are, in Poundian terms, ultimately subjective. Images arise within the mind. Their causes, whether remote and possibly hidden from consciousness or more immediate and available to scrutiny, are variously transformed with different degrees of abstraction, idealization and formal representation on what might be called a continuum of subjectivity.

If the first tenet of imagism is theoretically challenging and open to speculative interpretation, the other two are tame in comparison, though not entirely without ambiguity. The second, 'To use absolutely no word that does not contribute to the presentation', is, as subsequent glosses and commentaries make clear, not just a stricture about economy of expression, but a coded acknowledgement of a particular tradition. In the 1915 paper Pound notes: 'Our second contention was that poetry should be at least as well written as good prose' (*SP*, p. 345). This idea, usually attributed, at least in embryo, to Ford Madox Ford, was frequently invoked by Pound in a wide range of contexts: theoretical papers, reviews, letters. It is more often than not accompanied by a reference to 'a school of prose writers, and of verse writers for that matter, whose forerunner was Stendhal and whose founder was Flaubert. The followers of Flaubert deal in exact presentation' (*LE*, p. 399). The use of the term 'presentation' is not coincidental here: it is short-hand for the stylistic realization of a literary tradition that Pound identified with the great French prose writers and wished to embody in imagist poetry. Beyond its literal meaning he has invested the word with a set of connotations that he clearly takes as read. They are best conveyed negatively along the lines of: 'presentation' implies an absence or lack of interest in explanation, discursive comment-ary, superfluous verbal ornamentation, empty rhetoric, elaborate moral reflections and any other characteristics identified by Pound as typical of 'bad' writing.

The third tenet, 'As regarding rhythm: to compose in sequence of the musical phrase, not in sequence of the metronome', is not particularly well expressed: 'in sequence of' is more or less mean-ingless in relation to metronomes, if not musical phrases. However, it is clear enough in intent: the rhythmic organization of imagist poetry must be grounded in musicality rather than the mechanis-tic requirements of metrical conformity. Primarily, Pound saw this as a move away from the stranglehold, as he saw it, that the iambic pentameter had on English verse: 'to break the pentameter, that was the first heave', as he said in retrospect from Pisa (*CAN*, p. 532). But it also reflects his commitment to the lyric tradition of the troubadours and his belief in 'a sort of poetry where music, sheer melody, seems as if it were just bursting into speech' (*GB*, p. 82). For someone with such a gifted poetic ear and a rigorous apprenticeship in metrical forms, 'composing in sequence of the musical phrase' was a liberation. However, in the 1915 paper there is some sense of disillusion with the more widespread results of applying tenet number three. Pound notes that

> it is of course much easier to make something which looks like 'verse' by reason of having a given number of syllables, or even of accents, per line, than ... to invent a music or rhythm-structure. Hence the prevalence of 'regular' metric. Hence also bad *vers libre*.

> (*SP*, p. 346)

By 1917 he was quoting Eliot's dictum that 'No *vers* is *libre* for the man who wants to do a good job' (*LE*, p. 12), confirming his own view that the 'right' musical phrase is arrived at according to the needs of each specific poetic impulse.

Perversely perhaps, the three tenets make no attempt to define the concept of 'image' as it is understood by the new school. However, in the opening paragraph of 'A Few Don'ts', the collection of practical tips for prospective imagists which immediately follows Flint's statement of principles, Pound provides his now famous definition: 'An "Image" is that which presents an intellectual and emotional complex in an instant of time' (*LE*, p. 4). He derives his use of the term 'complex' from recent psychology: its meaning here approximates to a cluster of ideas or feelings. As far as poetry is concerned, then, an image is a verbal manifestation of a conceptual cluster that is both intellectual, which we can gloss as 'open to rational scrutiny', and emotional, i.e. 'appealing to emotions, attitudes or otherwise possibly irrational feelings'.

This definition, even with my interpretative gloss specific to poetry, remains impressionistic, partly because the ideas involved are both complicated and relatively untried. One route to a sounder theoretical framework may be afforded by applying certain concepts from linguistics. In particular, the theories of Ferdinand de Saussure, the founder of modern linguistic science, may prove helpful in clarifying Pound's imagist conceptions. De Saussure delivered a series of seminal lectures on the nature of the linguistic sign on three occasions at his university in Geneva in the early 1900s. Saussure's students made a compilation of his lectures which were published posthumously in 1916. What follows here are suggestions as to how his theories might be applied to imagist principles.

In very simple terms Saussure's theory may be outlined as follows: the linguistic sign consists of two aspects, a signifier (some concrete verbal manifestation) and a signified (some meaning or concept, though not any particular referent). For example, the sound pattern and its written form indicated by the word 'tree' is a signifier whose signified is the concept 'tree'. Together signifier and signified constitute a linguistic sign which may be used to refer to particular trees in specific contexts. Roland Barthes, working in a broadly post-Saussurean framework, characterizes the sign as follows: 'What is a sign? It is a piece of an image, a fragment of something murmured which I can recognize: without recognition there is no sign' (Blonsky (ed.), 1985, p. 54). Inverting Barthes's formulation, we can say that an image is a series or cluster of signs. Pound's notion of the image is readily explicable in these terms as just such a series or cluster of linguistic signs. Given its presentational, instantaneous and generally charged nature, we could even call it the poetic sign. The signifiers of Pound's image or poetic sign are thus recognizable verbal manifestations whose signifieds constitute an intellectual and emotional complex.

Perhaps it is worth trying to arrive at some more elegant characterization of Pound's notions of 'intellectual' and 'emotional' than my earlier glosses. Two further ideas from linguistic theory may be useful in this respect, those of 'denotation' and 'connotation'. Denotation is that aspect of meaning that relies on relatively stable semantic components or features. For example, the denotation of the word 'girl' may be seen to rely on such basic features as: +human, +female, −adult. Change one of these basic semantic components and a different denotation is implied: e.g. +human, +male, −adult gives 'boy'. It is possible, however tentatively, to draw a parallel between denotation and what Pound might mean by the intellectual aspect of his 'complex'. Connotation is that aspect of meaning that relies on variable features related to context, association, figuration and the like which override, complicate or render ambiguous the basic denotation. For example, a connotation of the word 'girl', when used to refer to a mature woman, may be a sexist put-down. At the very least, the semantic feature −adult is misapplied for whatever purpose. Connotations, as this simple example shows, are more likely to apply in the expression of emotions, attitudes and feelings. Again, it is possible to suggest that the emotional aspect of Pound's 'complex' has some affinity with connotation. Integrating the various linguistic strands outlined here, we can arrive at an elaboration of Pound's definition of the image along the following lines: an image is a series of signs whose signifiers present a complex of denotational and connotational signifieds in an instant of time. This definition has at least the possibility of being applied analytically to samples of text with a view to gaining some insight into how images achieve their effects in a poetic context.

There was some advantage to not having a particularly well-defined concept of the image. When events overtook the doctrines they were associated with and ideological positions shifted, it was possible to refine key concepts accordingly or redefine them under another name. Early in 1914 Pound attended a lecture by T.E. Hulme in which he advocated the progress of art towards more abstract forms and complex geometrical designs reflecting the machine age. As Butler notes, Hulme was 'on the move from a Bergsonian subjectivism towards the classical defence of an anti-humanist geometrical art against ego-centred Romanticism' (Butler, 1994, p. 227). This shift was part of a larger reaction to the success of Post-Impressionism which was rapidly being seen as the dominant artistic movement after the second of its famous pre-war exhibitions. Gaudier-Brzeska, Epstein, Lewis and other artists were exemplifying Hulme's philosophy in their sculpture and painting. In particular, Lewis's work in the period leading up to the first number of *Blast* took on an angular but strikingly dynamic quality. What was not immediately obvious to Pound was how this work might relate to poetry. There was some correlation in terms of the imagist doctrine of hard clear lines and direct presentation of the thing, but these concepts at least gave the impression that the image was essentially self-contained. However, his artist friends were capturing movement and energy in plastic forms and any new manifesto would have to accommodate this development. At a talk in the Rebel Art Centre, later elaborated in print, Pound managed to extend his concept of the image as follows:

> The image is not an idea. It is a radiant node or cluster; it is what I can, and must perforce, call a VORTEX, from which, and through which, and into which, ideas are constantly rushing.
>
> (*GB*, p. 92)

This redefinition of image as vortex is, I think, both practically unconvincing and theoretically mistaken. If an image is a radiant node or cluster which presents an intellectual and emotional complex in an instant of time, then its redefinition as a whirlpool of ever-changing ideas is hardly credible. In practical terms it is difficult to imagine, for example, a short imagist poem which would meet the requirements of a vortex. Theoretically, the equation of image and vortex discards the possibility of interesting distinctions and insights. The concept of the vortex as conduit for ideas and dynamic centre of simultaneity and change is a brilliant one into which the ebb and flow of images could have been explicitly incorporated, if the distinction between image and vortex had been preserved. As a spokesperson for the more radical avant-garde, Pound clearly felt some responsibility 'to establish a language of criticism which was not connected with Post-Impressionist standards and preoccupations' (Tillyard, 1988, p. 240). This may have pressured him into the vorticist formulation of 1914, which failed, as Tillyard notes, along with Lewis's own pronouncements, to establish a critically distinctive and coherent basis for vorticism as a lasting artistic movement.

Vorticism did not survive the First World War. Some of those most closely associated with it were killed and the frenetic energy of the *Blast* era was dissipated. Furthermore, once Pound had re-exiled himself in 1920 after twelve years in London, he was no longer within the immediate influence of Wyndham Lewis nor under any sense of obligation to theorize on behalf of a particular movement. These may have been the factors which allowed him to arrive at a clearer and more coherent statement of his poetics. The basis for this was already there in his 1914 essay on vorticism which, as I noted above, identified poetry closest to music as 'lyric' and associated imagism with painting or sculpture in words. Over the next ten years or so these categories are refined. Beginning with a review of poems by Marianne Moore and Mina Loy in 1918, they were supplemented by a third into a much more convincing presentation, though at that stage the term 'imagism' was still retained. The definitive version of this appears in his 1927 essay, 'How to Read', later to be recycled in *The ABC of Reading* in 1934. Given that great literature is 'charged' language, Pound outlines the ways in which language can be so charged under coinages derived from classical Greek: melopoeia, phanopoeia, logopoeia. The following discussion quotes from, paraphrases and comments on his formulation in 'How to Read' (*LE*, p. 25).

Melopoeia is poetic language charged 'with some musical property' which affects, but goes beyond, its 'plain meaning'. The term not only relates to the idea of lyric poetry but also conceptualizes the practice advocated in the third tenet of imagism. Pound notes that melopoeia can be appreciated by someone who doesn't know the language the poem is in, but that it is more or less impossible to translate. These comments may be seen as a rationale for, or defence of, the direct quotation of different languages as an integral feature of his poetry. Moreover, the concept of melopoeia provides some justification for the belief, strongly held by Pound and Eliot, that poetry can be 'understood' outside of its conceptual meaning. Again, this offers some defence for the poem which has no 'plain meaning', which is semantically difficult or allusively obscure. It also has implications for reading strategies with regard to such poems.

Phanopoeia is characterized as the 'casting of images upon the visual imagination' and is, according to Pound, eminently translatable. Clearly, this formulation is his latest definition of imagism itself and is retained in various versions in *The ABC of Reading*. In an interesting passage in which he refers to phanopoeia as 'the throwing of an image on the mind's retina', Pound goes on to criticize those who took the image to be stationary and asserts, 'If you can't think of imagism or phanopoeia as including the moving image, you will have to make a really needless division of fixed image and praxis or action' (*ABC*, p. 52). This is in effect a reinforcement of the idea of image as vortex. Words like 'fixed' and 'stationary' are used pejoratively here to reject the idea of an image as a self-contained 'complex in an instant of time' and align it with the more dynamic vortex. The concept of the vortex as a locus of rapid change is, as I argued above, enhanced rather than challenged by the idea of images moving through it in a series of juxtapositions. Such a formulation satisfies the requirement for a sense of dynamism to be associated with the image without creating a dichotomy between stasis and praxis which Pound warns against. The use of a new label, phanopoeia, with its evocative new definitions, does nothing to resolve the theoretical problems created by the equation of image and vortex. As Pound himself comments, the use of the term phanopoeia is designed to distract from ideas associated with imagism in its pre-vorticist characterization. As such it is the least satisfactory aspect of his redrawn poetics.

Logopoeia is given the fancifully vague definition 'the dance of the intellect among words', but a fairly detailed gloss on this indicates that it refers to an emphasis on the interplay of meanings within language according to style, context, association, idiom and collocation. The effects of logopoeia, such as irony or ambiguity, cannot be translated directly, but linguistic equivalences or parallels may be found in different languages. Unlike phanopoeia, the term logopoeia is not merely the renaming of a previously theorized category: Pound's elaboration provides fresh insight into his poetic thinking. The idea can be traced to an essay written in 1917 where his tripartite division of poetic aspects is already rudimentarily in place. Referring to the French poet Laforgue as a 'verbalist', Pound goes on to say: 'Bad verbalism is rhetoric, or the use of cliché unconsciously, or a mere playing with phrases. But there is good verbalism, distinct from lyricism or imagism, and in this Laforgue is a master' (*LE*, p. 283). Here, bad verbalism is defined: within a year he had begun to define good verbalism as logopoeia.

Despite the problems which I recognize in the failure to distinguish between phanopoeia and vorticism, Pound's elaboration of his 'three kinds of poetry', relating to musical, visual and verbal qualities, is an important statement of his own poetic standpoint as well as a major contribution to the poetics of modernism. The terms have become a critical shorthand for elements of poetic endeavour and achievement rather than kinds of poetry as such. All three may be, and often are, present in a poem, though one may dominate or distinguish itself. The distinctions Pound has outlined help us to arrive at insights of the kind we understand when he says: 'it is mainly for the sake of the melopoeia that one investigates troubadour poetry' (*ABC*, p. 52).

The Chinese connection: language, poetry, philosophy

Pound's exposure to things Chinese, rather than an unlikely occurrence brought about by chance, was more or less inevitable in the climate of fashionable orientalism in pre-war London. The nineteenth century had been a period of western imperialist intervention and exploitation in China, culminating in the brutal suppression of the Boxer rebellion in 1900. This quasi-colonialism had also resulted in the appropriation of Chinese cultural artifacts and their imitations in the museums and salons of the west. Oriental iconography and its literary interpretation were part of a consciously acknowledged chinoiserie. But there was also genuine and more scholarly sinology, exemplified by Giles's *History of Chinese Literature* of 1901. This text was introduced to Pound by Allen Upward, traveller, colonial diplomat and anthropologist, whose work, judging by the numerous references to it in Pound's letters, clearly impressed him. Upward was also responsible for introducing Pound to Confucius and Mencius in French translations. As well there were Upward's 'Chinese' poems, entitled 'Scented Leaves from a Chinese Jar', which Pound promoted in *Poetry* in 1913. In a letter to Harriet Monroe regarding their publication he notes: 'Upward is a very interesting chap. He says, by the way, that the Chinese stuff is not a paraphrase, but that he made it up out of his head, using a certain amount of Chinese reminiscence. I think we should insert a note to that effect, as the one in the current number is misleading' (*SL*, p. 23). Extracts from Upward's work also appeared in the first imagist anthology, *Des Imagistes*, in 1914. His poems are short prose-like anecdotes of which the following is a typical example:

> The sailor boy who leant over the side of the Junk of Many Pearls, and combed the green tresses of the sea with his ivory fingers, believing that he heard the voice of a mermaid, cast his body down between the waves.
>
> (Jones (ed.), 1972, p. 98)

There was always a danger that such stuff would be read as a translation from the Chinese, something Pound was clearly aware of in his letter to Monroe. In this climate of orientalism it would have been easy for Pound to produce his own superior brand of chinoiserie. However, in an essay of 1914 he had already grasped the literary significance of Chinese verse: 'Undoubtedly pure colour is to be found in Chinese poetry, when we begin to know enough about it; indeed, a shadow of this perfection is already at hand in translations' (*LE*, p. 218). The translations referred to here may be those of Giles's history, but they are more likely to be the interlinears and cribs of the Fenollosa manuscripts that Pound was by this time working on.

The immediate creative result of being made literary executor of Ernest Fenollosa's remaining papers was the translation of a Japanese Noh play and the making of *Cathay*. However, Pound must have edited the draft of Fenollosa's essay on 'The Chinese Written Character as a Medium for Poetry' fairly quickly too, since a letter of 1915 notes that 'Fenollosa has left a most enlightening essay on the written character (a whole basis of aesthetic, in reality), but the adamantine stupidity of all magazine editors delays its appearance' (*SL*, p. 61). Subsequent letters over the next three or four years reiterate Pound's high esteem for the essay and express his frustration at its rejection by various magazine editors. It was eventually published in four instalments in *The Little Review* in 1919, but did not appear in separate book form until 1936.

The main impulse of Fenollosa's essay, as the title implies, is to present a linguistic and aesthetic theory regarding the ideograms of written Chinese, and it was these aspects which so excited Pound's attention. However, given that the essay must have been written at or shortly after the height of western imperialist aggression towards China noted above, it is worth mentioning that Fenollosa opens with an indictment of the way in which England and America have mistreated the Chinese. He goes on to say that 'The duty that faces us is not to batter down their forts or to exploit their markets, but to study and to come to sympathise with their humanity and their generous aspirations' (FEN, p. 8). Part of this cultural and racial disaffection, he claims, manifests itself in western trivialization of Chinese poetry, something he wishes to rectify on account of his own enthusiasm for the poems he has studied. This possibly unpopular humanitarian opening may have contributed to the resistance Pound encountered when trying to get the essay published.

Fenollosa's aesthetic is based on a number of convictions about Chinese ideograms which may be summarized as follows: 1. they are essentially pictorial; 2. they present natural processes as verbal action; 3. their formal configurations reside in natural metaphors; 4. these qualities make written Chinese an ideal medium for poetry. It is generally acknowledged that Fenollosa's treatment is based on partial understanding and somewhat flawed linguistic analysis. Although Chinese writing is ultimately derived from a pictographic system in which pictorial elements represent ideas, most Chinese characters actually represent words or parts of words and contain a phonetic indicator. While some characters remain ideogramic or even pictographic in quality, Chinese writing cannot be interpreted as a series of pictures. Modern linguistic theory has demonstrated how important metaphor is to semantic development and Chinese is probably no more metaphoric in this sense than any other language, though its writing may well capture its metaphoric evolution in more transparent ways than an alphabetic system. Fenollosa more or less disposes of the noun as conceptual indicator and grammatical category in his desire to promote the verb as 'the primary fact of nature' within a 'new chapter in the philosophy of language' (FEN, pp. 23–5) and the Chinese language as an archetypally verbal medium for poetry. Some of this discussion now seems no more than quaint. Moreover, the illustrative plates at the end of the essay, whose characters are glossed by Pound from Fenollosa's notes, contain more nouns than any other grammatical category: there are relatively few verbs. To a great extent none of these points matters very much with regard to the impact of the essay on Pound's thinking about poetic method. In broad terms Fenollosa laid emphasis on the verbal representation of things and actions: this was far more important than any insights about the Chinese language which might subsequently prove to be unsupported by 'the lexicographers'. He was much more impressed by the idea that Fenollosa's essay seemed to present an alternative version of imagism in which ideogram and image are virtually interchangeable. As such, it suggested a method which, Pound later asserted, Fenollosa would have gone on to elaborate if he had not died: the ideogramic method.

There are two aspects to Pound's conception of the ideogram. In so far as a single Chinese ideogram may consist of a number of graphic elements that constitute a poetic sign, it is readily identifiable with his conception of the image as the realization of an instantaneous intellectual and emotional complex. Pound is able to identify the ideogram as an ideal medium for 'direct treatment of the thing'. However, in terms of the image as vortex, into which ideas are constantly rushing, the ideogram is inadequate in my view. As with the term phanopoeia, the adoption of the ideogram does nothing to resolve the theoretical problems created by the equation of image and vortex. Again, the possibility of a wholly coherent aesthetic is allowed to drift away. However, if the idea of ideogram as vortex is untenable, the notion of an ideogramic method which embodies vorticist principles is an attractive alternative. Much later Pound was to arrive at a formulation which at least implicitly makes this connection between ideogramic method and vortex: 'The ideogramic method consists of presenting one facet and then another until at some point one gets off the dead and desensitized surface of the reader's mind, onto a part that will register' (*GK*, p. 51). Substitute idea for facet in this statement and the ideogramic method can be seen to be a way of promoting the constant rush of ideas through the vortex. If the equation of image and/or ideogram with vortex is discarded, then a general principle of ideogramic method/vorticism becomes possible along the following lines: the ideogramic method promotes the constant flow of ideas, images, ideograms, facets through an appropriate vortex. This formulation has the flexibility to accommodate the issues raised by Pound in his footnote to the paper on vorticism in his Gaudier-Brzeska memoir (*GB*, p. 94). For example, a long vorticist poem would be possible with an appropriate vortex or series of vortices. Also, poems without a vortex, not employing the ideogramic method, are equally possible: this would allow for imagist poems that were distinct from vorticism. It can also account for Pound's idea of a musical concert organized according to the ideogramic method, where each disparate piece is an ideogram in the vortex of the concert. However, it has to be remembered that the general principle outlined above is not Pound's. It is clear that he did, at least on some occasions, equate ideogram with vortex. For example, at the end of a chapter in *Guide to Kulchur* he notes: 'These disjunct paragraphs belong together . . . are parts of one ideogram . . .' (*GK*, p. 75).

The French translation which provided the starting point for Pound's interest in Confucius consisted of the so-called Four Books: the *Analects* or sayings of Confucius, the *Book of Mencius*, the *Ta Hio* or Great Learning, the *Chung Yung* or Doctrine of the Mean. He translated the *Ta Hio* from the French in 1928, but was eventually to make original translations of three of the books, excluding the *Mencius*, under the titles: *The Analects*, *The Great Digest*, *The Unwobbling Pivot*. Pound's interest in Confucian philosophy, as opposed to the inspiration he took from Chinese poetry and its language, appears superficially to be a much less predictable example of his eclecticism. In order to understand its appeal, we need to review some of the main aspects of Confucius's life and belief system in relation to what we know of Pound's predilections.

Confucius was primarily a teacher: a belief in the power of education is central to his philosophy. This aspect had great appeal to the pedagogue in Pound, whose railings against contemporary educational practice are predicated upon a belief that 'good' education is vital to the literary, cultural and moral health of the state. It is no accident that the beautifully written Confucian Canto 13 is mostly an account of a lesson taught in a manner that Pound could imagine himself emulating. The fact that Confucius went into self-imposed exile at one stage in his life may also have attracted Pound, who used exile as an oppositional strategy in what now looks like part of a wider modernist practice.

As far as Confucian philosophy itself is concerned, a major attraction is its sense of tradition, a need to revive the best of the old to create the new. The 'make it new' agenda of Poundian modernism presupposes an 'it' that is worth renovating, a live tradition, unlike more radical movements such as futurism which seemed to want to reject the past in its entirety. Another fundamental aspect is the idea of cultivation of the self as the basis of social order: for Confucius, the personal is unfailingly political. Pound had already conceptualized something along these lines with regard to literature in an essay of 1912: 'Having discovered his own virtue the artist will be more likely to discern and allow for a peculiar *virtu* in others. The erection of the microcosmos consists in discriminating these other powers and in holding them in orderly arrangement about one's own' (*SP*, p. 29). Pound's will to literary order can be seen to sit happily with Confucian notions of a wider social arrangement whose structure is familial, hierarchical and predominantly male. Such ethics are encapsulated in the Confucian canto:

> If a man have not order within him
> He cannot spread order about him;
> And if a man have not order within him
> His family will not act with due order;
>   And if the prince have not order within him
> He can not put order in his dominions.

(CAN, p. 59)

A further explanation for the appeal of Confucianism is that Pound saw it as an antidote to religion, and more specifically Christianity, whose establishment forms he had come to loathe. For example, in a letter from 1916 he asserts: 'Religion is the root of all evil, or damn near all' (*SL*, p. 98). Confucianism was seen as something very different from 'Xtian superstition'. Its emphasis on the cultivation of a responsible self rather than unquestioning obedience to a set of commandments was particularly attractive to Pound's notion of the serious artist. In the postwar years this rejection of Christianity, though not of Christ himself whom Pound saw as a kind of victim of his own religion, was expressed as part of a larger distrust of fundamentalist belief. In a letter from 1922 he deplores the fact that such things as alternative views of creation are banned from school textbooks in the US and asserts: 'I consider the Writings of Confucius and Ovid's Metamorphoses the only safe guides in religion ... I refuse to accept ANY monotheistic taboos whatsoever ... I consider the Metamorphoses a sacred book, and the Hebrew scriptures the record of a barbarian tribe, full of evil' (ibid., p. 182). The juxtaposition of Confucius and Ovid's *Metamorphoses* as a basis for religious belief is probably best seen as an application of the ideogramic method whereby Confucian humanism is illuminated by the reality of the old gods and their interaction with the human race. In a letter from 1939, Pound gave a more reasoned view of the relationship between Confucianism and Christianity: 'Kung and Mencius do not satisfy *all* the real belief of Europe. But all valid Christian ethics is in accord with them.' Valid Christian ethics were the basic teachings of Christ which had been obscured by 'the jungle of propaganda and fads that has overgrown Xtn theology' (ibid., p. 327).

The philosophy of Confucius as presented here might be char-

acterized as 'authoritarian humanism'. As such it is wholly un-
derstandable why it appealed to Pound. Central is the individual
person's inner development, the will to order and goodness, the
assertion of rightness that results in political stability. Such a philo-
sophy has no place for a deterministic, judgemental or punitive
deity. This humanism does, however, tend to focus on the indi-
vidual who is both privileged and obligated by position or birth,
the holder of office, the head of the family, the noble, the royal. As
such it implies both hierarchy and patriarchy. Pound was recept-
ive. In the literary domain, Confucianism could endorse the will
to excellence, the identification and promotion of the best, the
role of the poet in guarding society's linguistic, cultural and moral
health. In political terms, it could be made to endorse a presumedly
benevolent authoritarian leadership in an ordered world. Writing
in 1952, when Pound was still in St Elizabeth's and the events of
the Second World War were still very recent, Kathleen Raine re-
viewed his translation of the Confucian Analects. Her conclusion
begins: 'However wrong-headedly and illogically Pound may have
sought to identify this organic philosophy of social order with Mus-
solini's regime, we should not therefore overlook the fact that the
main elements of that philosophy are a penetrating and accurate
criticism of the worst heresies of our society' (Homberger (ed.), 1972,
p. 414). She goes on to say that by his translations Pound has cre-
ated yet another context of ideas within which contemporary poetry
can operate. Whether that is true of much contemporary poetry
today is doubtful, but it remains a valid assessment of Pound's Con-
fucian involvement: as long as his poetry, and in particular *The
Cantos*, is being read, he will remain the inventor of Confucius for
many of his readers.

Economic politics

Pound's poetry cannot be divorced from his politics. As we have
already seen, even his early work embodies attitudes towards and
comments on issues that are political in the broadest sense. This
political involvement becomes increasingly overt and more focused
as his poetry develops and is most obvious in *The Cantos*. The
political element in literature in English has a long tradition. The
popular political ballads and broadsheets of previous centuries
may be seen as forerunners of the performance poetry of today
which evinces a high level of political comment. In the Romantic
period, the poetry of Shelley provided a scathing attack on the in-
justices of his day. Auden's overtly political poetry of the 1930s was
part of a wider politically motivated literature. More recently, such
poetries as those written from a regional, post-colonial or feminist

perspective exemplify this tradition. Setting aside nationalistic propaganda of the kind dismissed by Pound in *Homage to Sextus Propertius*, what almost all of this poetry has in common is its oppositional nature. In very broad terms the main targets for such opposition are systems of power and privilege and their representatives which are seen to perpetuate a range of inequalities and injustices. Given the variously aristocratic, establishment, institutional or financially advantaged nature of these systems, it is inevitable that much politically motivated poetry in English has been associated with a liberal and Protestant tradition. In contemporary terms, this translates into an association with the left of the political spectrum, even if it does not express a specific allegiance. In this respect the oppositional element in Pound's poetry is a comparative novelty in being associated with authoritarian political structures on the right of the political spectrum and expressing specific allegiances to representatives of a reactionary political system. The fact that a version of this system was responsible for one of the most horrendous acts of genocide in human history makes an objective discussion of the political, social and economic factors relevant to Pound's life and work difficult, if not impossible. Some commentators on the poetry avoid these issues altogether: the number of lines one needs to overlook is very small. Others attack the poetry and the poet with a vehemence that is as unpleasant as anything Pound himself used in his most regretted moments. In this section I attempt to provide a contextual overview of these issues so that the poetry can be discussed without avoiding its political element and the poet assessed without resort to mere defamation.

In 1918, as he himself later recalled, Pound began an investigation into the causes of war in order to oppose them. This understandable reaction to the mass slaughter of the First World War, which was to have dire consequences for him personally, was not uncommon. However, it is his misgivings four years earlier about more global consequences that impress us with their prophetic concern:

> I wonder if England will spend the next ten years in internal squabble *after* Germany is beaten. It's all very well to see the troops flocking from the four corners of Empire . . . But, but, but, civilization, after the battle is over and everybody begins to call each other thieves and liars *inside* the Empire.

(*SL*, p. 46)

Despite the carefree image of the 1920s, 'internal squabble' was a fairly accurate prediction as far as England was concerned: the promises of victory went unfulfilled, at least for the lower classes, and there was widespread poverty linked to a low-wage economy and high unemployment. Disaffection was epitomized by the miners' strike of 1926 which for a few days became a more general strike, though still only involving one-fifth of the working population. In the aftermath of the Russian revolution there was some paranoia about revolutionary communism in Britain, something which Winston Churchill did nothing to dispel in his capacity as editor of the *British Gazette*, a rabidly anti-socialist government paper. Although armoured troops were used to move goods and other oppressive measures were taken, other factors ensured that the strike would never be the prelude to revolution. Most important was the fact that Britain was a long-standing democracy with a history of imperial success and a secure middle class who supported the government's stance. Pound's remark about the internal breakdown of empire was also apposite. In the 1920s the Empire became a Commonwealth: self-government and eventually independence were already the goals of many colonized states. However, the threat to civilization created by the First World War and its aftermath ultimately came from the defeated power.

Internal squabble was not exclusive to Britain: poverty, unemployment, strikes and paranoia about communism were also part of the German postwar scene. However, conditions in Germany were exacerbated by defeat and the penalties imposed by the Treaty of Versailles: loss of European territory, renunciation of overseas colonies, massive and unrealistic financial reparation. The consequent collapse of the German economy with its now legendary inflation and unprecedented levels of unemployment created a kind of national depression, a condition receptive to the promises of a strong leader. In Italy the situation was different, but led to similarly receptive conditions. Italy was one of the 'victorious' allies in the First World War, but saw itself as benefiting much less than the dominant democracies. The country was still predominantly a traditional rural economy with high levels of poverty and illiteracy: its involvement in the war had not radically changed these conditions. It had no empire to soak up its unemployed masses. Italy and Germany, then, 'victor and conquered together', in their different ways presented social and economic conditions that led their peoples to be susceptible to strongly nationalistic and authoritarian solutions to their problems and, specifically, to that political system now known as fascism.

The concept of fascism is so inextricably associated with the horrors perpetrated by Nazi Germany that it is virtually impossible to make a neutral appraisal of its political ideology. However, it is essential to the understanding of Pound's work, both as literary theorist and political activist as well as poet, to characterize the ideology which he supported for a substantial and creatively important period of his life. The following list is a fairly crude identification of elements:

1. A vision of the future based on the glories of an evoked, possibly mythical, past, for example, the glory that was Rome, Teutonic myth.

2. A will to power: essentially a male impulse in which action, military and/or violent if necessary, is idealized and conquest seen as vital.

3. Against democracy: the bourgeois liberal values promoted by democracy are seen as destructive of tradition: the masses should be engaged by an authoritarian hierarchy selected on the basis of leadership qualities rather than elected by popular vote.

4. The idea of nationhood in which the state is paramount: this idea embraces notions of race-identity and racial superiority.

5. The supreme leader: the nation invests its authority in a charismatic individual who exercises absolute power.

These elements suggest that in a number of ways fascist ideology had more in common with canonical literary modernism than other political systems such as liberal democracy or communism, though it is worth noting that some of the above elements apply to early radical socialist stances, for example the use of violence to oppose middle-class liberal values. Certainly, Pound's brand of modernism was a kind of radical traditionalism in which the new is based on the glories of an evoked past. The concept of the will was very important in Pound's thinking: we have already seen how he related ideas of literary order to Confucian philosophy. Its economic importance was highlighted in the *ABC of Economics* in 1933:

> The science of economics will not get very far until it grants the existence of will as a component; i.e. will toward order, will toward 'justice' or fairness, desire for civilization, amenities included.

(*SP*, p. 210)

This makes clear that Pound's concept of will to order is very different from the fascist will to power. Even so, the masculine impulse of these ideas may be related to male dominance within canonical modernism. Democracy was not attractive to Pound's sense of tradition and elitist distrust of mass culture. Where literature was concerned, this stance was developed relatively early in respect of anything he saw as mediocre. In a letter to Amy Lowell in 1917 he makes his position very clear: 'You tried to stampede me into accepting as my artistic equals various people whom it would have been rank hypocrisy for me to accept in any such manner. There is no democracy in the arts' (*SL*, p. 122). In the political arena his views were confirmed by the fact that democratic states perpetrated the destruction of civilization that he saw in the First World War. *Hugh Selwyn Mauberley* is particularly bitter about these issues.

Nationalism figures relatively little in Pound's thinking or his poetry. There is little doubt that he cared deeply for his American nationality, though it was the care of an exile who felt let down by his country's treatment. His vehement opposition to the Second World War stemmed from his sense of the tragedy of America fighting Italy. In this his loyalties were divided, though his outrage was directed towards his native land because he believed the cause was sited there. Pound's expressed anti-Semitism and views on racial difference probably originated in his early background, but they became much more focused with the development of his economic theories. His disenchantment with democracy was partly based on the view that it did not throw up strong, dynamic leaders. In this respect an ideology which centred on a charismatic leader must have been attractive to him. Pound may have been temperamentally inclined to hero-worship: perhaps there is an element of this in his support for Joyce, Eliot, Gaudier-Brzeska and the rest. In any case, it would seem that Mussolini was the political hero Pound had been waiting for.

The term 'fascist' is so indelibly linked to the perpetrators of Nazi atrocities that it is impossible in any considered way to label someone a fascist without associating them with genocide. This is the reasoning behind the approach taken by those who point out that Pound was never a member of any fascist party or organization and therefore never a fascist. Their reasoning may well be sound: the ideological elements of fascism outlined above suggest that a benevolent or even politically unthreatening fascist regime is a contradiction. However, we can only make these judgements with the analysis of hindsight and in the knowledge of historical events. If Mussolini had not invaded Ethiopia or formed the Berlin–Rome Axis or entered the Second World War in 1940, effectively becoming the satellite of Nazi Germany, the possibility of a tolerable fascism might have been a reality. By the time these regrettable events did take place, Pound was too emotionally involved with Mussolini and too committed to his cause to turn away. We may not be able to condone this misplaced loyalty to what turned out to be an ugly regime, but we can probably understand it. In this respect, it is worth noting that in 1926, when Pound was already an Italian resident, but still investigating the merits of Marx and Lenin in relation to his economic theories, Winston Churchill, fresh from his defeat of the miners, paid an official visit to Mussolini. As one of Churchill's biographers notes, the 'interview with the Duce went smoothly. He professed himself "charmed" by Mussolini's "gentle and simple bearing" and declared that in Italy he would have been a fascist' (Brendon, 1984, p. 106).

Pound's economic arguments all essentially contribute to what might be called 'a critique of capitalism'. The main motivation for this critique was, as we have seen, a profound sense of the futile waste of the First World War resulting in a desire to investigate the causes of war with a view to eradicating them. A literary motive for the critique was his disenchantment with the level of support given to artistic excellence by the so-called liberal democracies which he saw as another example of the way capitalism created unemployment. Both these motivations can be seen to have a personal dimension to them in terms of his loss of valued friends in the war and his failure to make a living from strictly literary activity. Pound's work for the socialist publication *The New Age* brought him into contact with the economic theories of Clifford Douglas whose ideas were serialized in the magazine and published in 1920 as *Economic Democracy*. It is worth trying to outline the main points of Douglas's economic theory in order to understand why they were particularly attractive to Pound:

1. The capitalist system does not pay its workers enough to buy the goods they have helped to manufacture.

2. Underpaid workers and excessive profits are accompanied by the manipulation of money by bankers, landlords and stockbrokers for further profit.

3. Unpurchasable goods promote aggressive export strategies: the competition for markets leads to war.

4. The solution to these problems is for the state to give people greater purchasing power by putting more money into circulation.

5. Various measures could be used to effect this including a government-controlled financial dividend to all citizens known as Social Credit.

Much of Douglas's monetary theory was a valid critique of purely *laissez-faire* capitalist policy. However, the practicalities of his interventionist programme were underdeveloped and at odds with mainstream economic theory. His ideas were never put into practice in any sustained or large-scale way. One of Pound's problems in promoting Douglas's ideas was to find examples of good monetary practice that he could claim were Douglasite. Such examples were invariably small-scale, localized and outside the scope of the modern industrialized world, such as the practice of the Monte dei Paschi bank in seventeenth-century Siena.

Apart from the attraction of Social Credit as a monetary solution to the world's economic problems, Pound was particularly interested in two aspects of Douglas's analysis: the manipulation of money for profit and its relation to the causes of war. It is possible to 'deconstruct' Pound's later obsession with money in terms of his grandfather's silver mines and lost fortunes, his father's post at the US Mint and, of course, his polysemic surname. More easily relatable, perhaps, is the fact that he experienced relying on allowances from his family and subsidies from his wife and for much of his life made relatively little from his writing, especially his poetry. At the same time he was generous by nature, spending what money he had as well as his time supporting others in their literary endeavours. Whatever the origins and reasons for his preoccupation with money, it had a deep effect on his later poetry to the extent that one might legitimately characterize *The Cantos* as, to parody his own formulation, 'a poem including the history of money' or even just 'a poem including money'. One aspect of this preoccupation was his concern for lawful ways of making money. He tends to idealize productive activities such as farming and crafts which result in direct recompense: included in this realm is the 'making' of literature. He more or less ignores what we would call mass production or service industries. More important for both his politics and his poetry are those forms of money-making which meet with his unflagging hatred: usury and arms sales.

Usury is Pound's general term for the manipulation of money for profit. In his poetry he favours the Latin 'usura' from which usury derives. In Latin there is a declension of meaning in the term from 'use' to 'use of money' to 'interest' to 'inordinate interest'. In England the medieval concept of excessive interest became the modern offence of charging an illegal rate of interest. In Koranic law the term still means 'any interest', the charging of which is officially forbidden. In strict Hebraic law usury is a sin. Pound, however, has his own working definition: 'Usury, a charge for the use of purchasing power, levied without regard to production, sometimes without regard even to the possibilities of production' (*SP*, p. 325). This definition is informed by Douglasite economic analysis and reflects Pound's preference for productive means of making money. Interestingly, it also renders usurious virtually all modern money market and international loan finance activity, while casting doubt on mortgage and credit facilities. Elsewhere, in relation to the Monte dei Paschi bank, for example, Pound makes clear that he does not class as usury the charging of minimal, cost-covering interest. However, in his detailed study of Pound's economic politics Nicholls suggests that 'In contrast to his earlier view of legitimate entrepreneurial gain, Pound's later writings mount a moral case against the very principle of monetary profit' (Nicholls, 1984, p. 152). This analysis seems to be confirmed by one of Pound's last public statements in 1972. In the foreword to Cookson's edition of his *Selected Prose* he notes: 're USURY: I was out of focus, taking a symptom

111

for a cause. The cause is AVARICE' (*SP*, p. 6). In acknowledging his own error Pound neatly characterized 'the politics of greed' several years before the phrase became commonplace.

To use Poundian terms of reference, the will to profit is a negation of the will to order, especially when that profit is made selling mass destruction. The arms trade and the economics of the military–industrial complex were aspects of the 'case' that Pound spent much time investigating and opposing. Although his interest stemmed from the horrors of the First World War, it extended to other arenas of conflict and imperial exploitation both historical and contemporary. The sale of weapons and the need to sell weapons, often to opposing sides by the same dealer and even by one side to another in the same conflict, incensed Pound. He identified the manufacture and sale of arms as a major cause of war and not merely its consequence. He railed against research foundations, particularly in the United States, which spent vast amounts of money investigating the effects of war while ignoring research into its causes and preventive strategies. His letters, economic pamphlets and political articles frequently refer to the issue, but a statement in the *ABC of Economics* is probably his most succinct indictment:

> An economic system in which it is more profitable to make guns to blow men to pieces than to grow grain or make useful machinery, is an outrage, and its supporters are enemies of the race.

> (*SP*, p. 233)

The striking irony in this discussion is that much of Pound's critique of capitalism, its distaste for rampant monetarism, its condemnation of military–industrialism, presents arguments that are broadly identifiable with a liberal standpoint. This irony serves to remind us that a lot of his economic views were not politically partisan. Social Credit policy could have been adapted to a wide range of party political systems. Throughout most of his Rapallo years Pound maintained an interest in American left-wing political movements and contributed to leftist magazines. His frustration with representatives of these organizations, as with mainstream 'demo-liberal' governments, was their refusal to contemplate the efficacy of Social Credit. Ultimately he chose to see Mussolini's dictatorship as the nearest thing to a nationwide implementation of Douglasite economics.

None of this quite prepares us for or provides adequate explanation of the way Pound associated his critique of capitalism with a vehement anti-Semitism. It is probably true that he was subject to a 'belief that bad things (wars, depressions) did not come about through folly, incompetence and accident, but were the result of deliberate plots laid by powerful and evil men for financial profit' (Stead, 1986, p. 249). This is hardly an outrageous or even a decidedly minority view. However, a conspiracy theory which seems to associate the conspirators with a racially identifiable minority needs further examination.

In this respect, as in so many other things, Pound proves to be both the upholder of tradition and a man of his time, most obviously influenced by events and attitudes forged in the latter part of the nineteenth century. The history of anti-Semitism is, of course, a long one. For much of that time its chief basis was religious and Jews were particularly vulnerable to attack around Easter time. However, in Germany and eastern Europe racial and political motives led to more organized persecution in the second half of the nineteenth century. In Russia, pogroms led to the mass emigration of Jews to the west: this undoubtedly provided the context for popular anti-Semitic sentiments of the kind Pound may well have heard or expressed as a boy in Wyncote. Ideas of racial superiority accompanied such sentiments. In the eastern states of America these were expressed with regard to the Anglo-Saxon stock of the 'original' settlers and aimed against a wide range of other ethnic immigrant groups, not just Jews. These attitudes were assimilated by Pound to some extent: they are referred to in his American sketches of 1912, *Patria Mia*, though they do not figure in his early poetry. However, they were clearly not rejected or rebelled against and laid the foundation for later, more focused prejudice. In the aftermath of the First World War and the advent of Douglasite economics that focus may have been triggered by a document known as 'The Protocols of the Elders of Zion'. This purported to be a programme for world dominance drawn up by Jewish leaders in which the funding of war, revolution and the arms trade all figured as strategies. The document was concocted by the secret police of Tsarist Russia as a ploy to forestall revolution by inciting anti-Semitism. Pound probably did not read the document itself in postwar London, but would certainly have known of it and its implications. By the time its forgery had been conclusively proved, he had moved on to more entrenched positions. The document's apparent confirmation of a Jewish conspiracy together with the erroneous conviction that the majority of arms manufacturers, dealers and 'usurers' were Jewish proved irresistible to Pound's 'suburban prejudice'.

In dealing with the subject of Pound's anti-Semitism several counter-arguments may be rehearsed in mitigation. Firstly, it is true that he had a number of lifelong friends and/or important literary associates who were Jewish, none of whom seems to have been subject to personal prejudice or individual abuse on account of their race. The most significant of these was Louis Zukofsky, who testified that he 'never felt the least trace of anti-Semitism in his presence. Nothing he ever said to me made me feel the embarrassment I always have for the "Goy" in whom a residue of antagonism to "Jews" remains. If we had occasion to use the words "Jew" and "Goy" they were no more or less ethnological in their sense than "Chinese" and "Italian"' (Carpenter, 1990, p. 561). This serves as a useful reminder that terms like 'Jew' have a range of connotations whose meanings vary with context and that we have to be careful to read the appropriate connotation when judging such sensitive issues.

Secondly, it is argued that his use of racially loaded expressions was a kind of indiscriminate shorthand for groups who were not necessarily racially delineated, such as arms dealers, international loan capitalists and the like. In this light, his use of the term 'Jewspapers', for example, could be seen as a general term for the western capitalist press he so despised. Even so, this is anti-Semitic in effect, if not in intent. The idea that Pound was unaware that he was being anti-Semitic cannot really be entertained. He was constantly being warned of the negative reception his remarks were getting, especially in America. For example, his friend and publisher James Laughlin, himself opposed to anti-Semitism and concerned for the effect Pound's reputation was having on his publishing ventures, was particularly explicit in a letter of 1939: 'I will not run an anti-Semitic sheet or be in any way connected with one . . . I think anti-Semitism is contemptible and despicable and I will not put my hand to it. I cannot tell you how it grieves me to see you taking up with it' (Gordon (ed.), 1994, p. 109). However, Pound's response to this and other more accusatory expressions was invariably one of denial. In personal letters, in more official communications, in numerous articles and even in some of his radio speeches, he repeatedly claimed he was not anti-Semitic.

This conviction constitutes the third and most serious counterargument: effectively, Pound argues that if a Jew is also an arms dealer, an international money marketeer or a capitalist newspaper magnate, then he should not be beyond criticism by virtue of being Jewish and that such criticism is not anti-Semitic. If Pound had been consistently scrupulous in the application of this argument, then his denials would have had some credence. However, it is clear from previous discussion that his anti-Semitism had much deeper roots and was less discriminating than this argument suggests. Perusal of Pound's more vehement writing on the topic as well as the Rome Radio transcripts tends to nullify all the above mitigations. One cannot avoid concluding that his language is anti-Semitic in effect. In so far as such language spills over into the poetry and contaminates his poetic voice, the quality of the poetry is diminished. For example, Canto 52 opens with what may be intended to be further notes from the hell of contemporary usurious practice. Righteous invective, even where it is disagreeable, can be admired for the power of its conviction, the expressive force of its language. However, some of the lines in this passage seem to be crucially different:

> Stinkschuld's sin drawing vengeance, poor yitts paying for
> Stinkschuld
> paying for a few big jews' vendetta on goyim

> (*CAN*, p. 257)

Apologists for lines of this kind argue that Pound's sympathy is with most Jews, who are not wealthy usurers. They may be right. Pound used similar arguments when defending himself against charges of anti-Semitism of the kind outlined above. However, the lines seem to confirm that Pound was at least aware that large numbers of Jews were being persecuted in Nazi Germany, although the nature of that persecution was still a secret. Indeed, it would have been hard not to know of such persecution, 'anno sedici', that is, in year sixteen of the fascist calendar, 1938, since it was widely reported in the international press. It was also the year when anti-Jewish legislation was introduced in Italy. If Pound was genuinely not anti-Semitic, then the above lines are at best ambiguous in their sympathy and certainly do nothing to condemn those carrying out the 'vengeance'. Incredibly, if one were not accustomed to Pound's poetic mood swings, these quite distasteful lines precede one of the most beautiful passages in *The Cantos*, Pound's adaptation of part of the *Li Ki* or Chinese book of rites. Conceptually, the presentation of this natural and socially ordered world juxtaposes a vision of what may be achieved against the preceding hell. But the possible implication of the poet in that hell through the language he uses within the poem may well damage our reading of that vision as much as, if not more than, any of his pronouncements outside of the poetic text.

Sexual politics

That early modernism was a monolithic cultural phenomenon with a unified aesthetic is increasingly a questionable and questioned notion. For example, even the title of Nicholls's survey, *Modernisms*, is suggestive of a plurality and diversity that the singular form denies. Referring to so-called canonical modernism, Nicholls says that his aim was 'to show that such a modernism, caricatured as it now frequently was, could be seen to constitute only one strand of a highly complex set of cultural developments at the beginning

115

of the twentieth century' (Nicholls, 1995, p. vii). One of the characterizations of that modernism highlighted by much recent feminist analysis is that it is gendered in a highly or even exclusively masculine way. The aesthetic and political stances represented by canonical modernism suggest that this is not mere caricature. The purpose of this section is to outline the social and political context in which that modernism's gendered nature developed and to appraise the significance of Pound's theoretical and poetic contribution to that development.

The position of women in society was one of the main focuses for debate in the twenty years preceding the outbreak of the First World War. Women were challenging the roles traditionally assigned them by patriarchy with an increasingly energetic liberal feminism particularized in the second half of this period by the movement for women's suffrage. In her discussion of 'the Woman Question' in the last decade of the nineteenth century, Showalter outlines a number of relevant issues, some of which I summarize here. Male fear of women's sexual and economic liberation was related to their conception as a potentially chaotic force whose freedom from patriarchal constraint could even herald the decline of western civilization. The perception of this threat was also symptomatic of a crisis in masculine identity. Feminism was matched by renewed anti-feminist and anti-suffrage movements. Virile values and notions of male supremacy were promoted. At the same time, among avant-garde artists, reformers and intellectuals there were a significant number of male pro-feminists (Showalter, 1991, pp. 7–11). It was during this period that Pound spent his adolescence and early manhood in more or less exclusively male educational institutions and then later found himself in London at the height of suffragist activity.

In the summer of 1914 Pound wrote an article in *The Egoist* entitled 'Suffragettes'. The use of this term does not in itself betoken disparagement: although the term had been invented by the *Daily Mail* as a label of derision, it was by this time being used by feminists with some pride. The article, written under one of Pound's pseudonyms, Bastien von Helmholtz, is satiric in nature and clearly meant to offend the establishment and its practices. Taken as a parody of 'magnanimous' male chauvinism which uses the context of supporting women's suffrage to assert male superiority, it can be read with some entertainment. The article's anti-democratic sentiments are the mainstay of the writer's satiric point that, while women's right to the vote is a perfectly just one, they are stupid to want it, since it is a useless facet of democracy. The article ends with the suggestion that the House of Commons and the House of Lords should be abolished and replaced by male and female chambers. The tone of the article may be judged from the following extract where the writer lists some of the forces on the side of women's suffrage:

> They have the mob's tacit approval of violence, of anything that causes excitement, they have their own conviction, their own love of adventure, their hatred of traditional forms of feminine ennui, they have the force of male sentimentality or chivalry working in their favour.
>
> (Scott (ed.), 1990, p. 370)

It would be rather humourless to take the whole article as a serious, unironic representation of Pound's views. However, as one of his prose personae, perhaps von Helmholtz does mask some of his own attitudes, the tenor of which is hardly supremacist, though there is an assumed air of male superiority. This male chauvinism, such as it is, has to be read in the context of its time and the magazine in which it was published. *The Egoist* was owned and edited by a woman who wished to present a wider range of humanist and individualist views rather than a narrow suffragist agenda. A satirical article which defended the justice of women's suffrage and attacked its opponents while suggesting that there was more to civilization than the vote, would at least have had editorial approval.

The role of women in a democratic process for which he had little time seems to have been of marginal interest to Pound. Of much greater interest was the role of women in literary production. There are two issues here. One is the nature of the male–female relationship as it relates to artistic creativity, or rather male artistic creativity. The other is the woman as writer and the extent to which women writers were able to validate and promote their work in the context of early modernism. These issues are both grounded in a common ideology, though one is of a more aesthetic nature and the other has more practical consequences. These issues are central to the sexual politics of modernism and it is Pound's contribution to them that has received most attention and negative criticism.

With regard to the significance of sex in artistic creativity, there are two phases in Pound's theoretical development, one related to the troubadour tradition, the other to the ideas of the French writer Rémy de Gourmont. From his Provençal studies as a young man at university Pound absorbed the tradition of courtly love. In the course of preparing his book *The Spirit of Romance,* in his early years in London, he began to develop theories about that tradition which were eventually articulated in the interpolated chapter of his book, known as 'Psychology and Troubadours'. He suggests that the troubadour's complex poetry encodes ritual and visionary experience that is evidence of a surviving Hellenistic paganism. Courtly love is thus a trace religion whose objects of worship are lovers rather than gods. This cult is a refinement of sexually based mysteries in which 'the charged surface is produced between the predominant natural poles of two human mechanisms' (*SR*, p. 94). The presentation of these ideas is regaled in scientific metaphor and is somewhat obscure, either because the subject matter was indelicate for the times or because Pound was genuinely tentative about what he was getting at, or possibly both. His hypothesis that rites such as the Eleusinian mysteries, a fertility cult of ancient Greece, survived via the troubadours into the present remains just that. But his beliefs have poetic consequences in that the old gods inhabit his poems and in particular play a vital role at numinous moments in *The Cantos*. Although the sexual element in his discussion is dealt with in an oblique way, it can probably be reduced to: (a) sex is a potentially mystical and illuminating experience; (b) when it is, great poetry may be its verbal concomitant.

In themselves these ideas are neither startlingly original nor controversial, though their publication may have been in early twentieth-century London. Pound reiterated his belief in the first idea (a) with his mantra 'Sacrum, sacrum, inluminatio coitu' in *The Cantos*. The second may be seen as a variant of the poetic muse. What is relevant to the present discussion is the fact that Pound's ideas are implicitly gendered. Although the above quotation refers to 'two human mechanisms', it is clear from surrounding argument that 'the charged surface' benefits the male participant. The lover/priest/poet transforms his experience with (or should it be of?) the lady/goddess/muse into religion or poetry. How the female participant benefits from 'the charged surface' or otherwise transforms her experience is not taken into account. Again, there is nothing remarkably new here: sexual explicitness aside, Pound's ideas conform to a fairly traditional masculinist aesthetic. However, his adoption of such ideas did mean that this aesthetic had its place in the development of early modernism.

The obliqueness of Pound's discussion in 'Psychology and Troubadours' gave way to much more explicit statements in later years. There is also an addition to his aesthetic perception of woman as muse and object of adoration, namely, woman as a chaotic principle. This idea first surfaces in a now notorious letter to Marianne Moore written in 1919. In the context of a correspondence in which Pound is helpful and supportive of Moore's early attempts to get her work published, he wrote a rambling poem-like piece some of which is a kind of masculine apologetics, some of which may be read as a rather crass epistolary sexual advance. The piece opens with the statement: 'The female is a chaos'. Apart from its incongruity, of which Pound reveals no awareness at all, the piece is confused and contradictory. For example, the male 'is a fixed point of stupidity' but also 'more expansive and demands other and varied contacts', while the chaotic female is content 'with prolonged conversation with but one sole creature of its own sex' (*SL*, p. 146). It is likely that Pound was conscious of quoting himself when he elaborates on this theme in Canto 29:

> Chiefest of these the second, the female
> Is an element, the female
> Is a chaos
> An octopus
> A biological process
>
> (*CAN*, p. 144)

It is also likely that Marianne Moore was conscious of the allusion to his letter to her when, in an otherwise fulsome review, she dismissed his characterization of the female as archaic. This particular line in Pound's thinking can be seen as an aesthetic version of the wider male fear of women's sexual and economic freedom I mentioned earlier. It had its practical and legal realizations in the culture of dependency that most women were still subject to in the first half of the twentieth century.

In the aftermath of the First World War Pound was beginning his search for radical solutions to actual and potential chaos of a military and political kind. Since war and politics were so obviously male domains, it is both disappointing and difficult to explain why he should find so powerful a metaphor for chaos in the feminine. As we have seen, the 'chaos theory' of woman can arise as part of a masculine backlash against perceived feminist threats to patriarchal arrangements. The war had provided a wider range of roles for women, had in fact promoted their 'liberation' in ways the suffragists had not achieved. There was postwar concern that women would not return to their time-honoured roles, but continue to prove their competence in male domains, so threatening the patriarchal order of things. Pound, who had expressed great anxiety about what 'civilization' might be like after the war, may have seen this as a contribution to the chaos. In so far as the notion of 'will to order' was a nostalgic appeal for the restoration of essentially male systems of hierarchy, a belief in the female as chaos would give even greater impulse to that will.

In a 1915 letter to Harriet Monroe Pound announced: 'De Gourmont is dead and the world's light is darkened' (*SL*, p. 64). The promised obituary which appeared in *Poetry* began with the same sentence and asserted that de Gourmont had died because the war had grieved him to death. Pound praised the French writer's poetry and prose, recalled his correspondence with the older man who had retained a youthful outlook and quoted his belief that a writer's only pleasure is to write frankly what he thinks (*SP*, pp. 390–3). Perhaps it was in this spirit that Pound some years later translated de Gourmont's essay 'Physique de l'Amour' as *The Natural Philosophy of Love*, published in 1922. This is a more or less scientific survey of the sex lives of animals and humans which also reflects upon the psychological and developmental significance of sex and sexuality. Explicit sexual detail and positively expressed attitudes, for example, with regard to the value of sexual pleasure, must have given de Gourmont's essay and Pound's translation of it quasi-pornographic status in its time. In a slightly earlier essay on the writer Pound had written with reference to 'Physique de l'Amour': 'Sex, in so far as it is not a purely physiological reproductive mechanism, lies in the domain of aesthetics, the junction of tactile and magnetic senses.' The ideas and the language they are couched in are not dissimilar to those in 'Psychology and Troubadours'. Their gendered perception is revealed in Pound's follow-up comment that in the realm of sex 'some desire the trivial, some the processional, the stately, the master-work' (*LE*, p. 341). It would be difficult to argue here that the term 'master-work' merely denotes excellence without connotating an exclusively male act which renders invisible the other, presumably female, participant. The term effectively metaphorizes sex as sculpture or, more relevantly in Pound's case, poetry, from the perspective of the male artist.

The tenor and vehicle of this comparison are reversed in the postscript that Pound wrote to his translation of 'Physique de l'Amour'. Here the creative process is explicitly likened to an act of procreative sex: 'creative thought is an act like fecundation, like the male cast of the human seed . . .' (RG, p. x). Again, the comparison here between male orgasm and procreation typifies Pound's masculinist perception of sexuality. The much-quoted postscript takes up de Gourmont's remark that there is 'some correlation between complete, profound copulation and cerebral development' and hypothesizes that the brain is, at least in its origins, 'a sort of great clot of genital fluid held in suspense or reserve' (RG, p. vii). Language of this kind may be seen as an, albeit fairly crude, attempt to express ideas about the relation between cognition, brain mechanisms and hormonal activity at a time when the sciences of neurology and neurophysiology were in their infancy. Pound also wanted to put a scientific gloss on those age-old beliefs in the power of sex to enlighten, inspire and expand the mind, which we have already seen him exploring in relation to the troubadours. In both respects the male orientation of the ideas is very clear: the genital fluid is 'spermatozoic', the ancient religions are 'phallic', and man is 'the phallus or spermatozoide charging, head-on, the female chaos . . .' (RG, p. viii). This last remark amounts to an expression of 'the will to order' in sexual terms. When these ideas are translated into a literary context, the possibilities for women seem to be inevitably ancillary. Besides the role of muse, a sexual/emotional/spiritual inspiration to male creativity, woman is likely to be a receptacle of literature, a source of feedback and support, possibly the high priestess of a literary cult. Her own literary productions will be the obvious offspring of the 'master-work'. Pound himself outlines woman's literary function in these kinds of terms: 'the conservator, the inheritor of past gestures, clever, practical, as Gourmont says, not inventive, always the best disciple of any inventor' (RG, p. xvi). Yet in the very same sentence Pound characterizes woman as 'the enemy of the dead or laborious form of compilation, abstraction'. He was clearly aware that his main hypotheses, however quirky they might appear, were open to charges of male chauvinism, since at one point in the postscript he asserts: 'as I am certainly neither writing an anti-feminist tract, nor claiming disproportionate privilege for the spermatozoide, for the sake of symmetry ascribe a cognate role to the ovule, though I can hardly be expected to introspect it' (RG, p. viii).

One might expect from the above ideological positions that in practical and critical terms women writers would receive little support from Pound. However, in this as in other matters, his rhetoric was not always the best predictor of his response to individuals and his desire to promote literary talent mostly outweighed other considerations. However, his critical support was also tailored to promoting his own version of the modernist agenda and, to that extent, was motivated by his sexual politics. For example, in the case of H.D. we have already seen in the biographical section how his perception of her early work helped to launch not only the first wave of imagist poetry but also her career as one of the finest modernist poets. Pound's support of H.D. was, of course, complicated by their entangled relationship, but the cavalier way in which he was perceived to have treated her work may be seen as symptomatic of a wider literary male chauvinism. On the other hand, Pound's dispute with Amy Lowell seems to be much more about the demarcation of literary territory than sexual politics. Lowell came to London in 1913 with the express purpose of meeting Pound and becoming an imagist poet. Pound welcomed her and helped her to change her poetic technique: his editorial work on her poems was similar to the critical coaching he applied to other poets who sought his help, including Yeats. Lowell's poems appeared in the first imagist anthology, but she was dissatisfied with

121

Pound's tight control over its range of poets and poetry. She wished to institute an annual collection in which the poems were self-selected by each poet represented. Pound was no doubt put out at losing editorial control, but also concerned that the imagist principles underlying the movement's collective poetics would be abandoned. Although he did not want to be published in the new anthology, in a letter of 1914 he welcomed the opportunity it would provide for poets to get into print, and suggested, 'If you want to drag in the word Imagisme you can use a subtitle "an anthology devoted to Imagisme, vers libre and modern movements in verse" or something of that sort' (*SL*, p. 39). Lowell ignored his objections and called each yearly edition of the anthology *Some Imagist Poets*. The dispute deteriorated into name-calling and acrimony. Pound coined the term 'Amygism' for what he saw as the flabby substitute for imagism's hard clarity. Lowell proved equally stubborn and the rift was never healed. The anthologies successfully exposed a number of modernist poets to a wider audience on both sides of the Atlantic and Pound probably did himself more harm than good by not being represented in them. In addition, he was lampooned mercilessly in distinctly unflabby rhyming couplets by Lowell in her poem 'A Critical Fable', where she says that he no longer writes poems, 'just spleen on the loose', that he 'knows nothing at all, but has frequently guessed it', and that he 'struts like a cock, self-adored, self-deluding' (Gilbert and Gubar, 1988, p. 219).

One of Pound's specific aims in promoting literary talent was to identify work that was distinctively American. Possibly because of his more or less permanent exile and despite his disenchantment with American literary and educational institutions, there remained an element of literary partisanship in his outlook. It is not surprising, therefore, that his 1918 review of the early poems of Marianne Moore and Mina Loy should accentuate this aspect: 'without any pretences and without clamours about nationality, these girls have written a distinctly national product, they have written something which could not have come out of any other country . . .' (*SP*, p. 394). Although Loy was English born, she was effectively an American writer, working out of New York. This distinctive American quality is human rather than scenic, of the mind rather than the heart, and associated with an 'arid clarity'. Pound locates the two poets as unwitting followers of Laforgue and this could be interpreted as an unwarranted appropriation. However, as I noted in an earlier section, Pound was in the process of refining his definition of Laforgue's verbalism around this time. The fact that this review sees his first use of the word logopoeia as 'a dance of the intelligence among words and ideas' would suggest that certain linguistic qualities in the poems helped to crystallize his thinking. It would be unfair, I think, to see his subsequent readings of their work as exponents of logopoeia in crudely chauvinistic terms. On the other hand, his failure to detect emotion in Loy's poems suggests that he was unable to engage fully with her obliquely confessional feminist voice. Nevertheless, in identifying their work as distinctively American, Pound can now be seen to have anticipated their formative role in American modernist poetry and its postmodernist developments.

The poets mentioned above were by no means the only women writers to receive Pound's help in terms of favourable reviews, practical criticism and promotion through publication. One feminist account of modernist women writers says this of Pound: 'Where he perceived talent, he pursued and encouraged it and was, in addition, canny enough to know how to manipulate the appropriate publishing vehicles, so that women's work was not only fostered, but also printed' (Hanscombe and Smyers, 1987, p. 170). This willingness to promote the work of women writers contributed to the establishment of what is now recognized as a literary movement that presented a feminine-gendered alternative to male canonical modernism. On the evidence available, his promotion of women writers was based on their perceived qualities as writers with little sense that those qualities might in some way reflect or be related to their gender. In this respect his contribution to that alternative modernism was entirely without design. Indeed, he would probably have shunned a more consciously female-orientated movement as contrary to his own modernist agenda. For example, in a letter to John Quinn in 1915 he even proposed setting up one literary magazine from which women contributors were excluded (Materer (ed.), 1991, p. 53). Pound thus presents us with the fairly extreme paradox of someone whose ideology is male-orientated achieving pro-feminist goals.

This section has suggested that Pound's sexual politics have to be appraised in their social and historical context. He was born, brought up and educated in a highly patriarchal society which was beginning to see that patriarchy challenged. Many of his views were symptomatic of positions held more generally by women as well as men. We have seen that in the context of wider debate about the changing status of women in society and the challenge to patriarchy, uncertainties about male roles and crises of masculine identity tend to surface. These give rise to movements for the promotion of virile values and the reassertion of male supremacy. Pound's sexual ideology may be seen as a version of these wider concerns, focusing specifically on literary production and incorporating esoteric elements derived from his learning. The climate of literary London before the First World War is also worth looking at as a contributory factor. The over-assertion of a masculinist poetics may have been a reaction to uncertainties about the status of the poet as male. Bell notes the opinions expressed by Ford Madox Ford that in London 'a man of letters is regarded as something less than a man' and is 'at least effeminate if not a decent kind of eunuch'. Commenting on Pound's struggle to find acceptance in his first year in London, Bell adds: 'The societal problem that Ford suggested would have been particularly acute for the early confusions of Pound's exile, which were social as well as aesthetic . . .' (Bell, 1981, p. 87). Clearly, factors of temperament and personality of a complex kind are also involved in the way Pound dealt with these problems.

The fact that Pound held a largely phallocentric view of poetic creativity has prompted some fairly hostile critical responses in recent years, some of which amounts to little more than *ad hominem* attack in terms that are more offensive than anything he wrote himself. In this section I have attempted to outline Pound's thinking in a relatively neutral way in the context of some possibly explanatory background information. I have tried to avoid both politically correct disapproval and undue defensiveness. There are some ways in which it is useful to have such a singularly male perspective articulated, however oddly at times, since, whether we like it or not, it may well reflect the emotional and creative impulses of many male writers. Feminist and, indeed, alternative masculinist positions can then take into account, but not merely discount, Pound's views.

Pound was, by today's standards and in today's terminology, sexist. He could unthinkingly refer to two women poets of his own age as 'these girls'. That usage had a long history, was commonplace and acceptable then, is commonplace and often goes unchallenged now. Of course, it is not always meant or taken as a patronizing put-down, depending on the register in which it is used. More symptomatic is Pound's use of 'man' to generalize about poets or other writers. This is very rarely even generic and therefore potentially inclusive of women: it invariably implies a male enterprise. In judging Pound to be sexist we have to remind ourselves that the term 'sexism' was only coined in 1968. The phenomenon is age-old, but its conceptualization is relatively recent and there is always some unfairness in applying such terms retrospectively, even when our understanding of social and historical factors should prompt us to do so in a balanced way. Perhaps that balance is best kept by quoting May Sinclair, another of the modernist women Pound supported and, in this case, drew support from in a review of 1920: 'For the last seven years he has been more concerned to obtain recognition for other people than to capture any sort of hearing for himself. In this he has shown an absolutely incorruptible devotion to his craft' (Scott (ed.), 1990, p. 469). The fact that a substantial number of the 'other people' were women writers suggests that, where sexual politics were concerned, Pound's ideology was less important than his care for literature.

Part Two
Critical Survey

In my earlier discussion of Pound's concept of the persona it was clear that he applied the term specifically to poems of a dramatic nature which involved the appropriation of a character in monologue. However, he also used the term 'personae' as a general term for slightly more miscellaneous groups of poems and as the title of one of his early books. The term's significance for Pound was highlighted when he called his collected shorter poems, first published in 1926, *Personae*. Even the longest of the poems in this collection is relatively short-spanned and Pound emerges from it as the master of a range of lyric, dramatic and satiric modes that are by turns amusing, powerful and psychologically perceptive. The major cycles, such as *Cathay* and *Mauberley*, are by definition sequences of short pieces which achieve unity by thematic and structural means. The quality of Pound's shorter poems does underline the fact that his talent was not suited to sustained narrative or periodic argument. Indeed, the problem of how to construct a long, if not endless, poem without a unifying narrative or philosophical thread preoccupied him at a relatively early stage. *The Cantos* are a realization of, possibly a solution to, that problem. In the critical survey that follows I adopt the term 'personae' as a heading under which a representative sample of shorter poems may be looked at, analyse some technical aspects of imagism, then give separate consideration to the major cycles of poems before attempting an overview of *The Cantos* with sample approaches to reading.

Personae

The poems Pound wrote before his more or less exclusive preoccupation with cantos are highly varied in both style and content. Outside of the unified cycles they are mostly self-contained single poems, though there are a number of smaller groups linked according to source or theme, such as 'Amities', wry disclaimers about friendship, 'Langue d'Oc', translations from the Provençal, and 'Moeurs Contemporaines', satiric comment on the morals of contemporary London. From the poems in *A Lume Spento* (1908) to those in and around *Lustra* (1916) there is a broad stylistic development from archaism to the language of colloquial speech. However, this development is neither linear nor entirely complete. Pound adopted the language he felt appropriate to purpose and context. For example, the 'Langue d'Oc' poems of 1918 resort to an archaism that perfectly captures the ambience of Provençal courtly love. Compounding this development is the stylistic impact of Pound's efforts to realize the tenets of imagism, and later vorticism, in linguistic form. The content of the 150 or so poems under consideration here is wide-ranging, but there are discernible categories. There are the personae proper, lyric and dramatic monologues, some of which are translations, that evoke the distant worlds and cultures of Rome, Provence, medieval Italy and the rest. Secondly, there are poems depicting and commenting on, usually in a satiric way involving colloquial language, the customs and attitudes of contemporary society and its members, sometimes in the guise of classical or other models. Thirdly, there are poems exemplifying imagist technique on a range of topics. Finally, despite theories of impersonality and the idea that Pound rarely writes without a persona, there are in fact a substantial number of poems written at least in half-mask and some where it would be perverse not to identify the textual 'I' with Pound himself. What follows is a more detailed look at poems from two of these categories.

'Na Audiart' (first published in A Lume Spento 1908: CSP, pp. 8–9)

In a letter to William Carlos Williams written from London in 1908 Pound is clearly defending the poems of his first collection against Williams's earlier criticism. In the course of doing so he says:

> To me the short so-called dramatic lyric – at any rate the sort
> of thing I do – is the poetic part of a drama the rest of which
> (to me the prose part) is left to the reader's imagination or
> implied or set in a short note.
>
> (*SL*, p. 3)

It is quite probable that Pound had 'Na Audiart' in mind, preceded
as it is by just such a prose note. The poem is best approached
via Pound's more general interest in the troubadours and his
specific attraction to Bertran de Born. In 1914 Pound published
his translation of 'Dompna pois de me nous cal', subtitled 'From
the Provençal of En Bertrans de Born'. In his essay on Arnaut
Daniel Pound makes it clear that he considers Daniel to be the
greatest Provençal poet. The other troubadours 'sang not so many
diverse kinds of music as En Arnaut, nor made so many good
poems in different fashions, nor thought them so carefully, though
En Bertrans sings with more vigour, it may be' (*LE*, p. 114). Yet
de Born, probably because of the perceived vigour in his life as
much as his poetry, is the more significant influence on Pound's
complex revision of the troubadour tradition and 'Dompna pois
de me nous cal' the most significant emblem of that influence. He
was familiar with the poem and the details of de Born's life from
his Provençal studies at Hamilton College. It is worth noting that
the 'facts' of the lives of the troubadours stem from the *vida*, some-
what embroidered biographical notes by Provençal commenta-
tors. These 'biographies' invite interpretative speculation and in de
Born's case Pound was spurred to such interpretation in poetic
form by the apparent contradictions he discerned in the warmon-
gering troubadour's character. Chaytor's account of 1912 (Chaytor,
1970, pp. 57–64), which Pound may well have known, tells us that
de Born lived from about 1140 to 1215, had his estates in the
Perigord region and held a castle at Hautefort. He took part in a
series of wars relating to power struggles in southern France dur-
ing the time of the crusades. He was closely involved with Henry
II and his sons, Henry 'the young king' and Richard the Lion
Heart. He wrote a famous lament on the death of 'the young king'
(which Pound also translated) and was apparently spared by Henry
II on account of this. He also married more than once and paid
court to various noblewomen in true troubadour fashion, though
he ended his days in a monastery. In Dante's *Inferno*, de Born is
depicted in hell carrying his own severed head like a lamp as pun-
ishment for sowing discord between father and son. Most of de
Born's poetry has a political and/or military theme, calling allies
to battle and praising the efforts of soldiers. In this respect 'Dompna
pois de me nous cal' seems anomalous, since it is apparently a

love poem, conjuring up a composite woman to compensate de Born for his rejection by Maent of Montignac, one of the ladies he courted. Pound later responded to his full translation of the poem by choosing not to see it purely as a piece of male fantasy but by speculating that it is in some devious way a coded political message with military implications: these ideas were explored in 'Near Perigord', a poem whose technical and formal qualities manage to capture the emotional and psychological shifts of its content.

'Na Audiart', written some time before these ideas were formulated, is a different kind of response to de Born's 'Dompna pois de me nous cal'. Pound seizes on the detail of one stanza and, within that, the phraseology of one line to construct an entirely new scenario. In the process of fantasizing his composite woman de Born refers to a certain Lady Audiart as 'sibem vol mal' ('though she wishes me ill'). In his complete translation of the poem Pound renders the stanza in which this reference occurs as follows:

> Of Audiart at Malemort,
> Though she with a full heart
> Wish me ill,
> I'd have her form that's laced
> So cunningly,
> Without blemish, for her love
> Breaks not nor turns aside.

> (*CSP*, p. 106)

In 'Na Audiart' Pound takes what amounts to a passing reference among a whole catalogue of Provençal women in de Born's original and explores the imagined relationship the words allow, if not imply. The archaic language of the poem with its pre-Raphaelite throwbacks is offset by two structural devices. Firstly, de Born's line, in Pound's slightly altered form 'Que be-m vols mal', is used as both epigraph and final line of the poem. In the latter case it is syntactically part of the English sentence which it concludes: 'For whose fairness one forgave Que be-m vols mal', which is best read as: 'For whose fairness I forgave the fact that you wished me ill'. Between the Provençal of the epigraph and the final line Pound repeats English variants as a kind of reprise: 'Though thou well dost wish me ill', 'Though thou hate me', and so on. Secondly, the name Audiart occurs fifteen times throughout the poem. On seven occasions it is immediately repeated, so that 'Audiart, Audiart' punctuates the poem like a chorus. Where it occurs at syntactic boundaries it has the effect of reinforcing structural design, but it also interrupts the syntax on occasions, as if the speaker cannot wait to say the name again. These devices not only give the poem an incantatory quality but also demonstrate what might be termed the semantics of melopoeia, since the speaker's obsession with Audiart and her ill-will towards him are presented through sound rather than described or explained.

Reading between de Born's lines and behind that one enigmatic clause, Pound adopts the troubadour's persona to present the imagined 'reality'. De Born is familiar enough to send Audiart 'a word kiss'. Did they once share actual kisses? He pretends to move on to another woman, the lady 'Miels-de-Ben', but soon returns for 'Just a word in thy praise, girl', that form of address not only inappropriate but also symptomatic of the sexism that underpins the whole institution of courtly love. Then comes the hint that their relationship was fully sexual: '. . . never a flaw was there/Where thy torse and limbs are met'. Here, possibly, is the cause of Audiart's hatred, a failed or betrayed intimacy, though de Born would be the last one to reflect upon it. Instead, he appropriates Audiart's fame to himself, since it will be his poetry that immortalizes her beauty, a theme Pound returned to in the persona of Propertius. The final part of the poem is hardly an expression of 'carpe diem' as it is sometimes thought to be. Rather, it is a cruel portrait of Audiart 'reincarnate' in old age, 'Broken of ancient pride' and thus willing to soften her attitude towards de Born who parades his magnanimity on account of her beauty to conclude the poem.

'Na Audiart', then, shows Pound in his early twenties exercising a remarkably mature ability to enter a remote world and present convincing insights about the psychology of individuals operating within that world. Its internal reality strikes us as true to the picture of de Born given by Pound in his prose note to the poem. De Born's ambivalent obsession with Audiart is in keeping with a character who fantasizes a process which, while appearing complimentary to the women whose features are selected, objectifies and depersonalizes them. Pound thus presents de Born as an extreme case of the troubadour ethos, both as warrior and courtly lover. Incidentally, he also prefigures other notable men of action in Pound's poetry, most obviously Sigismundo Malatesta in *The Cantos*.

The final point we might want to consider here is how a poem like 'Na Audiart' realizes Pound's concept of 'masks of the self'. The term's ambiguity embodies a paradox in that the wearing of a mask is a device for concealing, while the choice and interpretation of the mask is a process of revelation: hiding is unveiling. For example, the poet may choose a persona that apparently conceals perceived weakness and in so doing reveals unacknowledged violence: de Born's attraction for Pound is a case in point of which Pound himself was at least partially aware. Further, the poet may project onto the persona more complex feelings which 'unmask' the poet's own, possibly unacknowledged, repressed or not fully realized emotions. The troubadour's courtly esteem for his lady also implied a potentially oppressive claim: in 'Na Audiart' Pound elaborates on this in a way that is not only consistent with de Born's character but also reveals his own ambivalent and sometimes chauvinistic attitudes towards women. We must remember, of course, that these unveilings become available to the poet. As such they are part of a process of self-revelation for which Pound's notion of 'casting off complete masks of the self' is a metaphor. However, the concept of 'casting off' cannot be taken to mean that the emotions or attitudes thus unmasked are necessarily abandoned.

'Villanelle: The Psychological Hour' (first published in Poetry 1915: CSP, pp. 158–9)

Scattered throughout Pound's shorter works are poems where the textual 'I' is neither an identified persona nor attributable to an implied other. These range from the early rumination on the likely fate of his poetry, 'Famam Librosque Cano', to the many poems addressed to his 'songs' in *Lustra* which satirically and sometimes poignantly commission them to 'Greet the grave and the stodgy' and 'Be against all forms of oppression' (*CSP*, pp. 86, 89). Alongside such poems where an authorial first person is at least implied, in half-mask as it were, there are others which allow for an autobiographically situated reading. For example, 'In Durance', which was written in 1907 while Pound was at Wabash College, reminds us with its constant repetition of the line 'I am homesick after my own kind' (ibid., p. 20) of his disastrous attempt to teach in the Midwest. A number of vignettes of London life, such as 'The Garret', 'The Garden' and 'Black Slippers: Bellotti', also edge into this category, though none is entirely without the sense of authorial detachment that preserves the half-mask.

'Villanelle: The Psychological Hour' has a quite different feel to any of the above. Although it is elusive in places and its exact context of situation remains disputed, it is clearly a personal, self-referential response to actual events: in terms of Pound's metaphor it is 'maskless', emotionally bare in a manner that prefigures certain passages of *The Cantos*. In a poetic output such as Pound's these qualities alone make the poem worth closer attention, since it borders on the unique. However, it is also a fine example of his modernism at its best: presentational, non-discursive, fragmentary, yet somehow structurally complete and narratively satisfying. The title immediately intrigues, since we expect a villanelle, an intricate stanzaic form with a rigidly defined rhyme scheme and repeated lines. What we get is a loosely structured poem in three unevenly shaped sections. The idea put forward by some commentators that the poem is a failed attempt at a villanelle is quite untenable: if nothing else, Pound's pride in his knowledge of verse forms would not have allowed him to miss the mark so widely. Neither is the poem a deliberately mangled version of the form. The villanelle of the title, then, is clearly not the poem which follows. However, it is conceivable that extracts from a villanelle are quoted in the poem. Certain lines appear in italics. Two of these, 'Beauty is so rare a thing/So few drink of my fountain', are repeated. Is Pound reading a villanelle within the context of situation the poem presents? This is unlikely because the next italicized line, 'Between the night and morning', is a quotation from a poem by Yeats, signalled as such by Pound's additional quotation marks: the Yeats poem is no villanelle. However, Pound could be in the process of writing a villanelle in which he intends to quote, with true modernist intertextuality, Yeats's line. The villanelle form is restricted to two end rhymes and the 'morning' of Yeats's line could be a rhyme for the 'thing' of Pound's own two lines. The next italicized line, 'Beauty would drink of my mind', does not fit the projected rhyme scheme, but this need not rule out the idea that Pound is writing a villanelle, since it suggests the compositional process of inventing, revising and possibly rejecting potential lines. The villanelle of the title is what Pound is writing, seemingly for therapeutic purposes, in the 'psychological hour' of his disappointment and self-doubt: we get its fragments, a poem within a poem.

The source of the poet's disappointment is the failure of 'two friends' to make a prearranged visit. The opening of the poem captures the anxiety of the host awaiting the arrival of guests: 'I had laid out just the right books, I had almost turned down the pages.' With hindsight this over-preparation seems to have invited a let-down and the rest of the poem is an agonized post-mortem on his apparent inability to attract the friendship of younger contemporaries, interspersed with fragments of the villanelle he is writing. In its technical aspects the poem probably represents the culmination so far of Pound's use of poetic 'stream of consciousness'. This term is most often associated with the representation of speech and thought in fiction, but is entirely appropriate here. Even in his early dramatic monologues Pound had begun to experiment with the representation of thought on the page, most notably in 'La Fraisne':

> Once there was a woman . . .
> . . . but I forget . . . she was . . .
> . . . I hope she will not come again.

> (*CSP*, p. 5)

Although this may still be a relatively crude attempt to show a mind under pressure, it demonstrates the potential for the dramatic monologue to move towards the interior. In 'Villanelle: The Psychological Hour' that move is both complete and complex. Not only do we have the representation of a mind talking to itself but also, through the use of quotation marks, the depiction of someone solitary talking to himself out loud. The shifts from subvocal to vocal monologue and back again, together with the 'voice' of the villanelle, make for a convincing portrayal of *Angst*.

The provenance of this poem has been thought to be an early stage in Pound's friendship with Gaudier-Brzeska in 1913 when he was unable to get the artist and his wife, Sophie, to visit him at his Kensington flat. Given that the poem was first published in December 1915 and probably written in the latter half of that year, this would mean it is very much an exercise in reconstituting an emotional complex from some distance in time. However, the news of Gaudier-Brzeska's death in the trenches in the summer of 1915 could have triggered a need to write about the first time he suffered the artist's 'loss'. Although Pound was under 30 and Gaudier-Brzeska only a few years younger, he tended to play up his older years in the face of the latter's youthful anarchy. This might account for the 'middle-ageing care' of the poem. However, an alternative episode has also been identified as a cue for the poem by Omar Pound and Robert Spoo who assert that 'The "two friends" of "Villanelle" are T.S. Eliot and his fiancée Vivien Haigh-Wood' (Pound and Spoo, 1988, p. 143). In a footnote they cite a letter in which Pound himself is reported to have told a friend that he wrote the poem in response to the occasion when Eliot and his fiancée failed to turn up because they had suddenly decided to go and get married, in June 1915. The second explanation more readily accounts for the poem's sense of immediately felt emotions. On the other hand, Pound had known Eliot since the previous September, so the lines, 'Are people less friends because one has just, at last, found them?', seem more applicable to the situation with Gaudier-Brzeska. Eliot was also much nearer to Pound in age. However, in 'The Love Song of J. Alfred Prufrock', which Pound had spent a lot of time promoting, Eliot had offered a model of middle-ageing anxiety. Ultimately, the exact provenance of the poem is much less important than the text itself. If it is to some extent post-'Prufrock', it is even more pre-*The Waste Land*. It anticipates Eliot's logical discontinuities and elliptical dialogues, especially those of 'A Game of Chess'. In this respect, its possible connection with the occasion of Eliot's first marriage is both fitting and ironic.

Gaudier-Brzeska working on the 'Heiractic Head of Ezra Pound'.

Imagism in practice

In 1913 Pound published a number of poems which have a structural similarity in common. Each of the poems ends with a line which is syntactically detached from what has gone before, yet related to it by the punctuation marks colon or semi-colon. This detachment is reinforced by the fact that these end lines are not syntactically complete, but are in fact disembodied noun phrases. To exemplify the kinds of lines I am referring to, I quote three here:

> Grey olive leaves beneath a rain-cold sky ('Gentildonna')
> Petals on a wet, black bough ('In a station of the Metro')
> A wet leaf that clings to the threshold ('Liu Ch'e')
>
> (*CSP*, pp. 92, 109, 108)

These lines illustrate a technique that puts into verbal practice Pound's concept of the image in its most obvious form, the self-contained poetic sign that presents 'an intellectual and emotional complex in an instant of time'. In my earlier outline I offered some ways of approaching imagism from the standpoint of structural linguistics. It is worth trying to apply these insights from linguistic theory to one of the lines quoted above: 'Grey olive leaves beneath a rain-cold sky'. This image's denotation, the 'intellectual' aspect of its conceptual cluster, presents us with leaves of a particular kind of tree, of a certain colour, that are spatially lower than a sky typically associated with rain and low temperatures. We cannot tell if the leaves are still attached to branches of a tree or are fallen on the ground. Nevertheless, this rational scrutiny of the image tells us a lot. Turning to possible connotations, the image presents us with the dull, possibly lifeless, leaves of an evergreen tree bespattered by rain in bitterly cold conditions, the emotional complex of which may be glossed as 'bleakness'. The image, a series of verbal signifiers with a specific sound pattern and syntactic structure, thus 'presents' a complex of both literal signifieds and their emotional resonances.

The next step in this exploration of Pound's theory of the image in practice is to contextualize the line in its poem and see how it relates to the lines that precede it. The full poem is as follows:

'Gentildonna'

She passed and left no quiver in the veins, who now
Moving among the trees, and clinging

in the air she severed,
Fanning the grass she walked on then, endures:
Grey olive leaves beneath a rain-cold sky.

(CSP, p. 92)

The anonymous woman who is the subject of the poem has been and gone, but not without trace. Her presence lives on, pervades the trees, stays like scent on the air, still stirs the grass. It is unlikely, then, that the final line can in any way refer to this woman. Indeed, given the meaning we have allocated to the image, it would be absurd to see it as some kind of metaphor relating to the woman or her presence on the scene. No, the last line with its separate entity, its heavy closure cued by the colon at the end of the preceding line, must be engaged in some other purpose. To suggest what this might be, we need to recognize that there is another 'subject' in the poem for whom the woman and her presence are in fact objects. This subject lacks a textual 'I' that we can identify as person or persona. Adopting a concept from structuralist poetics, we can call this subject the implied poet, whose voice we assume to be speaking the poem and through whose sensibility the content of the poem is focalized. This voice may or may not approximate to that of Pound himself, but that is not of central importance to the present discussion. What is important is that the woman came and went for the implied poet: he witnessed her passing. But she 'left no quiver in the veins', i.e. his veins. However we interpret this line, sexually, spiritually, emotionally, a blend of all three, it is clear that the speaking subject suffers a sense of loss or perhaps more accurately the never attained. This sense is projected onto his surroundings to such an extent that they seem imbued with the woman's presence, signalled by the use of 'now' in line two. But they also serve as a constant reminder of her actual absence, reinforced by the 'then' of line four. From this angle, then, the final image makes perfectly good sense: it acts as an equation for the bleakness of the implied poet in the aftergloom of beauty's loss.

The second line quoted above comes from what might be called the perfect imagist poem, since it applies the imagist technique outlined above in a single, brief and striking way. It is also famous because Pound commented in some detail on its origin. The entire poem is as follows:

'In a station of the Metro'

The apparition of these faces in the crowd:
Petals on a wet, black bough.

(CSP, p. 109)

Line drawing of Pound by Henri Gaudier-Brzeska, 1914.

Pound published an explanation of the poem in several places. The following references are to the vorticism essay of 1914 as reprinted in his memoir to Gaudier-Brzeska (*GB*, pp. 86–9). He refers to the poem as 'a hokku-like sentence', meaning in the manner of a Japanese haiku. Since that form has three lines, it is probably best to read the title as the first line. The most striking thing about the

139

structure of the poem is its verbless juxtaposition of a prepositional phrase and two noun phrases. This grammatical incompleteness seems to be a linguistic presentation of truncated, momentary qualities of perception. Pound's account of the provenance and development of the poem confirms this. He explains that as he got out of a Metro train at La Concorde in Paris he saw a series of beautiful faces and 'tried all day to find words for what this had meant to me, and I could not find any words that seemed to me worthy, or as lovely as that sudden emotion'. He goes on to recount how he wrote a much longer poem, then reworked it in ever shorter forms until he eventually arrived at his 'one image poem', which he calls 'a form of superposition, that is to say, it is one idea set on top of another'. In the light of these comments and our previous reading of the final line of 'Gentildonna', we can suggest that 'Petals on a wet, black bough' is not just a straightforward metaphor or truncated simile for the faces in the crowd. The image is an attempt to find an equation for the intellectual and emotional experience Pound went through as the faces appeared to him. As he goes on to say in his commentary, 'one is trying to record the precise instant when a thing outward and objective transforms itself, or darts into a thing inward and subjective'.

The third isolated image quoted above comes from one of the versions of Chinese poems Pound produced prior to working on the poems for *Cathay*. These were probably derived from more literal translations in H.A. Giles's *History of Chinese Literature*, which had been published in 1901. The whole poem is as follows:

'Liu Ch'e'

The rustling of silk is discontinued,
Dust drifts over the courtyard,
There is no sound of footfall, and the leaves
Scurry into heaps and lie still,
And she the rejoicer of the heart is beneath them:

A wet leaf that clings to the threshold.

(CSP, p. 108)

The final line of this poem has the structural features noted above: it is punctuationally detached, the colon 'presenting' the line as it were, and consists of a single noun phrase that is not part of a larger sentence. In addition, Pound isolates the line spatially, an interesting development which he was to exploit in a variety of ways in later poetry, especially *The Cantos*. Applying the mode of analysis developed above to this line, we can suggest that the denotation of this image is one of a fallen leaf that has been stuck to a doorstep by soaking rain. Connotatively, a wet leaf is a sorry sight, bedraggled, at the end of its useful life, no more than litter: the word 'clings' almost personifies the leaf as something which is hanging on hopelessly. In line with previous discussion we would expect this image to encapsulate some psychological state or experience relating to the rest of the poem. A brief paraphrase reveals that this is the case. Liu Ch'e, a Chinese emperor of the second century BC, states that the rustling of his wife's dress and the sound of her footsteps are no longer heard; there is a general air of neglect around the place; in fact the wife he cherished is dead. Once again, it is clear that Pound's image in the final line cannot be a metaphor for the dead wife, as a superficial reading might imply. The image is an attempt to find an equation for 'the thing inward and subjective', which in this case is the emperor's grief and sense of hopelessness at his wife's loss. The power of this use of the image is strikingly demonstrated by contrasting Pound's line with the final line of Giles's translation from which Pound was probably working. After five lines which roughly coincide with Pound's in presenting the consequences of the death of the emperor's wife and the fact that she is gone, Giles's final line reads: 'And I am left, in hopeless anguish tossed' (Brooker, 1979, p. 98). This statement describes in direct and clear terms how the emperor is feeling, but it lacks any emotional charge because it makes no attempt to find an equation for that feeling whereby readers can imagine their way into or empathize with the feeling itself. Pound 'translates' the feeling by providing a concrete image of the emotional devastation felt by the emperor, carrying it across to the reader. Following his very first definition of the image at the beginning of 'A Few Don'ts' in 1913, Pound goes on to say that

> It is the presentation of such a 'complex' instantaneously which gives that sense of sudden liberation; that sense of freedom from time limits and space limits; that sense of sudden growth, which we experience in the presence of the greatest works of art.
>
> (*LE*, p. 4)

Whether a miniature like 'Liu Ch'e' can be counted a great work or not, it seems to me that its final image has the quality to prompt the kind of reader response Pound was trying to elucidate in this statement.

Cathay

The poem 'Liu Ch'e' and other poems derived from the Chinese in 1914 were a foretaste of a much more sustained collection of translations published the following year. The poems of *Cathay* were chosen by Pound, in the words of the acknowledgement, 'For the most part from the Chinese of Rihaku, from the notes of the late Ernest Fenollosa, and the decipherings of the Professors Mori and Ariga' (*CSP*, p. 126). This tells us that *Cathay* is not a translation from Chinese ideograms, of which Pound knew none at the time, but a poetic deciphering twice removed from its source, the Chinese already filtered through the interpretations of Fenollosa's Japanese teachers and the interlinear notes of Fenollosa himself. Pound's insistence on using the Japanese names for the poets is both scrupulous and perverse, but not done in ignorance. Rihaku is Japanese for Li Po, or Li Bai in its contemporary transliteration, AD 701–62, one of the greatest Chinese poets. There is, however, a major difference between these poems and Pound's previous 'Chinese' poems. In 'Liu Ch'e' he was freely adapting a previously published translation in verse form. Here, there is no poem to work from, only notes and cribs, so the act of translation is inventive as well as creative, much closer to writing an original poem. These are probably the first Chinese poems to be translated directly into free verse and their achievement as poems in English is as important as their quality as translations. Eliot was most perceptive about this. His notion that Pound was 'the inventor of Chinese poetry for our time' is much quoted, but he goes on to note that 'Pound's translation is interesting also because it is a phase in the development of Pound's poetry' (Schulman (ed.), 1974, pp. 82, 83). And, he might have added, a phase in the development of English poetry.

Two aspects of the collection are singled out for brief comment here: technical and thematic. The poems were the first unified group to be written in the light of Fenollosa's essay and its powerful endorsement, as Pound saw it, of imagist principles. Although poetic theory and practice rarely match up, the poems have a number of sustained characteristics that may be linked to this influence. Syntactically, the favoured sentence type is a single clause statement in the present tense, usually coterminous with the verse line, rendering the majority of lines end-stopped:

> Ko-Jin goes west from Ko-kaku-ro,
> The smoke-flowers are blurred over the river.
> His lone sail blots the far sky.
>   ('Separation on the River Kiang', *CSP*, p. 137)

These clauses are not necessarily finite and many become no more than phrases through constituent verb lack, reinforcing their presentational quality:

> A gracious spring, turned to blood-ravenous autumn,
> A turmoil of wars-men, spread over the middle kingdom,
> Three hundred and sixty thousand,
> And sorrow, sorrow like rain.
>   ('Lament of the Frontier Guard', *CSP*, p. 133)

The emphasis on simple statement and the absence of auxiliary verbs may stem from Fenollosa's essay, though they are more likely to reflect the raw material of the notes where key words appear in parataxis before the gloss of the commentary and grammatical elements such as tense and number are left vague. The poems are also notable for their wealth of natural detail and, with relevance to the Fenollosa influence, their images grounded in nature. Two examples from 'The River-Merchant's Wife: a Letter' are particularly striking:

> And you have been gone five months.
> The monkeys make sorrowful noise overhead.

> The paired butterflies are already yellow with August
> Over the grass in the West garden;
>   (*CSP*, pp. 130, 131)

In both cases the natural phenomena provide an equation for human emotion: it is the wife who projects sorrow onto the monkeys' noise, who pictures her need in the late summer coupling of the butterflies. This poem, in which Li Po adopts the persona of a young woman to chronicle the progress of an arranged marriage and express the sorrow of separation, is one of the finest in the collection: Pound wears this mask with simple poignancy.

Separation and its sorrows, whatever the cause, is the pervasive theme of *Cathay*. Domestic neglect or desertion, the call of commerce or public service, unwanted exile, all prompt moments of departure, loneliness, longing, nostalgia. The longest poem in the collection is a major realization of this theme: Li Po's 'Exile's Letter'. This account of friendship amid the vicissitudes of political success and failure in the form of a letter to a high-ranking friend

143

was highly thought of by Pound himself. In the first edition of *Cathay*, he inserted his version of 'The Seafarer' next to 'Exile's Letter', presumably because he thought they complemented each other in their treatment of exile and loss. Years later, he was to say, 'Apart from the Seafarer I know no other European poems of the period that you can hang up with the "Exile's Letter" of Li Po, displaying the West on a par with the Orient' (*ABC*, p. 51). It was of some interest to Pound that Li Po's poetry was roughly contemporaneous with the composition of the Anglo-Saxon poem.

In some cases the cause of separation and sorrow in *Cathay* is war. Pound's choice of poems was probably influenced by his response to the First World War, though the cycle as a whole is not an overt collection of war poems. Only three have a distinctly military setting. However, the details and attitudes conveyed are unequivocally anti-war. For example, the opening poem, 'Song of the Bowmen of Shu', both sets the overall tone for the collection and provides an indirect commentary on the deprivations of the First World War as Pound might have imagined them:

We grub the soft fern-shoots,
When anyone says 'Return', the others are full of sorrow.
Sorrowful minds, sorrow is strong, we are hungry and thirsty.

(CSP, p. 127)

This was one of the poems he sent to Gaudier-Brzeska in the trenches and to which his friend replied: 'The poems depict our situation in a wonderful way. We do not yet eat the young nor old fern shoots, but we cannot be over victualled where we stand' (*GB*, p. 58). As well as the plight of the common soldier, the war poems convey the privileges of generals and indict 'barbarous kings', details whose contemporary relevance must have been obvious to readers at the time.

It is worth noting that 'Song of the Bowmen of Shu' was translated again by Pound in his *Classic Anthology defined by Confucius*. In his introduction to that book Achilles Fang notes that 'the appreciable difference between the present version and the "Song of the Bowmen of Shu" is understandable because in the earlier version Pound was at the mercy of Ernest Fenollosa's notes' (*CON*, p. xiii). This implies that the earlier version is inferior. However, it is more helpful to see both versions as appropriate to their respective contexts. Although the two poems really need comparison as a whole, the equivalent passage to the above in the later version, with its bouncy nursery rhyme rhythm, is revealing in its contrasts. Here, the emphasis is on the song element, perhaps a marching song, whereby the soldiers cope with their misfortunes in a less introspective way:

Pick a fern, pick a fern, soft as they come,
I'll say 'Home.'
Hungry all of us, thirsty here,
no home news for nearly a year.

(CON, p. 86)

In the context of the First World War, this seems more like the Chinese equivalent of 'Tipperary' and inappropriate to the overall mood of *Cathay*. In providing two such different but equally valid versions of the same text Pound exemplifies Eliot's point that there is no 'Chinese poetry-in-itself, waiting some ideal translator who shall be only translator' (Schulman (ed.), 1974, p. 83). This point is more than relevant to Pound's other major translations and in particular to their critical reception.

Homage to Sextus Propertius

The Latin poet Sextus Aurelius Propertius was probably first introduced to Pound in his first year at the University of Pennsylvania. He became one of those poets Pound always recommended or included in exemplary lists both in his published pronouncements and in private advice. For example, in a letter to Iris Barry in 1916 which amounts to a guided reading course in the classics, he notes: 'Catullus, Propertius, Horace and Ovid are the people who matter. Catullus most. Martial somewhat. Propertius for beautiful cadence though he uses only one metre' (*SL*, p. 87). The metre was the Latin elegiac, strictly a term for couplets made up of alternating hexameter and pentameter lines. The association of this metre with subject matter of a personal, emotional or tender nature has some basis in classical poetic practice and Propertius does exemplify this. While our term 'elegy' does derive from the Latin usage, it has come to mean something rather more restricted, a poem of mourning. It was Pound's contention that Victorian/Edwardian interpretations of Propertius overemphasized and sentimentalized the elegiac mood of his poetry at the expense of its ironic and playful qualities, its logopoeia. This led him to the rather exaggerated view that there were no 'decent' translations of Propertius available and this seems to have been the initial spur for his own. However, another motivation emerged which radically affected the overall shape and tone of what became the *Homage to Sextus Propertius*. He retrospectively outlined this in a letter from 1931, asserting that the poem presented

> certain emotions as vital to me in 1917, faced with the infinite and ineffable imbecility of the British Empire, as they were to Propertius some centuries earlier, when faced with the infinite and ineffable imbecility of the Roman Empire.

> (*SL*, p. 231)

At the height of the First World War, then, Pound saw his translation, among other things, as a critique of the imperial enterprise and the demands it makes on its poets for literary propaganda.

The following discussion looks at the *Homage* in three ways: as one of Pound's major personae, as a translation and as a poem in its own right. The first two, if not the third, require a brief outline of Propertius and the context in which he lived and wrote poems. Propertius lived in the second half of the first century BC, though his exact dates are unknown. It is likely that he was entering adulthood around the time of Antony's defeat at the battle of Actium in 31 BC. Within a few years the victor, Octavian, had renamed himself Augustus, the first Roman emperor. Civil war, which had devastated Rome for much of the previous 100 years, was at an end. Unifying exploits against common, foreign enemies were the order of the day. Augustus, his achievements and his imperial plans had to be endorsed in as many ways as possible, including the use of literature. This political context coincided with a time when the status of poetry and poets had finally shifted from amateur to professional. Through patronage poets were able to achieve high social standing. However, such patronage could also have obligations that amounted to commissioned literary propaganda. Propertius appears to have been reasonably wealthy, with influential relatives and friends. However, it is clear from his poetry that patrons, such as Maecenas, one of Augustus's ministers, put him under some pressure to write an epic that would support the imperial enterprise. Propertius had no reason to do so: his family had suffered at the hands of Octavian in the civil wars. Furthermore, his poetic allegiance was to the Greek poets of the Alexandrian school who had written rich, verbally complex lyrics and repudiated the epic.

Pound adopts Propertius as a major persona, wearing his mask in a series of brilliant translations, paraphrases or imitations, depending on which criteria one applies. In order to do so, he is highly selective. Propertius's work is arranged in four books, the first two of which concentrate on his love for Cynthia. Pound takes the bulk of his material from books two and three, where Propertius expounds his Alexandrian allegiance and debates the role of the lyric poet in an imperial world. This debate anticipates to some extent the issues that Pound explores in his next major cycle of poems, *Hugh Selwyn Mauberley*, though with very different conclusions. Here the outcome is positive: the lyric triumphs and the epic is rejected. In terms of our theory of the persona, perhaps translating Propertius in this positive way helped Pound to cast off his exclusively lyric mask. He had, after all, already written drafts of the early cantos, but the nature of his 'epic' was still uncertain. *Mauberley* tackles the issue in a very different way. What conclusion there is, is negative: the exclusively lyric poet is in an aesthetic cul-de-sac. No alternative is offered within the poem, though the poem itself suggests a possible way forward, if the epic Propertius rejected can somehow be assumed. Pound's selectivity extends to rearranging his chosen extracts, sometimes within individual sections, to create his own patterns of emphasis and contrast. In drawing his political analogy, Pound implicitly equates the

147

past slaughter of civil war and the prospective damage of colonial conquest with the devastation of world war in all its apparency by 1917. The military epics of imperial Rome imply in theme, if not in genre, the jingoistic sonnet and the 'liars in public places' of wartime England. But, unlike *Mauberley*, this is not a bitter poem. This theme is lightened by its ironic treatment and balanced by others: love with its passions and jealousies, the triumph of poetry over death. These topics too are subject to the playful ironies of logopoeia.

The identification of Propertius as a master of logopoeia and the desire to convey this in translation was probably the main cause of the poem's negative reception by Latin scholars and critics. According to Pound's own formulation, 'Logopoeia does not translate; though the attitude of mind it expresses may pass through a paraphrase' (*LE*, p. 25). Even if translation at the literal end of the spectrum were desirable in a poem, then, it is ruled out in this case by the logopoeic nature of the original. Of course, one of the main criticisms of the *Homage* that has persisted to the present is that Pound misrepresents the amount of logopoeia in Propertius and introduces irony and verbal play where there are none. A contemporary translator of the complete poems of Propertius who clearly admires Pound's achievement, nevertheless is of the opinion that where Propertius is 'muted, suave, subtle', Pound has 'a verbal swagger', is 'a little vulgar, flamboyant' (Shepherd, 1985, p. 29). It may well be that Shepherd's translation provides 'Propertius-in-itself', having found some ideal translator who shall be only translator'. Even if that were the case, it would not invalidate the text that is *Homage to Sextus Propertius* which invents a Propertian world, not only for its time but for its readers, whenever they happen to be. The debates about the 'accuracy' of Pound's translation, the focus on perceived 'howlers', were and still are tinged with pedantry and oversensitive erudition. Of course, 'docta testudine', literally 'with a skilful tortoise-shell lyre', becomes 'Like a trained and performing tortoise', a brilliant simile for the time-serving propagandist poet. Of course, 'Wordsworthian' is used anachronistically to characterize a tedious ancient Greek poet. What is often overlooked when such instances are highlighted is the fact that many of Pound's lines are as literal as one could want in a poetic translation or convey the sense of the original far better than any literal version could. George Steiner includes in his definition of translation 'the writing of a poem in which a poem in another language (or in an earlier form of one's own language) is the vitalizing, shaping presence; a poem which can be read and responded to independently but which is not ontologically complete, a previous poem being its occasion, begetter, and in the literal sense, raison d'être' (Steiner (ed.), 1970, p. 34). *Homage to Sextus Propertius* is the archetype here and it is a shame that Pound was driven by reactionary 'scholarship' to deny its status as a translation altogether. Indeed, if *Cathay* is arguably the first modern translation, then the *Homage*, with its self-conscious intrusions and textual distortions, is the first one to be truly modernist.

As a poem in its own right the *Homage* has one outstanding difficulty: the range and density of its classical references and allusions. As a Latin poet in the Alexandrian tradition Propertius is prolific in this respect and it is a measure of Pound's faithfulness to the original that his translation fully reflects this. Although the problem for the reader is of Propertius's making in this case, it parallels one presented by some of Pound's other work and in particular *The Cantos*. One approach is to look up and absorb the significance of every reference. Its polar opposite is an unsupported reading: if an allusion means nothing, the reader infers whatever the verbal ambience of the text allows and moves on. With the *Homage* I favour a fairly minimalist reading. Some passages that are dense with references may be almost unintelligible as detail, but will usually make sense as illustrative wholes, for example, the passage in section V, 2 which lists lots of heroes Propertius won't be writing about, though ironically by compiling the list he is actually writing about them anyway. Unknown references can always be followed up for interest's sake, but that is not necessary for an overall understanding of the poem. However, some key bits of information are useful from the outset, even though most of them are embodied in the text: 1. Callimachus and Philetas are poets of the Alexandrian school favoured by Propertius; 2. Apollo is the god of poetry to whom the Muses are responsible and Calliope the Muse of epic poetry; 3. Cynthia, Propertius's lover, is a Roman 'new woman' in the line of Catullus's Lesbia, independent, though probably married, and 'in control' of the relationship: the name is probably a pseudonym for an actual person, though there is a possibility that Cynthia is fictitious; 4. Jove (Jupiter, Zeus) is the king of the gods and Juno the queen, while Persephone and Dis rule the underworld; 5. most other references are to mythological figures and deities, actual military and political leaders, places associated with these groups: this can usually be inferred from the surrounding text without knowing every reference in detail.

The poem is in twelve sections, some of them subdivided. What follows is an attempt to provide an overall picture of the arrangement Pound imposes on his material by giving brief characterizations of each section:

I. Propertius affirms the Alexandrian lyric over the epic: poetry cheats mortality.

II. Propertius debates his role as lyric or epic poet with Apollo and Calliope.

III. Cynthia: Propertius declines her invitation out of cowardice.

IV. Cynthia: Propertius receives news of her from the slave Lygdamus.

V. Propertius is pressurized to write epic propaganda by Maecenas and defends his preference for love poetry.

VI. A meditation on death: Propertius imagines his own funeral and Cynthia's mourning.

VII. Cynthia: a night of sexual bliss which prompts thoughts of mortality.

VIII. Cynthia's illness and possible death: an ironic plea for her safety.

IX. Cynthia's illness and recovery.

X. Cynthia: Propertius is kidnapped by cupids and taken to her: she is indignant at his intrusion.

XI. A meditation on Cynthia's infidelity: Propertius will forgive her anything.

XII. Propertius's friend Lynceus, a minor epic poet, is Cynthia's latest lover: despite this and the impending success of Virgil's epic, Propertius aligns himself with the great lyric love poets of the past.

This overview allows us to see how the main concerns of the poem are introduced, presented and interwoven. The relationship between Cynthia and Propertius is central to the greatest number of sections, one of which depicts their love-making with happy sensuality:

> Me happy, night, night full of brightness . . .
> Now with bared breasts she wrestled against me,
>   Tunic spread in delay;
> And she then opening my eyelids fallen in sleep,
> Her lips upon them; and it was her mouth saying:
> Sluggard!
>
> (*CSP*, p. 220)

Even here, though, the poem shifts to the 'carpe diem' theme in a manner that clearly invokes Catullus:

> Today we take the great breath of lovers,
>   tomorrow fate shuts us in.
> Though you give all your kisses
>   you give but few.
>
> (*CSP*, p. 221)

In this way the Cynthia sections provide contexts for other themes, such as jealousy, death, the immortality of poetry. The poem is structured to allow these themes to offset the major concern for

150

the role of the artist in an imperial society which is proclaimed
in the opening sections:

> Annalists will continue to record Roman reputations,
> Celebrities from the Trans-Caucasus will belaud Roman
>   celebrities
> And expound the distentions of Empire,
> But for something to read in normal circumstances?
> For a few pages brought down from the forked hill
>   unsullied?
> I ask a wreath which will not crush my head.
>
> (*CSP*, p. 207)

In contrast, these debates are followed by the accessible anecdote
of section III where Propertius reveals his feet of clay. Cleverly,
a light-hearted depiction of his death and funeral is introduced
which foreshadows the much more sombre meditation of section
VI:

> When, when, and whenever death closes our eyelids,
> Moving naked over Acheron
> Upon the one raft, victor and conquered together,
> Marius and Jugurtha together,
> one tangle of shadows.
>
> (*CSP*, p. 218)

These are only a few examples of the way thematic foreshadowing
and textual reprise create a convincing and integral Propertian
world whose final section ends in lyric solidarity:

> And in the dyed pages of Calvus,
>   Calvus mourning Quintilia,
> And but now Gallus had sung of Lycoris.
>   Fair, fairest Lycoris –
> The waters of Styx poured over the wound:
> And now Propertius of Cynthia, taking his stand
>   among these.
>
> (*CSP*, p. 230)

Hugh Selwyn Mauberley

Pound considered that *Mauberley* was an up-to-date and more specific presentation of the anti-imperialist message of *Propertius*. Although that may be the case, just as *Propertius* is about other things, so also *Mauberley* explores a wider range of issues. Furthermore, they differ not just in the poetic worlds they portray, historical Rome against contemporary London, but also in matters of style. Where *Propertius* is free and expansive, its wit and pathos presented by a consistent voice, *Mauberley* is forced and tight, its irony and anger delivered by uncertain and anonymous voices. This difference in the sureness of the persona partly derives from the translated nature of *Propertius*, but also signals the shift towards the much more fragmented multiplicity of voices in *The Cantos*. The transitional place of *Mauberley* in this respect is complicated by autobiographical ambiguities which render uncertain the status of the character Mauberley as a persona. Whereas *Propertius* presents a circumscribed classical world some of whose references, I argued, could be overlooked without loss of sense, *Mauberley* presents a wider range of references and allusions in a manner that foreshadows the encyclopaedic nature of *The Cantos*. In a few sections of the poem these features take on a cryptographic quality where the point is lost without decoding. These structural and linguistic aspects of *Mauberley* undoubtedly make it more difficult to read than much of Pound's previous work: its first anonymous reviewer praised its 'qualities of structure, rhythm and sincerity' but considered it 'needlessly obscure' (Homberger (ed.), 1972, p. 194). Some of the obscurity in the poem is probably needless in the eyes of a reviewer who was unaware of Pound and Eliot's literary political motivation to combat the pastoral simplicities of the Georgian school of verse. A reasonable level of obscurity helped to make modernist poetry distinctive.

Even this poem's 'surface structure', to use or probably misuse Chomsky's now universal phrase, needs careful scrutiny. It consists of eighteen short poems with the overall title *Hugh Selwyn Mauberley*, which carries the subtitle 'Life and Contacts' and a Latin epigraph. They are divided into two uneven sections of thirteen poems then five, some of which are numbered while others have upper case titles. The section with five poems has its own title, 'Mauberley 1920', and its own Latin epigraph, which suggests that the first Latin epigraph might really only belong to the first section and not the poem as a whole. The longer first section has no title of its own. Apart from the occasional use of block capitals and Greek lettering, the graphics are unremarkable, but there is one poem printed entirely in italics. Most of the poems are set out in four-line stanzas, though the actual line lengths and rhyme schemes are variable. This more or less casual perusal of layout, graphics, titles and the like suggests two major ways of getting beneath the poem's surface. First, the poem's physical organization into two sections seems to be attempting some form of balance or even symmetry which fails or is subverted in some way. In what ways does this two-part arrangement reflect the thematic or narrative meaning of the poem? Second, why is Pound, the master of imagist free verse, using the quatrain as a structural prop for one of his major works and how does this relate to the language of the poem as a whole?

The second of these questions is more readily answered, since in 1932 Pound gave the following retrospective account:

> At a particular date in a particular room two authors . . . decided that the dilution of vers libre, Amygism . . . general floppiness had gone too far and that some counter-current must be set going . . . Remedy prescribed, *Emaux et Camées* (or The Bay State Hymn Book). Rhyme and regular strophes. Results: Poems in Mr. Eliot's second volume . . . also 'H.S. Mauberley'.
>
> (Brooker, 1979, p. 185)

Pound and Eliot, then, in the year or so after the First World War, collaborated on poetry which was meant to redress what they saw as the slackness that had crept into free-for-all verse. Pound's poetic antennae were particularly sensitive to language that he considered slithery, sloppy, slack, muzzy or soft. This was partly an overreaction to his own early poetry, but mainly had a doctrinaire aspect: the rejection of the qualities indicated by such labels was a corollary of the imagist/vorticist preference for hard clear lines. Particularly relevant here is an article from 1918 entitled 'The Hard and Soft in French Poetry'. In this Pound asserts that hardness is always a virtue in poetry, though he concedes that softness need not always be a fault. He goes on to say: 'Anyone who dislikes these textural terms may lay the blame on Théophile Gautier, who certainly suggests them in *Emaux et Camées*; it is his hardness that I first had in mind' (*LE*, p. 285). Pound thought that the French poet's work, especially the quatrains of his 1852 volume, literally 'Enamels and Cameos', presented a model for the linguistic equivalent of hard-surfaced designs or portraits cut in hard stone, though the qualities of this language are never given any precise exemplification. There is a hint in a letter of 1916 in which Pound says of Gautier: 'perfectly plain statements like his "Carmen est maigre" should teach one a number of things' (*SL*, p. 89). On this evidence, simple one-clause sentences with a finite verb and the minimal amount of adjectival or adverbial adornment are the preferred medium, just the kind of language I suggested would fulfil the imagist requirement for 'direct treatment of the thing'. There are a large number of such sentences in *Mauberley*, sometimes in coordination, sometimes with a qualifying adverbial phrase, but often syntactically self-contained. A good example of their cumulative use is in poem III of section one, where six quatrains pile up instances of bitter disappointment in 'perfectly plain statements'. In the climactic seventh stanza the poetic voice's exasperation at these instances is reinforced by the syntactic shift into exclamatory question. Variants on the basic unit of finite statement are most obviously elaborations through compounding and subordination. However, there are examples where Pound retains the single unit but creates a sense of complexity by means of phrasal elaboration. In poem III of the second section we get:

> The glow of porcelain
> Brought no reforming sense
> To his perception
> Of the social inconsequence.

> > (*CSP*, p. 201)

The sense of elaboration within this syntactically simple statement is further reinforced by the fact that it realizes an entire rhyming quatrain.

Variants in the direction of syntactic minimalism pose a different kind of problem for the reader. The non-realization of one or more elements in the basic unit results in an elliptical sentence that requires some kind of verbal reconstitution. For example, the final poem begins: 'Luini in porcelain!' (ibid., p. 204). Outside of any cultural reference, this isolated unit's meaning is syntactically challenged: possible verbal realizations that might resolve its meaning remain indeterminate, depend contextually on the whole poem. That context allows us to arrive at something like: this woman singing at the piano looks like/is reminiscent of Luini in porcelain. Without any further culturally determined knowledge, that is enough for us to appreciate the decorative ceramic quality of her looks and relate them to the poem's title, 'Medallion'. The element of cryptography in such phrases is at least sensitive to syntactic and contextual resolution. More extreme minimalization leads to examples like the syntactically detached 'Capaneus' in the first poem of the sequence (ibid., p. 187). Syntactically the status of this word is entirely indeterminate. Its meaning is insensitive to contextual resolution. If we do not know who Capaneus is, we can treat the word as a phonic filler within the verse line. If we do know, we can try to make sense of the significance of the name within the poem. The problems of syntactic and contextual indeterminacy I have touched on here reflect Pound's desire to create a modern realization of Gautier's enamelled verse, but they were always implicit and sometimes explicit in his earlier poetry and become even more challenging in range and scale in *The Cantos*.

As well as Gautier's polished quatrains, the other model for 'rhymes and regular strophes' was an American hymnal. In Christian hymnody at any rate, a large proportion of verses are quatrains rhymed 'abab' or 'abcb'. Most of the poems in *Mauberley* have one of these stanzaic patterns as their framework, though the way they break out of or otherwise vary the pattern is one of the technical delights of the sequence. Contrasts in length and density are used to realize physically the meanings of lines. For example, in poem III of the second section Mauberley's ineffectual mental drift is catalogued with tedious abstraction:

> Incapable of the least utterance or composition,
> Emendation, conservation of the 'better tradition',
> Refinement of medium, elimination of superfluities,
> August attraction or concentration.
>
> (*CSP*, p. 202)

The abandonment of perfectly plain statements reinforces this weariness: the syntax is no more than a parataxis of noun phrases dependent on the initial adjective. By contrast, in the very next poem, Mauberley's terse suicide note consists of three simple statements embodied in a quite remarkable variant of the quatrain form:

> 'I was
> And I no more exist;
> Here drifted
> An hedonist.'
>
> (*CSP*, p. 203)

These two stanzas also illustrate variation in rhyme scheme and the use of weak and half rhyme. Such devices are used to great effect throughout the sequence. For example, poem XI in section one has a strict 'abba' pattern incorporating polysyllabic rhymes, one of which, 'Milesien' against 'Englishmen', is really just graphic similarity, since the actual sounds do not match at all. This is only one example of Pound's use of rhyme between different languages. Perhaps the most startling occurs in the climax to poem III of section one, where an ancient Greek phrase pronounced 'tin-a-the-on' is matched with 'tin wreath upon'. These examples, and many others, of the way Pound manipulates stanza forms, rhyme schemes and the phonic properties of language contribute to the melopoeic intensity of the whole. But, more than in any of his previous work, this attention to phonic, rhythmic and melodic qualities is so much at the service of the poem's bitter ironies that the integration of melopoeia and logopoeia seems fully achieved.

This preliminary look at its language has given us a feel for *Mauberley* as a poetic text and a few glimpses at the densely allusive world it creates. My first question, about the poem's organization and how this might reflect its thematic or narrative meaning, concerns the relation of its surface structure to its deep structure, to preserve the Chomskyan analogy. Again, Pound himself can help us initially. In almost all printings of *Mauberley* the subtitle appears as 'Life and Contacts'. However, for a reprinting in 1957, Pound told his publisher to invert it so as to reflect 'the actual order of the subject matter' (Ruthven, 1969, p. 127). Applying this to the organization of the poem suggests that the first section is about Mauberley's 'contacts', those he knew or knew of, and the second a kind of potted biography. This application characterizes the second section very well. Its first four poems are written in third person, past tense narrative in which the 'he' whose story is told can be assumed to be Mauberley, though he is never named. There is one narrator intrusion, 'we admit', in poem III, but this does not disturb the narrative or affect its status. The fifth poem, 'Medallion', is a portrait of a woman singing at a piano, written in the present tense. Given that Mauberley emerges from the narrative as a poet, we can take the last poem as a sample of his work. The first section, unfortunately, does not accept the above application in any straightforward way. The first poem is an obituary, real or mock, for 'E. P.'. None of the other poems is a third person narrative where the 'he' can be assumed to be Mauberley. Some of the poems which are most obviously accounts of 'contacts' are written in the first person, as is the final poem whose voice, on the basis of what we learn in section two, could never be that of Mauberley. Are these first person voices that of the intrusive narrator in section two? These uncertainties and questions cast doubt on the clear-cut organization indicated by 'Contacts and Life' and most of all render the status of Mauberley as character and/or persona problematical.

Even though it has raised some problems, Pound's own comment has proved a useful guide to the poem's apparent two-part structure. It is worth, therefore, following up his other pronouncements on *Mauberley*. In a letter of 1922 he said: 'Of course, I'm no more Mauberley than Eliot is Prufrock ... Mauberley is a mere surface. Again a study in form, an attempt to condense the James

novel' (*SL*, p. 180). In the first part of this comment Pound dis-
tances himself from the character of Mauberley, suggesting per-
haps that he was aware it was being seen as a persona of himself
in ways he never intended. He should not have been surprised at
this, since the problems inherent in the poem's schema more or
less invite confusion. These formal subtleties may be a direct con-
sequence of Pound's aim, expressed in the second part of his com-
ment, to write a condensed Jamesian novel. Pound admired Henry
James and we can get a good idea of what he considered to be
the hallmarks of James's fiction from his essay of 1918, where he
expressed the following opinion: 'If one were advocate instead of
critic, one would definitely claim that these atmospheres, nuances,
impressions of personal tone and quality are his subject' (*LE*, p. 324).
A condensed homage to James's fiction, as Pound saw it, is therefore
more likely to be concerned with creating ambience and revealing
psychological insight than presenting a fully coherent narrative struc-
ture. Pound's sense of the fictional nature of *Mauberley* was not a
passing defence against criticism. In his *Paris Review* interview of
1960 he reasserted his belief that 'Mauberley . . . was the definite
attempt to get the novel cut down to the size of verse' (Dick (ed.),
1972, p. 100). While it is clear that *Mauberley* is not a narrative
poem in the conventional sense, perhaps we ought to take the poet
at his word and treat it as an experimental verse novel.

Seeing the poem as a novel prompts us to ask questions that
are more usually associated with the reading of fiction than poetry,
questions of authorial voice, number and status of narrators, focal-
ization, character development, plot, temporal organization. Ad-
dressing such questions might help to resolve problems raised by
the 'Contacts and Life' approach adopted above. We have already
seen that the second section is readily described in novelistic terms.
The narrative voice recounts in the third person the latter part of
Mauberley's life and leaves us with a sample of his work. There is
little plot as such: the narrative sketches its protagonist's aesthetic
loss of confidence, sexual failure, breakdown and suicide in the Far
East. No other characters are delineated. The woman Mauberley
is involved with is not only anonymous but perceived as almost
nebulous: 'He had moved amid her phantasmagoria'. Perhaps she
is the singer portrayed in his poem. All this is focalized omnisci-
ently by the narrator, who reveals himself once with a concessive
aside.

In contrast, the first section is inhabited by a wide range of
characters. Some are actual historical figures, like Gladstone in
poem VI and Dowson in poem VII. Others, such as Brennbaum
in poem VIII and The Lady Valentine in poem XII, are fictional.
There is no plot at all in this section. Some of the poems bemoan

the cultural decline of the times, others furiously lament the tragedy of the First World War. The historical figures are no more than emblems of the eras they lived in. There is some character revelation, if not development, of, for example, Mr. Nixon in poem IX and the textual 'I' of poem XII. The narrative voice of nine of the poems seems to match that of the second section and is allowed to intrude explicitly in poem III. The presence of a textual 'I' in four other poems needs more detailed comment.

In three of these poems, VII, IX and XII, the narrator meets and converses with fictional characters. One way of dealing with this is to propose that the narrator here is Mauberley, that the 'I' is properly a persona, though unidentified except by implication. This lack of identification does, as I noted in my earlier discussion of the persona as a device, invite an autobiographically situated reading. Given the potential similarity between Mauberley's 'contacts' and Pound's real-life experience, this ambiguity between poet and persona is inevitable. In addition the 'voice' of these poems is not obviously differentiated from the narrative voice implicit elsewhere. These uncertainties may be seen as part of the modernist syndrome of textual relativity and narrator unreliability. However, it is also fair, I think, in the case of *Mauberley*, to suggest that Pound the 'novelist' is not fully in control of the fictional techniques he means to employ. Certainly, a later remark of his, meant to enlighten his confused critics, suggests a level of confusion of his own: 'The worst muddle they make is in failing to see that Mauberley buries E. P. in the first poem; gets rid of all his troublesome energies' (Brooker, 1979, p. 188). If the voice that buries E. P. in the first poem is attributed to Mauberley, then the narrator of the other poems in the sequence would revert to him too, resulting in the dead Mauberley narrating his own life and reading his own suicide note. While this is not impossible in fictional terms, it makes for an unsatisfactory reading of the poem as a whole. It also loosens the concept of persona to the point where it means any kind of coincidental similarity between author and character, rather than the well-defined literary phenomenon it is. Pound may have made this remark in exasperation, rather like some of his over-defensive claims about the translation of Propertius. Whatever the case, I find this particular piece of insider information misleading.

The final poem in the first section, entitled 'Envoi (1919)', is the poetic, and moral, centre of the sequence. It is a first person lyric address to what has gone before, affirming the positive beauty of poetry against the catalogue of negativity in the 'dumb-born book'. The quality of this lyric exemplifies the beauty it affirms in a voice that cannot possibly be that of the persona, the textual 'I' that is

Mauberley. Neither does it belong to the narrative voice of the poem as a whole. Its language is distinguished by that kind of archaism which Pound had refined in his earlier poetry and which in *The Cantos* is the stylistic marker of lyric and emotional intensity, as it is here:

> Hadst thou but song
> As thou hast subjects known . . .
> Recking naught else but that her graces give
> Life to the moment . . .
> Till change hath broken down
> All things save Beauty alone.

(*CSP*, p. 197)

This distinctive style is graphically reinforced by the italicized presentation on the page. Together with its title and date this emphasizes its detachment from the preceding poems to the extent that it is more like a separate section of its own. This is the novelistic equivalent of those passages or chapters where authors temporarily detach themselves from their fiction to reflect on some theoretical, philosophical or structural aspect of their work. But Pound's modernism will not allow him to do so without a touch of ambiguity: 'Envoi (1919)' refers to a female singer and therefore anticipates 'Medallion' which in its turn becomes the other poem's echo. This kind of cross-referencing between sections and voices occurs throughout *Mauberley*, blurring identities, creating uncertainties in a play of foreshadowing and reprise.

This brief look at the poem as verse novel suggests that its overall organization is dependent on the interplay of different voices and characters rather than narrative structures. Three voices are implicated in the schema that I find most helpful to an overall understanding of the poem. First, there is Pound himself, or, in the more careful terminology of theoretical poetics, the implied poet of the text: this is the voice of 'Envoi (1919)'. Second, there is the voice which narrates much of the sequence. My reading identifies this voice as that of E. P. In so far as E. P. occasionally intrudes in the first person, he may be considered a persona, though his identity is only implied: clearly, the psychological and experiential proximity of E. P. to Pound himself renders this persona highly complex and ambiguous. Third, there is Mauberley, whose voice is heard in three poems in section one: he too is only an implied persona, since the textual 'I' is not identified as such. Mauberley is also the major character in section two.

With this schema as a guide to the poetic and narrative voices in *Mauberley*, the brief summary which follows is meant only to give an overview of the sequence with some indicative examples of its allusive richness and cross-referencing. Guides, such as Ruthven (1969) and Brooker (1979), give definitions of, or explanations for, virtually every word or phrase requiring additional comment and these are recommended to support more thorough reading.

Epigraph: Pound's conception of *Mauberley* as a 'farewell to London' may well explain this. The Latin's literal meaning, 'The heat calls us into the shade', reminds us of a much more trenchant contemporary motto: 'If you can't stand the heat, get out of the kitchen.' Just as E. P. 'passed from men's memory' and Mauberley 'drifted precipitate', so Pound turned his back on the hostile literary environment of postwar London.

I: E. P. ODE POUR L'ELECTION DE SON SEPULCHRE: E. P. offers an ironic ode on his own literary career and demise, projecting onto himself the patronizing assessment of the London literary establishment. The quotation from, and references to, Homer's *Odyssey* probably show the influence of Joyce, whose *Ulysses* Pound was busy promoting at this time, as well as his own work on the early cantos.

II: E. P. characterizes the age he has lived through in London by its preference for facile art with mass appeal.

III: Continuing the elitism of poem II, E. P. compares an ancient past of fine art and pagan ritual with a degenerate present and expresses anti-democratic sentiments: the vote allows us to choose 'a knave or an eunuch' as our leader.

IV: E. P. dwells on the wastage of the First World War and the disillusionment of its aftermath with some bitterness. In this context Pound first uses the term 'usury' in a poem.

V: E. P. angrily laments the sacrifices of the trenches for the 'botched civilization' typified in poems II and III.

YEUX GLAUQUES: E. P. presents a condensed portrait of the pre-Raphaelite age. The main focus is Elizabeth Siddall, lover and wife of Dante Gabriel Rossetti, who was the model for many famous pre-Raphaelite paintings, including Burne-Jones's 'Cophetua and the beggar maid'. Siddall committed suicide. E. P. comments on her fate by invoking 'Jenny', a prostitute in one of Rossetti's poems. 'Yeux Glauques' is the first in a sequence of retrospective snapshots depicting historical and contemporary aspects of the English literary scene.

'SIENA MI FE; DISFECEMI MAREMMA': Mauberley recalls meeting Monsieur Verog, who tells him about the poets of the Nineties: Mauberley shows no awareness that their aesthetic decadence may be pertinent to his own career. For this poem Pound used details learned from Yeats at Stone Cottage as well as the memoirs of his friend Victor Plarr, another Nineties poet.

BRENNBAUM: E. P. portrays a Jewish writer whose externally

immaculate appearance acts as a protective cover for his Judaic preoccupations.

MR. NIXON: Mauberley is given advice on how to advance his career by a successful, but cynical, writer. He is told to write for nothing at first, 'butter reviewers' and 'give up verse'. Perhaps Mauberley takes the last bit of advice to heart with the result shown in section two.

X: E. P. offers a picture of a so-called 'stylist' who has paid for his artistic integrity with lack of recognition and financial reward, in contrast to the manipulative Mr. Nixon.

XI: E. P. dismisses the possibility that a suburban woman writer may even be working in a worthwhile tradition, given constraints of marriage and upbringing. The influence of Rémy de Gourmont on Pound's thinking is evident here.

XII: Mauberley reflects upon the literary patronage of an upper-class society woman and incidentally reveals his lack of sexual confidence: at least the lady has an interest in poetry which, Mauberley concludes in an afterthought, can hardly be said of the popular press.

ENVOI (1919): In a lyric that matches its original model, Edmund Waller's seventeenth-century lovesong 'Go, Lovely Rose', the poet commands his 'dumb-born book' to take a message about the transcendent beauty of song to the woman who once sang for him 'that song of Lawes'. There is no poetic reason why this singer should have been 'real' and Pound himself rightly dismissed any enquiries as to the identity of the 'her that sheds Such treasure in the air'. Raymonde Collignon, Pound's favourite 'diseuse' during his years as William Atheling, the music critic of *The New Age*, is usually cited. This is only of critical interest in that it leads us to one of Atheling's reviews from 1918 in which he says: 'Raymonde Collignon's art is exquisite and her own, minute as the enamelling on snuff-boxes . . .' (Shafer (ed.), 1978, p. 119). This is an unusual enough comparison in itself, but its interest here is the link it suggests in Pound's mind between Collignon's art and Gautier's verse 'emaux', the medium he was working with in *Mauberley*, the medium in which he would compose the only sample of Mauberley's poetry, the enamelled portrait of a 'diseuse' that is 'Medallion'.

The Latin epigraph that accompanies 'Mauberley (1920)' refers to the frustration of a mythical dog when trying to bite an elusive monster: in Ovid's account both dog and monster are turned to stone. This signals the frustration of Mauberley's failed sexual relationship and his atrophy as person and poet: its translation is the basis of the final quatrain of the second poem.

I: E. P.'s ironic assessment of his own commitment to Flaubertian exactitude in the initial ode really does apply to Mauberley and

is quoted straight: 'His true Penelope Was Flaubert'. E. P. char-
acterizes Mauberley's art as colourless aestheticism.

II: For three years (probably the same three years that E. P.
was striving to resuscitate the dead art of poetry), Mauberley
has failed to consummate his relationship with a woman who has
never become more than intellectual ambrosia. By the time he has
woken up to her sexual signals, his 'mandate Of Eros' is 'a retro-
spect'. This ineptitude parallels an artistic incompetence.

'THE AGE DEMANDED': it is clear that Mauberley is quite
incapable of responding to demands for the kind of populist art
E. P. outlined in poem II of the first section. This 'chapter' records
with a tedious concatenation of abstract nouns Mauberley's de-
cline into apathy and resignation from the London literary scene.

IV: Mauberley escapes from English life and letters; in a meta-
phorical fantasy, perhaps. From a novelistic point of view I prefer
to read this poem as E. P.'s account of Mauberley's actual retreat
to the South Seas and his appropriately indecisive drift into self-
slaughter.

MEDALLION: a sample result of Mauberley's 'urge to convey
the relation Of eye-lid to cheek-bone By verbal manifestation'. Its
descriptions are derived from books and art galleries, precise but
passionless.

This summary has, I think, given us a clear picture of the
poem's overall shape and progression from one interpretative point
of view. Other readings allocate the distribution of voices differ-
ently, discern different shifts in the narrative, and we have seen
that Pound had his own interpretative stance in this respect. I
conclude from this that the poem has a degree of in-built structural
uncertainty and it is this that caused it to be seen as needlessly
obscure rather than any problems raised by its range of references
and allusions. Structurally, then, the work has a design fault which,
if it were a 'prose kinema' rather than tightly packed quatrains,
would still remain. Seeing each poem as a chapter in a novel does
help with this structural problem. Modernist fictional technique
makes quite commonplace such things as multiple narrators, the
unreliable narrator and the first person narrator who becomes a
third person character in alternate chapters. Focusing on the cine-
matic aspect of the above term may also help us to live more
easily with the poem's structure. The intercutting of images, voices,
scenes and narrative perspectives can be viewed as filmic montage.
These approaches will be equally useful, if not more so, for read-
ing *The Cantos*.

In focusing on the language and structure of Mauberley I
have said very little about its overall significance in Pound's poetic
career and life. It is an intensely personal poem in which Pound pub-

licly and courageously assesses his situation as a poet in post-First World War London. His dismay at what he sees as the injustice of that situation with regard to recent political and literary contexts is not concealed and the contexts themselves are treated with an angry bitterness. Paradoxically, this intense personal involvement is handled by means of a more complex use of masks than any of his previous work which stretches the concept of the persona to breaking point. If E. P. and Mauberley are yet more elaborate masks of the self (and it is hard to conceive of them otherwise), then only one is cast off in the farewell to London. Mauberley is thoroughly killed off in the poem, though in the life and the future work the aesthete would never wholly capitulate to the man putting ideas into action. E. P. is more problematical because he is more obviously Pound's alter ego than a persona as such. E. P. expresses the dismay, carries the anger, hints at racism, implies attitudes of male chauvinism. And survives the poem.

The Cantos

In 1949 Basil Bunting wrote a brief verse commentary entitled 'On the Fly-leaf of Pound's Cantos' in which he likens the poems to the Alps, phenomena which simply exist:

They don't make sense. Fatal glaciers, crags cranks climb,
jumbled boulder and weed, pasture and boulder, scree . . .
There they are, you will have to go a long way round
if you want to avoid them.

(Bunting, 1978, p. 110)

Bunting's analogy may be fanciful, but it is worth pursuing as a first way of thinking about Pound's ultimate work which runs in its latest edition to well over 800 pages. The Alps do not have to make sense in the commonly understood meaning of that term, though they may be said to 'make sense' in terms of the geological development of the planet or, for some, as a manifestation of divine creativity. However, there is some expectation that poems will make sense, not just in terms of general poetic development or as examples of the poet's creativity, but as coherent text. The idea that *The Cantos*, like the Alps, do not make sense in any way that term commonly implies has been part of the critical reception of the poem from the time of its early instalments to the present day. Pound himself also made various statements over the years about the manner in which the poem did and did not make sense, so the idea needs to be taken seriously. Bunting's analogy also points to some of the problems confronting the reader of *The Cantos* and suggests that there is rather less poetic pasture than desired even in a verbal mountain range. The idea that *The Cantos* are unavoidable is the weak point of the analogy. No-one has to visit the Alps. Indeed, some would argue they are out of bounds. You can always fly over them or read a rough guide instead of sampling the real thing. But if you do not want to avoid them, then the analogy holds good. People motor through the Alps, tour round the famous sights, go on more detailed tours and even go climbing, but rarely every mountain. Those who get a taste for the Alps usually visit them over and over again.

The analogy suggests a number of approaches to reading *The Cantos*. First, there is the skim and skip approach. In a letter of 1934, when admittedly far less than half *The Cantos* had been written, Pound advised a reader: 'Skip anything you don't understand

and go on till you pick it up again' (*SL*, p. 250). This is one way of fairly rapidly reading the whole work as a first look at the poem, getting a feel for it and finding bits you like for yourself. A *Selected Cantos* was first published in 1967 and there is also a selection of cantos in the *Selected Poems* of 1975. At one level such selections have already done some skipping for you, but you can also read these preselected cantos or passages with the method advocated by Pound. The second main approach is often called 'the annotated index method', after the first detailed guide to *The Cantos* by Edwards and Vasse published in 1957. This involves looking up every unknown word, reference, allusion, item of foreign language as one reads. The most comprehensive guide for this purpose is now Terrell's *A Companion to the Cantos of Ezra Pound* (1993).

In practice, the best approach will probably involve both some rapid reading and skipping as well as detailed annotation. Knowledge of certain key personages, references, foreign phrases and Chinese ideograms is essential even for an introductory reading. Pound was rather cavalier in his estimate of the demands for referential understanding placed on the reader, though he was largely correct when he said in a 1939 letter: 'I believe that when finished, *all* foreign words in the *Cantos*, Gk., etc., will be underlinings, not necessary to the sense, in one way. I mean a complete sense will exist without them; it will be there in the American text . . .' (*SL*, p. 322). Even so, more than most texts, *The Cantos* resist what might be called 'passive' reading. Theoretically helpful in this respect is Barthes's distinction between 'readerly' and 'writerly' texts. In his seminal work, *S/Z*, first published in 1974, Barthes characterizes the readerly text as one in which the reader is 'plunged into a kind of idleness . . . left with no more than the poor freedom either to accept or reject the text' (Barthes, 1990, p. 4). He suggests that classic texts are readerly, presumably because they have achieved some inviolate status, but also goes on to note that they constitute the majority of textual production. One could add that a large number of popular texts within genre fiction, soap opera and formulaic movies, for example, are designed to be readerly in just the way Barthes outlines. In contrast, the writerly text invites the reader to become its producer, to (re)write it out of desire. Barthes characterizes the ideal writerly text in terms of its plurality: interacting networks, galaxy of signifiers, without beginning, reversible, multiple entry points, infinite and indeterminate codes. He concludes that 'for the plural text, there cannot be a narrative structure, a grammar, a logic; thus, if one or another of these are sometimes permitted to come forward, it is *in proportion* . . . as we are dealing with incompletely plural texts, texts whose plural is more or less parsimonious' (ibid., pp. 5, 6).

Although Barthes's ideal writerly text is a theoretical construct, the characteristics I have paraphrased here are wholly appropriate to *The Cantos*. In terms of Barthes's concept of plurality we can also say that they constitute one of the least parsimonious texts in literature. One could argue that Pound anticipates the concept of the writerly text in his use of the term 'palimpsest' to refer to *The Cantos*. In ancient Greece and Rome a palimpsest was a parchment that could be rubbed clean and written on again. There was always a possibility that traces of previous writings would be read as part of the text. *The Cantos* are a kind of giant palimpsest in this sense as they are full of traces of previous writings, a record, as Pound glosses it in Canto 116. In the same canto he asks: 'And as to who will copy this palimpsest?' (*CAN*, p. 811): who, in my Barthesian interpretation, will (re)write, by reading, this very writerly text? Far from being plunged into a kind of idleness, then, the reader of *The Cantos* has to be highly active, a retracer of traces, a filler of gaps. This can be both compelling and off-putting. On the one hand, following up a detail of the poem can be an educative process, often enlivened by the excitement of new learning. On the other hand, the density and sometimes obscurity of the detail can be overwhelming. In this respect *The Cantos* are something to turn to and return to over a long period, visiting new sections in detail, revisiting favoured narrative or lyric passages or even savouring single lines of particular poetic quality. The threads of Pound's discourse begin to emerge from this process, traced by echoes, repeats and cross-references, always with the possibility that each reading will result in, for better or worse, a new writing of meanings that reflects the greater knowledge and personal 'periplum' of the reader involved.

The rest of this section attempts to support that possibly long-term reading process in four ways. Firstly, I discuss some general and specific issues regarding the nature of *The Cantos* as a poetic enterprise. Secondly, there is a brief characterization of each section of the poem in order of publication. Thirdly, I discuss the language of *The Cantos* and illustrate how a particular kind of linguistic analysis can provide insights about the way that language operates. Fourthly, thematic and conceptual aspects of the poem are identified and commented on from the perspective of one particular view of its structure.

The nature of The Cantos

The sheer size of *The Cantos* leads us to think of the poem as an epic, in scale if not in quality. However, the status of the poem as epic is debatable. Certainly, it is very different from those works which normally exemplify the epic tradition in Western literature. These stereotypically involve a central hero in a thematically unified quest or conquest, usually with a single overriding goal, punctuated by episodes of varying size and importance. This heroic matter is related in narrative mode, preferably in a single verse form, and with suitably grand poetic conventions. The fact that Pound's poem does not conform to this blueprint need not automatically rule out its epic status. The traditional epic has been challenged in a variety of ways, both formally, by the use of prose or the introduction of lyric and dramatic elements, and thematically by, for example, having a predominantly comic purpose. Pound's own much quoted definition of the epic as 'a poem including history' is at best partial and more designed to characterize *The Cantos* than make a general point about epic poetry. However, it seems less perverse in the light of a statement from his *Paris Review* interview: 'I have tried to make the *Cantos* historic . . . but not fiction' (Dick (ed.), 1972, p. 93). Pound, then, is using the term 'history' to emphasize the factual nature of the work and reject notions that it is 'mere fiction'. In this respect the concept of a poem including history is a rejection of the poem as condensed novel, one rationale for *Hugh Selwyn Mauberley*. Yet, as we saw, the fiction of *Mauberley* included a number of episodes that were historically and factually based. These elements are carried forward into *The Cantos* but with a new emphasis, that of documentation. The history is no longer simply reported but presented as archive material. *The Cantos* are, then, a poem including documented history, and it may be this emphasis that Pound was seeking in his definition of epic. Nevertheless, Donald Davie is correct to assert that 'The definition will not serve; more than this must be asked of a poem before it can qualify as an epic . . .' (Davie, 1991, p. 354). To this end, it is worth looking at the poem in terms of the traditional elements outlined above.

There is no central hero in *The Cantos*. There are a number of figures whose actions, ideas or a combination of the two are central to the poem, such as Odysseus, Confucius, Dante, John Adams. Of these, Odysseus comes closest to realizing the role of epic hero in supporting the poem's narrative elements. However, since there is no single sustained narrative, this role is marginalized and fragmented. It is possible to see Pound himself as the, ultimately tragic, hero of his own poem. Because some of the history Pound included in the poem was in the making, the situation of the poet, his evaluations and self-evaluations, are inevitably part of its texture. However, an overemphasis on the autobiographical elements can lead to its erroneous characterization as 'an autobiographical poem'. That term would imply a central focus on the life history and/or personal experience of the author: Pound's concerns are far wider and much less egocentric.

The poem is not episodic in any conventional sense, though certain passages, individual cantos and even whole sections present historical documentary material in a relatively self-contained way that parallels the narrative episodes of traditional epic poems. Much of this material contributes directly to the theory of sound economics that underpins the quest for terrestrial paradise. In that respect the poem achieves a degree of thematic unity which Pound himself characterized as 'the tale of the tribe' (*GK*, p. 194). While substantial passages of *The Cantos* are written in narrative mode, at its most straightforward marked by a simple past tense third person syntax, the poem also adopts a wide range of styles, such as diary entries, personal and formal letters, public records, journalese. There are passages of intense lyricism and interludes that have the quality of song. The first person is used in stretches of dramatic monologue with identified personae, as the voice of the poet, and sometimes as an anonymous or ambiguous textual marker. In the light of this discussion it seems fair to say that *The Cantos* do have epic qualities, even by the standards of classical literary epics. However, these qualities are parodied, subverted and otherwise modernized by the imperatives of Pound's compositional techniques and the structure, or lack of structure, they promote.

If *Hugh Selwyn Mauberley* can be seen as a highly structured poem with a design fault, the major concern with regard to the structure of *The Cantos* is whether there is any design at all. The expectation raised by the concept of typical epic structure is for a large-scale work organized into 'books' or other clearly demarcated sections which are coherent in themselves as well as logically and/or chronologically related to other books or sections. Even the convention that the epic should start *in medias res* presupposes a linear narrative with a middle to start in. Since there is no single sustained narrative within *The Cantos*, attempts to see this convention at work in the opening section are fanciful. It is clear that Pound must have considered and rejected the traditional epic at quite an early stage in his poetic development. As he noted much later, when all he was going to write of *The Cantos* was more or less done:

I began the Cantos about 1904, I suppose. I had various schemes, starting in 1904 or 1905. The problem was to get a form – something elastic enough to take the necessary material. It had to be a form that wouldn't exclude something because it didn't fit. In the first sketches, a draft of the present first canto was the third.

(Dick (ed.), 1972, p. 93)

At first, as the three early cantos written at Stone Cottage show, Pound made his search for form an explicit topic of the poem. The problems of that search were addressed to Robert Browning and particularly influenced by his poem *Sordello*, an epic retelling of the life of an Italian troubadour, written in 1840, early in Browning's poetic development when he was still searching for his own formal solutions to the problems of presenting the psychological reality of his characters through dramatic monologue. *Sordello* quickly became synonymous with poetic difficulty and obscurity. In later editions Browning added an explanatory preface, but the poem's elliptical syntax, bookish diction, condensed narrative and discursive interludes remained too much for even the elitist Victorian reading public. Pound had been familiar with *Sordello* since his student days at Hamilton College and remained impressed by its experimental daring. Years later, Pound quoted a substantial extract from Sordello in his *ABC of Reading* and castigated 'Victorian halfwits' who claimed it was obscure. He went on to highlight the poem's 'limpidity of narration . . . lucidity of sound . . . clarity of outline without clog and *verbal* impediment' (*ABC*, p. 191). Some of this sounds slightly perverse in the light of the poem's reputation and may be partly motivated by Pound's desire to promote what he saw as a neglected masterpiece. However, *Sordello* is clearly organized in six books of rhyming couplets from which a paraphrasable narrative emerges, as Browning himself showed, so Pound's remarks may have some point. When I read the poem for the purpose of writing this section, I concluded that the main source of its difficulty was linguistic, and primarily syntactic. Ellipses, not always obviously supported by context, figured in often quite complex chains of subordinate as well as coordinate clauses. The resulting sentences were lucid enough as sound on the mental ear, but the complex grammatical relations within sentences and the discourse relations between sentences were a strain on comprehension. Therefore, as a reader, I did find specifically verbal impediment. Despite his later remarks, I think Pound learned from Browning's style in *Sordello* that the syntax of *The Cantos* would have to be dominated by coordination at both clause and phrase level, resulting in the parataxis that is the main syntactic feature of the whole of the poem, rather than the 'Browningesque' language that figures in the early abandoned cantos, as this extract shows:

> Hang it all, there can be but one 'Sordello'!
> But say I want to, say I take your whole bag of tricks,
> Let in your quirks and tweeks, and say the thing's
>   an artform,

> Your Sordello, and that the modern world
> Needs such a rag-bag to stuff all its thought in;
> (Cookson, 1985, p. xxiii)

If Pound largely abandons this kind of convolution in *The Cantos*, he does so in order to create a syntactic medium that will facilitate stuffing the modern world's thought into his poetic rag-bag. Pound chose the above extract as the 'best introduction' to his own selection of *The Cantos*, indicating what had been grasped from Browning, but also showing by example what had been discarded.

If Pound conceived of a *Cantos*-like poem at an early stage in his poetic development, it is also likely that the form of its apparent formlessness, or at least a rationale for that form, was a fairly early preoccupation. In a series of articles published in *The New Age* in 1911/12 under the title 'I gather the limbs of Osiris', Pound writes of an ancient scholarly 'method of Luminous Detail' and contrasts it with the current 'method of multitudinous detail' which does not discriminate between detail that is enlightening and the mundane welter of historical facts. In passing, he suggests that there is a similar contrast in literature (*SP*, pp. 21–3). While there is nothing explicit here about poetic technique, one can see how the concept of luminous detail as a method could underpin the poetic juxtaposition of apparently miscellaneous elements without explanatory comment, which is a major feature of *The Cantos*. Discussing the troubadour model of the 'borrowed lady' or 'donna ideale' which I outlined in relation to 'Na Audiart' earlier, McDougal suggests that Pound's method in *The Cantos* ultimately derives from that model by 'the creation of an ideal through the accumulation of fragments' (McDougal, 1972, p. 147). Extending that idea, we can characterize the resulting poetic structure as a 'poema ideale' or, to translate the equivalent Provençal, a 'borrowed poem'. Just as de Born selected the best features of famous ladies, so Pound would select the most luminous details for his poetic enterprise.

Two points are worth raising here. First, selection implies preference, bias, possible prejudice. Second, are all Pound's details really luminous and not merely multitudinous? In other words, is one basis for criticizing *The Cantos* not the juxtaposition of details, but the quality of the details juxtaposed? In the *ABC of Reading* (*ABC*, p. 92) and elsewhere Pound makes much of the German–Latin equation *dichten = condensare*, that is, to write poetry is to make something that is very dense, very concentrated. The idea is readily applicable to, for example, *Hugh Selwyn Mauberley*, but it can only be applied to *The Cantos* with some degree of paradox: the subject matter they condense is so vast that the overwhelming impression on the reader is one of superabundance and diversity of detail rather than its concentration. This paradox seems to have been lost on Pound himself. In a letter of 1939, he remarks: 'There is *no intentional* obscurity. There is condensation to maximum attainable. It is impossible to make the deep as quickly comprehensible as the shallow' (*SL*, p. 322). This maximum condensation results in vast amounts of detail, with few pointers as to what is luminous and what is not: the problem is often not comprehending the deep as locating it. One could argue, of course, that the juxtaposition of the mundane and trivial with the luminous and epiphanic reveals a modernist sensibility at work. Certainly, Joyce's *Ulysses* manages to give the reader vast amounts of mundane and trivial detail, sometimes with a meticulousness that engenders tedium, which provide a seamless backdrop to visionary and revelatory experience. But Joyce's 'rag-bag', as it were, is a highly organized one which clearly signals its structural arrangement of the thoughts of the modern world. To that extent Joyce maintains, prior to *Finnegans Wake* at any rate, a sense of audience. *The Cantos* are more ambitious than *Ulysses*, but also, depending on one's view of Pound's method, more reckless or lacking in organizational skill. If Pound had a rather weaker sense of audience than Joyce, his numerous attempts in letters and articles to clarify his methods show that he was not entirely insensitive to the way in which his work was received. Nevertheless, his determination to present, rather than arrange or organize, his material according to the tenets of the ideogram and the vortex override any concessions that might have been made to the reader, who must become writerly, an active participant in the pleasure of the text.

More than any other concept, apart from his desire to write a 'chryselephantine' poem on vorticist principles, Pound's notion of simultaneity probably confirmed his need for the form of *The Cantos*, both at macro-level, in terms of sections and individual cantos, and at micro-level, with regard to the parataxis of syntactic units. At the time when he was searching for a form, the concept of simultaneity had virtual doctrinal status among avantgarde visual artists, particularly the cubists. The representation of simultaneous images in two- and three-dimensional work contributed to the vibrant dynamism of art. For Pound, working in an essentially linear medium where only one item in the syntagmatic chain can occur at a time, simultaneity is unachievable. Its closest approximation is the rapid and sudden juxtaposition of linguistic material, a reason, I think, for a predominantly paratactic syntax in *The Cantos*. But a poem including history would also have, somehow, to represent the simultaneity of past and present events, for 'We do NOT know the past in chronological sequence . . . what we know we know by ripples and spirals eddying out from us and from our own time' (*GK*, p. 60). The temporal universe of *The Cantos* is not linear, but one which encircles our awareness. The present recycles the past and one past relives another. Old myths are repeated in history. The old gods are re-experienced, because they have always been with us. Again, in a linear medium this level of simultaneity can only be represented by the juxtapositions of discourse, by overlap and reprise. Perhaps because simultaneity is both a natural possibility and an artistic device in music, Pound invoked a musical analogy for the structure of *The Cantos* on a number of occasions. In 1927 he wrote, ambiguously, that the poem was 'Rather like, or unlike, subject and response and counter subject in fugue' (*SL*, p. 210). Ten years later, he was still citing the fugal analogy: 'Take a fugue: theme, response, contresujet. *Not* that I mean to make an exact analogy of structure' (ibid., p. 294). A more startling musical analogy occurred in *Guide to Kulchur*, where he remarks that 'Bartók's Fifth Quartet . . . is the record of a personal struggle, possible only to a man born in the 1880s. It has the defects or disadvantages of my Cantos' (*GK*, p. 134). This statement was made on the basis of a single hearing of the quartet at a concert in Rapallo. It is to Pound's great credit that he was listening to and actively promoting such new and 'difficult' music and entirely understandable that he should interpret Bartók's spiky rhythms and abrasive harmonies as a record of struggle. What Pound was unable to discern, without the benefit of repeated hearings and the prop of analytical notes, was that Bartók's Fifth Quartet is one of his most formally perfect compositions: every note contributes to its flawless symmetry. Ironically, then, in the light of Pound's statement, only someone hostile to the ideogramic method of *The Cantos* would want them to possess the qualities of Bartók's music, even if that were possible.

Pound's explanatory and/or defensive comments of the kind quoted in this section were prompted by the hostile reaction of critics and the concerned responses of more trusted friends. Such comments are undoubtedly problematical. They suggest that *The Cantos* are structurally something other than the author wanted, in need of a remedy that will eventually be forthcoming, as confirmed by a letter of 1939: 'As to the *form* of *The Cantos*: All I can say or pray is: *wait* till it's there. I mean wait till I get 'em written and then if it don't show, I will start exegesis' (*SL*, p. 323). Having set up this expectation, the almost inevitable conclusion becomes the 'It's a botch' comment referred to in the biographical section. If such evaluations and promised remedies were genuine, then we have to ask why Pound did not do something about the form of *The Cantos* fairly early on. Even in St Elizabeth's a major overhaul of the work to date would have been possible, perhaps at the sacrifice of other creative projects. I would find it hard to accept that Pound did not have the poetic, linguistic and editorial skills to transform *The Cantos* as they were into a syntactically tidier, more logically connected, less cluttered and obscure poem. This raises the possibility that the comments were not genuine, but smokescreen remarks of the kind Pound used in response to hostile criticism of *Propertius*. If so, they only work as a defensive tactic when they simply offer explanations that keep critics at bay. Once they make promises to reveal some grand and lucid design, they raise expectations that Pound had no real inclination to fulfil. Over such a long period it is probable that some of the remarks fall into each category. Nevertheless, my tentative conclusion is that most of *The Cantos* are the way they are because Pound wanted them that way. For me, this is a positive conclusion, since we can read and criticize them, assessing their positive and negative qualities, without continually thinking they are a failed version of some other poem.

The sections of The Cantos

A DRAFT OF XVI CANTOS (1925). The formal problems that were to bedevil Pound with respect to the totality of *The Cantos* present themselves in microcosm, if such a term may be used about what is already a substantial poetic undertaking, with respect to *A Draft of XVI Cantos*. In a letter of 1922 he wrote: 'The first 11 cantos are preparation of the palette. I have to get down all the colours or elements I want for the poem. Some perhaps too enigmatically and abbreviatedly. I hope, heaven help me, to bring them into some sort of design and architecture later' (*SL*, p. 180). The range of subject and period, diversity of reference and wealth of detail are indeed bewildering. Abrupt shifts in time and place, the juxtapositions of apparently unrelated material, challenge the reader's expectation that these cantos are organized according to some structural principles, however indeterminate. The notion of a palette is quite useful in this respect, since there are blocks of subject matter that provide the thematic and conceptual equivalents of primary colours. The following is an indicative list:

1. The Homeric world of the Troy legend and Odysseus, who is established as a major persona of the poem. In particular, the Odyssean journey home, via the underworld and in the face of earthly horrors, prefigures the poetic journey of *The Cantos* as a whole.

2. The gods of classical mythology. For Pound, these are very much alive, they 'float in the azure air'. Important gods in his pantheon are introduced, such as Aphrodite/Venus, Dionysus/Zagreus,

Diana/Artemis and Persephone. Their significance in fertility rites, mysteries and metamorphic wonders is established.

3. The world of the troubadours. In this context one of the heroic women of *The Cantos*, Cunizza da Romano, is introduced.

4. The man of action. A substantial section, Cantos 8–11, exemplifies this type in the form of Sigismundo Malatesta. Pound researched details of Malatesta's intrigues and achievements on trips to Siena and Rimini.

5. Confucius. The philosophical world of Confucian thought is introduced in Canto 13.

6. Dantescan Hell and Purgatory. This features bankers, usurers and politicians in obscene detail, moving into a final canto where Pound ponders, among other things, the dead of the First World War.

7. Venice. The city is established as one of the most significant locations in *The Cantos* both for its historical importance and its contemporary relevance to the poet himself.

8. The voice of the poet. Personal recollections and authorial asides establish Pound's presence in the poem.

This palette of themes, personages and places is, from the perspective of *The Cantos* as a whole, remarkably appropriate to their subsequent development. They are elaborated upon, recycled and varied in their own right, but also provide frameworks and precedents for new material of a related or contrastive nature. *A Draft of XVI Cantos* has some characteristically stunning lines and passages, moments of great power and beauty, for example, the sequence which opens Canto 4, beginning with the lines:

> Palace in smoky light,
> Troy but a heap of smouldering boundary stones,
>
> > (*CAN*, p. 13)

The alternation of such passages with, for example, Canto 9's raw extracts from Sigismundo's postbag discovered in the Siena Archives, is an early indication of the heterogeneous material *The Cantos* will present. From the start it probably gave rise to a particular view of the poem as a mass of largely unpoetic matter in which 'real poetry' may sometimes be found.

A DRAFT OF XXX CANTOS (1930). Pound added to and extended the range of his previously published group of cantos to form a new collection. The first sixteen cantos thus lose their separate identity, while Cantos 17–30 have no real status as a distinct batch. Nevertheless, there are good reasons for seeing them as 'A Draft of XIV Cantos', since they do more than elaborate on, re-exemplify and integrate previous material.

In these cantos there are scenes of mythic and pagan splendour. These act as glimpses of an earthly paradise presided over by the gods and suggest the possibility of a more ethereal paradise where Artemis, 'the goddess of the fair knees', casts a light 'not of the sun' (ibid., p. 76). Athene, guardian of Odysseus and one of the most significant deities of later cantos, also asserts her divine presence in Canto 17. In the final canto of the sequence Artemis returns in a very different role as the scourge of pity. The goddess attributes a list of wrongs to the false application of this emotion. While the initial stimulus for this was probably Chaucer's 'Complaint unto Pity', the lines actually prefigure the litany of the Usura canto. They also become ironic in the light of Pound's self-reproaches in *The Pisan Cantos* regarding his own lack of pity.

The achievements of the Italian Renaissance again demonstrate ideas in action. There are anecdotes of Niccolo d'Este of Ferrara. The Medicis in Florence contrive to impose peace through the control of money. The annals of Venice are mined for details of the building of the Ducal Palace. These elements all serve to show that constructivity has its price in pettiness, betrayal, intrigue, madness, murder. Pound is at least ambiguous about all this. In Canto 20 he clearly celebrates the artists whose talents were sponsored by such men of action and the will they exerted. Elsewhere there is no adverse comment on the behaviour of Renaissance men of action, but the selection of detail hardly shows them in a good light. For example, in Canto 25 an extension to the Ducal Palace is built so that the Doge can avoid the stench of rotting prisoners, with the following result:

> they built out over the arches
> and the palace hangs there in the dawn, the mist,
> in that dimness,
> or as one rows in from past the murazzi
> the barge slow after moon-rise
> and the voice sounding under the sail.

> (*CAN*, p. 117)

Pound captures the exquisiteness of Venice as it is for him and as it still is for us, but the ultimate motivation for that exquisiteness, 'the stink of the dungeons', is only a few lines away. If the exploits of Renaissance men of action were less than laudable, at least they left magnificent cultural products. Pound presents us with that possibly quite unpalatable truth without hypocrisy.

One further element in these cantos is the depiction of modern corruption and exploitation in a narrative form that supplements the rather abstract generalities of the previous Hell cantos. The inanities of what might be called imperialist tourism are exposed to satiric effect in Canto 28. More distastefully, in Cantos 18 and 19 we have the exploits of financiers and arms dealers. The ability of men to start wars is contrasted with a symbol of their practical ineptitude:

> War, one war after another,
> Men start 'em who couldn't put up a good hen-roost.
>
> (*CAN*, p. 83)

These elements contrast with and comment upon each other only by virtue of juxtaposition. It was in defence of this that Pound began to suggest that the structure of the poem as a whole was fugal and that the various elements were subjects in a counterpoint that would be resolved when the vast design of the work was complete.

Reviews of *A Draft of XXX Cantos* were polarized. For example, a reviewer of 1933 castigates the poem's use of contemporary references and bareness of statement and predictably criticizes its lack of structure: '. . . spatial adjacency, mere contiguity, is not enough. There must be continuity' (Sullivan (ed.), 1970, p. 135). Marianne Moore, on the other hand, in her 1931 review, is full of admiration for Pound's practitioner technique, but also notes an ethical concern: 'Why cannot money and life go for beauty instead of for war and intellectual oppression? This question is asked more than once by the *Cantos*.' In a second review of 1934 Moore goes on to say, 'We have in some of these metrical effects a wisdom as remarkable as anything since Bach' (Willis (ed.), 1987, pp. 271, 323). These reviews by a fine poet whose attitude to art and life was, to say the least, intolerant of any kind of nonsense, remind us that *A Draft of XXX Cantos* is a major achievement in its own right, something that can be overlooked in the context of the poem in all its final fragmented entirety.

ELEVEN NEW CANTOS XXXI–XLI (1934). These cantos reflect Pound's growing interest in the early presidents and so-called founding fathers of the United States. Much of the material is documentary in quality and anticipates the Adams cantos in subject, using some of the same source material, and to some extent the same technique, though here the material is less condensed and gives the reader more supportive markers of discourse. Other main sources are the writings of Thomas Jefferson and his correspondence with John Adams, the diary of John Quincy Adams, and the autobiography of Martin Van Buren. The main topics which emerge from this documentary synthesis are the necessity for enlightened political leadership and the need for sound economic policies to combat the depredations of bankers and financiers. However, Pound's selection of details affords us glimpses of his protagonists' personalities which humanizes what could be a rather arid exposition. For example, in the period covered by Canto 31 Jefferson was ambassador to France, from where he writes:

> I can further say with safety there is not a crowned head
> in Europe whose talents or merits would entitle him
> to be elected a vestryman by any American parish.
>
> (*CAN*, p. 155)

Interwoven and contrasted with the details of these champions of American independence and civic freedom are pictures of capitalist corruption and the machinations of arms dealers and warmongers. This material elaborates on and recycles Pound's exposure of the military–industrial complex in previous cantos. The voyage of Hanno the Carthaginian in Canto 40 represents a physical and temporal escape from such depressing concerns. The sequence also introduces Mussolini, first by quoting his reaction to Pound's *A Draft of XXX Cantos* at their meeting in 1933:

> 'Ma questo,'
>   said the Boss, 'e divertente.'
> catching the point before the aesthetes had got there;
>
> (*CAN*, p. 202)

Canto 41 continues with instances of the leader's achievements, his brush with financiers and evidence of the loyalty he inspires 'XI of our era', that is in the eleventh year of the Italian fascist regime, a form of calendar Pound had adopted in his prose of the time. The canto, and the section, ends with a return to the cynicism of arms dealers.

Two cantos stand apart from these mundane matters. Canto 36 gives us Pound's second complete translation of Cavalcanti's 'Donna mi priegha' with its complex, more or less coded, unfolding of the relationship between the spiritual and the erotic. In the aftermath of the translation Pound reinforces his own interpretation of this relationship. He invokes the thrones of Dante's *Paradiso*, later to preside over Cantos 96–109, and Scotus Erigena, the Neoplatonist theologian, as proponents of spiritual light. Alongside these he quotes the Latin tag 'Sacrum, sacrum, inluminatio coitu', which extols the sacred enlightenment to be found in sexual intercourse. Canto 39 presents the power of sex in its mythical and mysterious enactments. First, there is the sexually explicit and erotic depiction of Odysseus and his men in Circe's bower. This is offset in the second half of the canto by the evocation of spring from the half-dark of Flora's night which may be read as a scenario for, or an imagined transcript of, an Eleusinian rite.

THE FIFTH DECAD OF CANTOS (1937). In a letter evidently responding
to queries about the coherence of his work, Pound asserted, 'When
I get to end, pattern *ought* to be discoverable . . . Part of the job is
finally to get all the necessary notes into the text itself . . . 42–51
are in page proof. Should be out any day. I believe they are clearer
than the preceding ones' (*SL*, p. 294). In writing this Pound
conceded that no pattern was discernible as yet, that he was not
working to any blueprint and that explanatory notes were required,
even if they became part of the poem rather than addenda, like
Eliot's notes to *The Waste Land*. His comment about the new sec-
tion is fair, however. These ten cantos achieve a degree of unity
and coherence by means of reprise and repetition of both phrase
and theme.

The section begins with a new example of good economic prac-
tice, the Monte dei Paschi bank of Siena. The establishment and
subsequent history of this bank is presented by means of Pound's
engaging mixture of narrative, documentary and comment. The
main sources for these cantos were a nine-volume Italian history
of the bank and documents in the state archives at Siena. Pound
holds up this 'damn good bank' as an example of what a financial
institution that supports the people should be. His endorsement of
the bank makes clear that both the charging and receipt of
interest is not considered usurious in itself:

> any citizen shall have right to deposit
> and to fruits therefrom resultant at five percent annual
> interest
> and that borrowers pay a bit over that
> for services (dei ministri) that is for running expenses
> (*CAN*, p. 209)

Details of this bank without greed provide the backdrop to the
litany of the powerful 'Usura' Canto 45 and its reprise in Canto
51. The infamies of usurious capitalism are also exposed through
empirical detail as Pound hammers his 'case' home. In particular,
the Bank of England is held up as the opposite of the Monte dei
Paschi, because it manufactures money 'out of nothing' for its own
profit, without any sense of the relation between money and work.
The results of this are all around us:

> Look at the Manchester slums, look at Brazilian coffee
> or Chilean nitrates. This case is the first case
> Si requieres monumentum? [If you need a reminder]
> (*CAN*, p. 234)

As in the previous section, two cantos provide relief from this
concern with the debased world. Canto 47 is a reprise of Canto

39 in that it returns to Circe's bower where Odysseus gains release and is given instructions for his journey to the underworld. Similarly, and with a similarly male-orientated version of sexuality, the canto moves into a celebration of fertility rites associated with the myth of Adonis.

Canto 49, the so-called 'Seven Lakes' canto, is an idyllic vision of ancient China, based in part on a sixteenth-century Japanese manuscript owned by Pound's parents. The syntactically simple presentations of natural detail are an undoubted reminder of *Cathay*:

> Wild geese swoop to the sand-bar,
> Clouds gather about the hole of the window
>
> (*CAN*, p. 244)

This canto, as Pound himself suggests at its end, captures the quality of his fourth dimension, that of stillness. Overall, this section is both compact and well-balanced and contains lines that are as fine as anything Pound wrote. All the more depressing, therefore, are the anti-Semitic details: the totally unsupported claim that Bismarck blamed the Jews for the American Civil War, the reference to Wellington as a 'Jew's pimp'. However few of these there are in the context of so many lines, their presence cannot help but stain the rest. Ironic also, therefore, that the section ends with the first two Chinese ideograms to be printed in *The Cantos*, 'cheng ming', literally 'correct names', elsewhere glossed by Pound as 'true definition'.

CANTOS LII–LXXI (1940). Unlike the previous group with its compact intertextuality, these cantos fall into two distinct sections. Cantos 53–61 summarize vast stretches of Chinese history; Cantos 62–71 itemize elements in the life and opinions of John Adams, the second president of the United States. The composition of these long sections was comparatively quick. Pound employed roughly the same method for both groups, selecting from and condensing a prose treatment of his topics.

Before the Chinese history cantos get underway there is Canto 52, which opens with a further diatribe against usury among other things. As I noted in a previous section, this gives way to a second part which is based on a French rendition of the *Li Ki*, an ancient Chinese book of rites. The echoes of *Cathay*, and now the 'Seven Lakes' Canto, are again apparent in the finely crafted lines:

> Now is cicada's time,
> the sparrow hawk offers birds to the spirits.
> Emperor goes out in war car, he is drawn by white horses,
>
> (*CAN*, p. 260)

For the Chinese history cantos themselves Pound's source was an eighteenth-century French history of China by de Mailla. He transforms this thirteen-volume work into a series of abbreviated and sometimes cryptic annals covering more than 4,000 years, from the more or less mythic early emperors through the great dynasties to the impact of Christianity in the seventeenth and eighteenth centuries. Pound's expressed purpose was to redress the West's profound ignorance, as he saw it, of Chinese culture and civilization, which had many valuable lessons. In a chapter of *Guide to Kulchur* entitled 'Kung' he noted: 'Our history has been parochial . . . to call a book 'General History', and omit the great emperors, is as stupid as to omit Constantine or Justinian' (*GK*, p. 275). This rewriting of Chinese history is achieved with linguistic dexterity, often employing an incongruously colloquial style in which, for example, Kublai Khan is 'a buggar for taxes' (*CAN*, p. 304).

In the case of the Adams cantos Pound's source was the ten-volume *Works of John Adams*, edited in the nineteenth century by the president's grandson. The chronological organization of the Chinese history cantos gives them some coherence and momentum, but the Adams cantos have a much more desultory and patch-work quality. The language is almost exclusively direct quotation or near quotation from the original source without much 'poetic' intervention on Pound's part. In places both Adams's humour and compassion break through and there is a Poundian bite to his politics:

> Every bank of discount is downright corruption
> taxing the public for private individuals' gain.
>   and if I say this in my will
> the American people wd/ pronounce I died crazy.
>   (*CAN*, p. 416)

However, at least one otherwise sympathetic reviewer of the time concluded: 'there are here long passages shuffled in chronology, composed wholly of snipped lines from Adams's letters, isolated curiosities of detail, cryptic, contemporary references and a liberal use or implication of et cetera. These passages seem to me not merely arid, but, in effect, perfunctory and thoroughly dull' (Homberger (ed.), 1972, p. 352). Dullness, of course, is in the eye of the beholder. Pound's treatment of the material is not radically different from other documentary sections, though it is more condensed and sustained over a longer stretch of cantos than elsewhere, a combination that does tax the reader's stamina. As far as the content goes, the Adams cantos succeed in giving a vivid picture of America's second president in a way that, say, an entry in a biographical encyclopedia would not. Whether this appears dull probably depends on two factors: (a) the level of interest or potential interest the reader has in American history, and (b) the degree to which the reader finds Adams's rather fastidious personality attractive. Dull or not, besides the two written in Italian, there were to be no more cantos till the cage in Pisa.

THE ITALIAN CANTOS (1944). It was not until the 1987 edition of *The Cantos* that numbers 72 and 73 appeared in collected form. In previous editions the gap between cantos 71 and 74 was not remarked upon. Some commentaries ignore the Italian cantos or merely mention their existence in passing. Even the 1993 edition of Terrell's *Companion* omits any reference to them. They were written during the period of the so-called Salo Republic and are more overtly propagandist than anything Pound wrote elsewhere in *The Cantos*. Both poems involve encounters with ghosts who speak to Pound of the betrayal of the fascist state and the destruction caused by the invading Allied forces. In Canto 72 a skull sings in the desert:

> E non par stanco, ma canta, e canta: [and doesn't tire,
>   but sings and sings]
>   – Alamein! Alamein!
>   Noi torneremo! [We will return]
>   *Noi* torneremo
>
>   (*CAN*, p. 427)

This promise to redress the defeat at El Alamein in North Africa, a crucial reversal of the Axis fortunes, is a rather desperate attempt to give comfort to the side which, for better or worse, Pound supported. In Canto 73 the poet encounters the ghost of Cavalcanti who castigates Churchill and Roosevelt in language reminiscent of Pound's Rome Radio speeches. Cavalcanti then goes on to relate the story of an Italian girl who, having been raped by Canadian troops, leads them to their deaths in a minefield, killing herself in the process. Whether this story is based on true events is clearly an important consideration as far as its status as propaganda is concerned. Nevertheless, it is a powerful instantiation of war's brutal tragedy regardless of partisan allegiance. No side in war is innocent, as Pound's fellow inmates at the DTC in Pisa were to show later. The canto does, however, show how far the poet of *Hugh Selwyn Mauberley* had travelled in his thinking. Instead of condemning 'the old lie' that it is 'dulce et decorum' to die for one's country, we find this:

> Cantava, cantava   [she sang, she sang
>   incantata di gioia,   [a chant of joy]

Or' ora per la strada	[just now on the road]
che va verso 'l mare.	[that goes towards the sea]
Gloria della patria!	[Glory of the fatherland!]
Gloria! gloria	[Glory! glory]
Morir per la patria	[to die for the fatherland]
	(*CAN*, p. 434)

THE PISAN CANTOS (1948). Pound wrote these cantos in the Detention Training Centre at Pisa in 1945. The circumstances in which he found himself were described at the beginning of the biographical outline. These poems have an immediacy rarely achieved elsewhere in *The Cantos* because the situation of the poet is a significant part of their verbal texture. There is very much the sense of a man in shock, stunned by the news of Mussolini's death and the lamentable manner in which he died. From the outset the lines have the feel of mental spillage, notes from a tormented mind. In the first canto Pound feels he has become anonymous. However, his claim to be 'noman' is much more serious than that of Odysseus when playing a trick on Polyphemus. This anonymity is much closer to non-existence. Noman is 'a man on whom the sun has gone down', who more properly belongs with the dead: 'we who have passed over Lethe'. (ibid., pp. 440, 444, 463). Yet there is still the stubborn defiance, a desire to go out with a bang, not a whimper, as Eliot would have it, and still the righteous obsessions:

> and gun sales lead to more gun sales
> they do not clutter the market for gunnery
> there is no saturation
>
> (*CAN*, p. 443)

Impinging upon this mind in turmoil are the sensory impressions of Pound's surroundings, 'a smell of mint under the tent flaps', 'a white ox on the road toward Pisa', 'dark sheep in the drill field' (ibid., p. 442). There are also details of camp personnel, such as the prisoner Till who is reported hanged 'for murder and rape with trimmings'. These external elements provide a context for Pound's references to earlier cantos and powerfully nostalgic memories, which I have chosen to see as predominantly purgatorial in a later section. Nevertheless, it would be surprising if Pound's mind were suddenly rid of details appropriate to a Dantescan inferno, and there are such things in *The Pisan Cantos*:

> Geneva the usurers' dunghill
> Frogs, brits, with a few dutch pimps
> as top dressing to preface extortions
> and the usual filthiness
>
> (*CAN*, p. 495)

What is more surprising, I think, are the paradisal elements, not only those of memory and recall but also the mythic evocations, such as the remarkable lyrics to the lynx of Dionysus at the end of Canto 79, the ecstatic visions of light and the visitations of the gods: 'there came new subtlety of eyes into my tent' (ibid., p. 534).

Although there were few sources of written material available to Pound during his stay in Pisa, he made use of what was to hand. In Canto 80 he reports finding a copy of Speare's *The Pocket Book of Verse* 'on the jo-house seat at that'. This book gave Pound sources for subsequent reference to and quotation from, among others, fifteenth-century lyrics, Ben Jonson and Robert Burns. Pound also came to have access to editions of *Time* magazine which gave him news of, for example, Bartók's death as well as events in the political world. Again in Canto 80 he makes much of the defeat of Churchill in the British general election with a parody of Browning's 'Home Thoughts from Abroad':

> Oh to be in England now that Winston's out
> Now that there's room for doubt
> And the bank may be the nation's
> (*CAN*, p. 528)

The most important literary source, however, was the Confucian text and Chinese dictionary which Pound brought with him on his arrest. These allowed him to give Chinese ideograms as glosses to some of his statements, as in Canto 77, which includes one Pound translates as 'bi gosh' in an 'explication' at the end of the canto. But most of all the incidence of Chinese ideograms is a proclamation of Confucian ethics in abbreviated form. For example, 'chung' occurs three times. This is Confucius's point of balance, pivot or centre. In Canto 76 it is somewhere even the enlightened find hard to stay for long, yet always a place of gravitation in Canto 77, 'whether upright or horizontal'. Finally in Canto 84 it is 'our norm of spirit', approximate to that of John Adams. Most of all 'chung' may be seen as the still centre in Pound's chaotic personal and political world.

SECTION: ROCK-DRILL DE LOS CANTARES (1955). The title Pound gave to his next group of cantos refers to Jacob Epstein's sculpture of a man with a pneumatic drill which he had seen in its original form in 1913. When Paige's selection of Pound's letters was first published in England in 1951, Wyndham Lewis's review was headed 'The Rock Drill', referring to Pound's rock-drill action in promoting his ideas, and Pound was attracted by the metaphor. He confirmed this in his *Paris Review* interview: '*Rock Drill* was intended to imply the necessary resistance in getting a certain main thesis

across – hammering' (Dick (ed.), 1972, p. 112). To the extent that
these cantos go over old ground, such as Chinese history and philo-
sophy, usury and aspects of American history, the notion of ham-
mering or drilling away at central themes is pertinent, though it
is much less appropriate for the paradisal elements in the poem.

The rock drill metaphor may also apply to Pound's act of get-
ting back into *The Cantos*. The section was written eight or so years
after Pisa. If we except the specially situated world of *The Pisan
Cantos* with their largely unsupported reliance on memory and
recall, then *Rock-Drill* can be seen to be picking up where the mas-
sive blocks of the Chinese history/Adams cantos left off in 1940.
Certainly, the first five cantos give the impression of following a
similar pattern by juxtaposing ancient Chinese history with exem-
plary American heroes. By the time he was writing *Rock-Drill* in St
Elizabeth's Hospital, Pound again had access to secondary sources.
He extracted the Chinese material mainly from Couvreur's French
version of *Chou King*, a classic of early Chinese history, while the
American elements were derived in part from Benton's *Thirty Years
View*, a treatment of American governance in the first half of the
nineteenth century. However, unlike the earlier Chinese cantos, there
is no sustained narrative in these, nor are they exclusively Chinese
in subject matter. The opening line of Canto 85 seems to promise
a narrative: 'Our dynasty came in because of a great sensibility'
(*CAN*, p. 557). But this is lost in references to Galileo's prohibition,
Wellington's just peace after Waterloo, Elizabeth I's scholarship
and Cleopatra's interest in economics. In contrast, Canto 88 does
present us with an account of a duel between one of Pound's
American heroes, Senator Randolph of Virginia, and Henry Clay,
Secretary of State, as narrated in Benton's book. The episode was
representative of conflict between anti-bank and pro-bank factions
and therefore served as an illustration of Pound's own allegiances.
However, even this account is left incomplete and we need the
original source or Terrell's *Companion* to tell us that the duel ended
rather farcically without anyone getting hurt.

The second half of the section turns towards the paradisal,
though nothing can be left behind: even here, there must be usury,
munitions, Mussolini and 'Democracies electing their sewage'
(ibid., p. 627). Paradisal material is culled from a wide range of
sources, but two centres of interest stand out. One is mysticism,
whether pagan, Neoplatonist or Christian, represented by the say-
ings of the twelfth-century theologian Richard of St Victor and
the life of Apollonius of Tyana, first-century AD pagan mystic. The
second is ancient Egypt. In particular, Pound evokes the goddess
Ra-Set, a synthesis of the sun and moon gods of Egyptian theo-
logy. He also quotes the wisdom of the ancient Egyptian king, Kati,

derived from scholarly books by his son-in-law, Boris de Rachewiltz. For example, Canto 93 opens with a graphic string of hieroglyphics followed by:

> 'A man's paradise is his good nature'
>   sd/ Kati.
>   (*CAN*, p. 637)

The Egyptian hieroglyphics as well as the square notes of medieval musical notation used in Canto 91 add to the visual richness afforded by the frequent use of Chinese ideograms. With these and many other ingredients Pound constructs a vortex of linguistic and conceptual fragments which points to past infamies and highlights ancient splendours. However, the degree of fragmentation to which all this material is subjected is a serious challenge to the reader and attracted much adverse criticism. There are also passages of sustained lyricism which one sympathetic reviewer, A. Alvarez, suggested were 'some of the most perfect poetry of this century'. Alvarez also put forward the idea that the oblique, code-like style may be the result of Pound's incarceration: 'If he has in places abandoned his art for code messages in foreign languages, the blame lies as much with his circumstances as with his powers . . . perhaps Ancient Greece and China are the best way of escaping the public ward of St Elizabeth's Hospital' (Homberger (ed.), 1972, p. 442). And, one might add, the attentions of hangers-on. Pound seems to testify as much in Canto 94:

> To Kung, to avoid their encirclement,
> To the Odes to escape abstract yatter,
>   (*CAN*, p. 649)

THRONES DE LOS CANTARES XCVI–CIX (1959). Alongside those matters that will never go away, monetary corruption, political wrongs, these cantos celebrate law-givers and makers of good government from a range of civilizations and histories and so constitute an attempt to redeem some aspects of earthly rightness, if not paradise. The title of the section refers to the seventh material heaven of Dante's *Paradiso*, a heaven of Saturnine temperance, presided over by Thrones, an order of angels, and inhabited by contemplative spirits. In his *Paris Review* interview Pound associates such spirits with those 'who have been responsible for good government', a cue for his own *Thrones* to try 'to establish some definition of an order possible or at any rate conceivable on earth' (Dick (ed.), 1972, p. 112). To this end, as well as recycling instances of benevolent rule, contemplative philosophy and right living, Pound introduces new material appropriate to his aim. The most important new sources are: *The Book of the Eparch*, a Byzantine legal treatise on good conduct in the marketplace; *The Sacred Edict*, a book of eighteenth-century Chinese neo-Confucianism; an account of the Na-khi, an ancient Chinese civilization, by Joseph Rock; and the *Institutes* of Sir Edward Coke, a statesman under Elizabeth I, whose defence of common justice and the Magna Carta led to his imprisonment by James I. Perhaps it is the range and obscurity of these disparate secondary sources that Pound has in mind when he inserts the following prose apologia into Canto 96:

> If we never write anything save what is already understood, the field of understanding will never be extended. One demands the right, now and again, to write for a few people with special interests and whose curiosity reaches into greater detail.
>
> (*CAN*, p. 673)

As a rationale for the intellectual content of *The Cantos* this seems unimpeachable, but it says nothing about the manner in which that content is presented to the reader.

These cantos more than ever reflect the environment in which they were composed. There is a buzz of inchoate voices, multilingual and multitextual. The vortex of ideas and abstractions operates at an even greater level of fragmentary detail. As in *The Pisan Cantos*, fellow inmates intrude upon Pound's deliberations:

> Said Yo-Yo:
> 'What part ob yu iz deh poEM??'
>
> (*CAN*, p. 755)

This may well be a projection of Pound's own anxiety about the multiplicity of tongues and talkers that invade the work. Nevertheless, there is both humour and lyricism running through the poems. The humour, typical of that throughout *The Cantos*, is less related to amusing anecdotes or jokes, than the style in which incongruous details are presented, as in this juxtaposition of St Anselm's gastric problems with his theological acumen:

> brother Anselm is pessimistic,
> digestion weak,
> but had a clear line on the Trinity
>
> (*CAN*, p. 764)

Moments of lyrical vision are briefer, less sustained, yet in his evocation of the gods and their correlates in nature Pound still gives us passages of great beauty that stay in the mind:

> Gold light, in veined phyllotaxis.
> By hundred blue-gray over their rock-pool,

Or the king-wings in migration
            And in thy mind beauty, O Artemis
    Over asphodel, over broom-plant,
            faun's ear a-level that blossom.

(*CAN*, p. 768)

The strength of this is in its deployment of imagism in a more or less pure form. The details are directly presented. The language, technical, precise, allows us to see gold light through leaf formations and masses of butterflies, allows us to share the perceptions a goddess has of the beauty around her, subject to her. And in some strange way what the lines are 'about' is our experience of reading them.

DRAFTS AND FRAGMENTS OF CANTOS CX–CXVII (1969). Much of the work in these cantos was almost ten years old at the time of publication. When it became clear that there would be no further clarification of obscurities, definite ideas or dissociations, these drafts and fragments became the open-ended ending of *The Cantos*. However, it would be hard to contrive a more appropriate and moving halt to the rush of ideas through the vortex of the poem. Their valedictory tone, the mixture of regret and affirmation, the evocation of friends and loved ones both human and divine, also read, with hindsight, like a farewell to Pound's own life.

There is, however, some danger of assuming that the *Drafts and Fragments* are fundamentally different from what has gone before. On the contrary, they are true to the provisional spirit and fragmentary nature of *The Cantos* as a whole. Their content has thematic continuity: the political and economic motivation is apparent to the last. They also employ the techniques of intertextual allusion, anaphoric reference and incongruous juxtapositions that Pound had taken to extremes in the previous two sections of his work. In their condensation of Joseph Rock's legends of the Na-khi they even rework secondary source material for the last time. They do, however, allow the poet's own voice to speak directly in a way that is reminiscent of *The Pisan Cantos*. Though they do not have a single location, they also reveal the situation of the poet from time to time, for example, in Canto 113's unspecified garden where the poet's memories and reflections are intercut by personal detail.

It is, then, in this context of continuity with the rest of *The Cantos* that Pound turns to evaluation of self and work. That evaluation is very much an act of balancing, of weighing and weighting error and achievement. It is not, as some commentators seem to think, an admission of total failure. The weighing in the balance is often linguistically realized, as in the following examples:

187

> A blown husk that is finished
>> but the light sings eternal . . .
> And of man seeking good,
>> doing evil . . .
> a little light
>> in great darkness . . .
> Many errors,
>> a little rightness . . .
>> (*CAN*, pp. 808, 809, 811)

These contrasts reveal Pound facing the realities of his work and life, whether public or private, and giving a balanced, though more negative than positive, evaluation. The poetry predates his more devastating self-judgements and, in poetic terms, this is just as well. Despite the lack of closure in the *Drafts and Fragments*, there is finally a sense of letting go, even though several further additions and slight reorderings have been made to the palimpsest in later editions. Excepting the postposed dedication, however, the poem still ends with the syntactically uncertain structure that may be either stricture or statement of ideal: 'To be men not destroyers.'

The language of The Cantos

If *The Cantos* are the product of Pound's poetic wilfulness, whether that is viewed positively or negatively, then it is in the language of the poem that such wilfulness is embodied. There are three main issues here: the variety of languages, the variety of Englishes and the syntax of the poet's own language. *The Cantos* are a polyglot poem with quotations in a variety of modern European languages, classical Latin and Greek, Egyptian hieroglyphics and, of course, Chinese ideograms. Pound's claim that most of this is glossed in the English is largely true, but it was said more in defensive apology than as a justification of linguistic richness. In any case, all items of language other than English are now fully translated in the guide books, and even approximate pronunciations of the common Chinese ideograms can be assimilated. But if we do not always wish to take the 'annotated index' approach, we can treat text that is unreadable to us as iconic rather than symbolic, something which impacts upon the eye only, part of the sculptural texture of the poem. Rather than seeing this feature as an obstacle or being daunted by its apparent erudition, we can then on any one occasion assert our right as readers to ignore that which is unreadable or, if our curiosity and need to know is spurred, we can write the text's meaning to us with the help of the guides and then, perhaps, 'forget what book'.

That Pound's English would never adhere to some monoglossic version of the standard variety is announced from the start of *The Cantos* with a passage of Homer's *Odyssey*, or at least a Latin version of it, translated in the manner of Anglo-Saxon alliterative verse:

> We set up mast and sail on that swart ship,
> Bore sheep aboard her, and our bodies also
> Heavy with weeping . . .
>
> (*CAN*, p. 3)

Deliberately archaic diction such as 'swart' above and syntactic inversions like 'Poured we libations' a few lines later serve to reinforce the age-old nature of the material and its epic provenance. Pound's English is nearly always appropriate in this way, even when it is in bad taste. It ranges from that high style to the very personal simplicity of the final cantos:

> Let the Gods forgive what I
>   have made
> Let those I love try to forgive
> what I have made.
>
> (*CAN*, p. 816)

The diversity of English varieties presented in the intervening pages is great. This diversity partly reflects the material that Pound wants to stuff into his poem, such as extracts from decrees concerning the building and decoration of the Ducal Palace in sixteenth-century Venice:

> It being convenient that there be an end to
> the painting of Titian, fourth frame from the door on
> the right of the hall of the greater council . . . We
> move that by authority of the Council maestro Tyciano
> aforesaid be constrained to finish said canvas . . .
>
> (*CAN*, p. 119)

This captures in translation the register of legal documentary text to the point of parody, but no matter how ingeniously it is cut up on the page, it isn't poetry. It certainly isn't verse, even free verse. In the context of Canto 25, however, such passages frame a lyric section pertaining to the Roman poet Sulpicia and an evocation of the gods, so their depiction of the casual, ephemeral world of money, legal wrangling, corruption and the like, has some contrastive point. At the other end of the linguistic spectrum from written legal jargon is Pound's representation of spoken vernaculars: the wide-boy voice of Baldy Bacon in Canto 12, whose only interest is money business: 'No interest in any other kind uv bisnis'; the tormented slang of Niccolo d'Este in Canto 20: 'I have broken the horn, bigod, I have broke the best ivory'; the American abroad in Canto 28: 'I'm er misshernary I am'; the African–American dialect of the prisoner at Pisa in Canto 81 who makes Pound a table from a packing case: 'doan yu tell no one I made it . . . It'll get you offn th' groun'' (ibid., pp. 53, 91, 136, 533). These voices are cleverly differentiated in themselves and make for a rich colloquial texture which is an undoubtedly innovative extension of poetry's verbal palette. The one criticism I would make here is that sometimes Pound incorporates features from these vernaculars into his own narrative or commentative style and the differentiation between character and narrator is blurred or lost. This may well be a deliberate ploy, but it can leave Pound's own poetic voice sounding too much like the exaggeratedly hill-billy Americanese he favoured in some of his letters, an inappropriate voice for most of the material in *The Cantos*.

One other variety of English needs to be mentioned here: Pound's archaism. I have previously discussed the significance that such language held for Pound, not only as a medium for replicating ancient styles in translation, but also as a mechanism for expressing emotional intensity. As we have seen, the style is marked by archaic diction, some syntactic inversions and, most obviously, by the adoption of obsolete verbal and pronominal forms, such as hath, lovest, thou and thy. In *The Cantos* this kind of language realizes the continuing voyage of Odysseus in Canto 47 and the complex philosophy of love translated from Cavalcanti in Canto 36. It embodies the anger against usury in Canto 45:

> Usura is a murrain, usura
> blunteth the needle in the maid's hand
> and stoppeth the spinner's cunning.
>
> > (*CAN*, p. 229)

Most notably, perhaps, it figures largely in both *The Pisan Cantos* and the final *Drafts and Fragments* where it is the vehicle for expressing a range of emotions from regret and grief to visionary conviction:

> What thou lovest well remains,
> > > the rest is dross
> What thou lov'st well shall not be reft from thee
> What thou lov'st well is thy true heritage
>
> > (*CAN*, p. 534)

Pound's syntax is the third aspect of the poem's language I want to look at briefly. We have already noted on several occasions how the syntax is paratactic, predominantly chaining together coordinate structures both at phrase and clause level. This is the

grammatical means which makes possible the juxtaposition of lumin-
ous details without the imposition of causal, temporal and other
relations signalled by subordination. Although ellipsis is not a
necessary consequence of such a syntax, it is more likely to occur.
It becomes the structural marker of Pound's maximal condensa-
tion. This is particularly true of so-called telegraphic ellipsis which
characterizes abbreviated or truncated structures such as telegrams,
notices, headlines and titles. To illustrate how an analysis of such
ellipses can help us to understand the way Pound's syntax works,
I have set out a short passage from Canto 17 with the elliptical
gaps marked by dashes:

<pre>
                              Between them,
__ Cave of Nerea,
             She __ like a great shell curved,
And the boat __ drawn without sound,
Without odour of ship-work,
Nor __ bird cry, nor __ any noise of wave moving,
Nor __ splash of porpoise, nor __ any noise of wave moving,
Within her cave, __ Nerea,
                      She __ like a great shell curved
In the suavity of the rock,
                      cliff __ green-gray in the far,
In the near, __ the gate-cliffs of amber,
And the wave
                      __ green clear, and blue clear,
And the cave __ salt white, and glare-purple,
                      cool, porphyry smooth,
                      the rock __ sea-worn.
__ No gull-cry, __ no sound of porpoise,
Sand __ as of malachite, and __ no cold there,
             the light __ not of the sun.
</pre>
(CAN, p. 76)

I have replicated the layout of this extract as faithfully as possible,
as the spatial arrangement is clearly important. Pound's half-lines
and spatial breaks reinforce rhythmic and cadential features as
well as structuring meaning. Syntactically the outstanding charac-
teristic is verblessness. The only verb forms are participial. Many of
them are adjectival rather than verbal in function, such as 'curved'
and 'sea-worn'. Pound does, however, achieve a sense of move-
ment into the specific scene with the truncated clause 'the boat
drawn without sound' which is readily analysed as a telegraphic ver-
sion of a finite passive clause: 'the boat is being/has been drawn
without sound'. The other kind of telegraphic structure in the extract
is the detached noun phrase. If we allocate all of the ellipses to

one or other of these categories, the distribution is: detached NPs 7, truncated clauses 12. This analysis suggests that Pound labels the physical properties of his scene by listing images in the form of noun phrases, but that there is more emphasis on truncated statements which have a narrative or descriptive function: the reader, like the boat, is drawn into the scene. Pound's syntax does indeed realize the imagist and vorticist principles upon which the language of *The Cantos* is based.

Aspects of The Cantos

DANTE AND/OR ODYSSEUS. Attempts to give an entirely Dantescan or Odyssean reading to *The Cantos* as a whole probably have their origins in Pound's own pronouncements, since he invoked both Dante's *Divine Comedy* and Homer's *Odyssey* as models of sorts for his own epic enterprise. I have adopted Pound's 'and/or' formula to suggest that Dante and Odysseus are both complementary and competing figures in the poem. Not only is their status and function different but their presence also creates differing expectations about the structural design of *The Cantos*. In order to assess these differences it is necessary to take a brief contrastive look at the figures and their respective poetic contexts.

Dante the poet is the first person narrator of his own story and the star of his own poem. The *Divine Comedy* is an account of a spiritual journey in which he is escorted to the bottom of Hell and then through Purgatory by Virgil, whose stature as a poet and exemplar of pagan moral excellence makes him eminently suitable for the task. Beatrice, Dante's object of chaste desire, then takes over to lead him into Paradise. Dante's Hell, Purgatory and Paradise are hierarchical structures, allowing for an orderly descent and an equally orderly ascent. Hell's nine circles are a negatively ordered hierarchy descending from the merely reckless via the violent and fraudulent to the depths of treachery. Purgatory rises through pre-purgatorial levels before reaching the terraces of purgation which are superseded by the earthly paradise. Paradise proper has ten heavens. The lowest is a lunar heaven of flawed spirits, the highest an ethereal and insubstantial heaven of pure divinity. Venus resides in heaven three with those who have loved 'not wisely but too well', while the seventh heaven is Saturnine, peopled by mystics and ruled by Thrones. The organization of Dante's dream world is reflected in the carefully structured arrangement of 100 cantos in three books, employing a uniform metrical pattern of *terza rima* throughout.

Odysseus, in contrast, is the hero of Homer's epic poem, a character manipulated by a master story-teller, a hero in the hands of wilful gods. The *Odyssey* is an account of the hero's struggle to return home after ten years fighting the Trojan War and a further ten years wandering the Mediterranean, experiencing all kinds of adventures including a trip to the underworld. His journey is not a guided tour through a highly ordered spiritual world, but an apparently haphazard one, extremely physical, dangerous, violent, erotically charged, and, without his knowledge, giving human form to the grievances and game-plans of the gods. Odysseus's periplum can be seen as the antidote to, or even the antonym of, Dante's mapped hierarchy. It is geography as experience and myth as enactment. Uncharted knowledge and the psychological insight it affords have to be pursued by sail. The way home and the restoration of domestic and political harmony are equally hard-won. All of this is told in 24 books of different lengths, by Homer as omniscient narrator and in flashback by the character of Odysseus himself. The *Odyssey*, then, has most of the characteristics of the classic epic genre which I outlined earlier in relation to the epic status of *The Cantos*, though it is particularly noteworthy for its dynamic sweep, temporal shifts and variety of settings. The *Divine Comedy* is less obviously an epic in the classical sense, though it is more clearly a poem including history, since the inhabitants of Dante's world are for the most part historical figures whose lives are recounted and reflected upon.

Pound draws on these contrasting features in quite different ways in *The Cantos*. Homer's Odysseus is very much a character, a persona, of Pound's poem, whereas Dante the poet is largely invisible as a personage, though his words and ideas pervade. On the other hand, the *Odyssey* as an epic structure does not inform Pound's organization in the same way as the divisions of Hell, Purgatory and Paradise which are at least structural principles, if not models for design. If we need not look for an Odyssean template in *The Cantos* in the manner of Joyce's *Ulysses*, nevertheless the poem as a whole is a cultural periplum for which Odysseus's voyages are a metaphor. Pound wanders around civilizations, sails past contemporary affairs, sees other lives like land from the sea, lands on historical events and explores philosophies. Odysseus's main purpose is to find his way home. He is full of longing for a lost centre, a return to base, the primary meaning of the term 'nostalgia'. Pound too is motivated by nostalgia, not for the exile's physical home, but for the idealist's perfect nation-state in a war-free world without the depredations of capitalism. Odysseus, of course, returns to Ithaca, reclaims his home, but for Pound there is really no base to return to, for in fighting the world, ironically on behalf of the world as he wanted it to be, he lost his centre in the process, as he acknowledges in the final fragments of his epic poem.

In an essay of 1944 Pound wrote that for 40 years he had schooled himself 'to write an epic poem which begins "In the Dark Forest", crosses the Purgatory of human error, and ends in the light' (*SP*, p. 137). This is one of many suggestions that the *Divine Comedy* provides some structural ground plan for *The Cantos*. However, the Odyssean periplum counteracts any neat replication of Dante's hierarchical world which in many ways presents a vision of things that is 'out of key' with Pound's time. The much older *Odyssey* is actually more 'modern' in the way it disturbs temporal sequence and shifts the perspectives of character and place. Pound acknowledges this, albeit without specifically mentioning the *Odyssey*, in his *Paris Review* interview: 'I was not following the three divisions of the Divine Comedy exactly. One can't follow the Dantesquan cosmos in an age of experiment' (Dick (ed.), 1972, p. 112). The Odyssean counterpulse to Dante's ordered progress is more explicitly revealed in Canto 74:

> By no means an orderly Dantescan rising
> but as the winds veer . . .
>> as the winds veer and the raft is driven . . .
>> as the winds veer in periplum
>>> (*CAN*, p. 457)

Here the reference is to Book 5 of the *Odyssey* where the hero, supported by the kindness of the nymph Calypso, builds a raft to continue his journey home, a journey that will be subject to the whim of Poseidon, controller of the winds. We can expect, then, an Odyssean trip through a Dantescan world. We will encounter instances of Hell, aspects of Purgatory and intimations of Paradise as they arise, unordered, juxtaposed as if simultaneous.

HELLS. The first hell that we are presented with in *The Cantos* is that which Odysseus must visit in order to consult Tiresias about his journey home. In Canto 47's reprise of this journey, this underworld is referred to as 'the bower of Ceres' daughter Proserpine' (ibid., p. 236). Although it is a place of 'overhanging dark', peopled by the shades of the dead, it is in some respects a very positive hell. It is a source of practical knowledge and potential enlightenment. Most of all, it is the mythic location for nature's recurrent fertility. Proserpine, elsewhere in *The Cantos* referred to by her other titles, Persephone, Kore and Flora, presides over this underworld for six months of the year only. As the daughter of Demeter or Ceres she returns to earth each spring to give new life to the world. Fertility rites celebrating her return are associated with the Eleusinian mysteries linked by Pound to the lovecults of the troubadours. There are parallels between her return and the emergence of Aphrodite or Venus from the waves. Both goddesses share the same lover, Adonis, at different times of the year. Nature's fertility and the experience of sexuality are thus metaphorized in interlinking myths. Accordingly, Pound associates Proserpine's emergence from the darkness of the underworld into the fertile light of earthly spring with a more or less mystical illumination afforded by sex, as exemplified in Canto 47:

> The light has entered the cave. Io! Io!
> The light has gone down into the cave,
> Splendour on splendour!
>
> (*CAN*, p. 238)

However, he also sees nature's annual revitalization in terms of a wider breakthrough to enlightenment. The culmination of this occurs in Canto 106 where details of the fertility myth are juxtaposed with Confucian virtues:

> Persephone in the cotton-field
>   granite next sea wave
>   is for clarity
>   deep waters reflecting all fire
>
> (*CAN*, p. 767)

This hell, then, is a cyclic context for aspects of paradise, derived from the Homeric world of ancient gods and mythic presences. As such, it pervades the whole poem.

Much more localized in terms of their referential scope and place in the poem are Pound's Hell cantos, numbers 14 and 15. These declare themselves Dantescan in conception by starting with a quotation from Canto 5 of the *Inferno*: 'I came upon a place bereft of all light'. But we are not in Dante's second circle about to encounter with pity the ill-fated lovers Paolo and Francesca da Rimini. Instead we are presented with Pound's vision of the London he had abandoned. He noted in a letter of 1924: 'You will readily see that the "hell" is a portrait of contemporary England, or at least Eng. as she wuz when I left her.' He was more precise in a letter of 1932: 'The hell cantos are specifically LONDON, the state of English mind in 1919 and 1920' (*SL*, pp. 191, 239). This hell is peopled with those categories of humans Pound particularly detests: arms dealers, politicians, perverted academics, corrupt newspaper magnates, imperialists, money-men. The treatment is coprographic, something which Pound consciously derived from Dante, most obviously Canto 18 of the *Inferno*, where there are details of 'people dipped in human dung' and 'someone whose head was so filthy with shit that you couldn't tell whether he was a layman or a priest'. Pound elaborates a hell that in its detail is a contemporary version of scenes from such paintings as Bosch's triptych of *The Last Judgement* or Bruegel's *The Fall of the Rebel Angels*. The intention of these cantos is to offer a hell, in the words of Canto 14, 'without dignity, without tragedy'. In a much later letter Pound comments: 'that *section* of hell precisely has *not* any dignity. Neither had Dante's fahrting devils. Hell is not amusing. Not a joke' (*SL*, p. 293). Here, I think, Pound shows some lack of awareness of the distasteful comicality of some of his depictions:

> And with them ....r,
>   a scrupulously clean table-napkin
> Tucked under his penis,
>
> the vice-crusaders, fahrting through silk,
>
>   head down, screwed into the swill,
> his legs waving and pustular,
>   a clerical jock strap hanging back over the navel
> his condom full of black beetles

(CAN, pp. 61, 63, 64)

Criticism of the Hell cantos as sophisticated toilet graffiti tend to overlook the precedent in medieval and Renaissance literature and art, the fascination with the obscene as both abominable and ill-omened. A fairly aggressive critique of Pound's hell was mounted by T.S. Eliot in his book *After Strange Gods*, published in 1934. Eliot occupies the theological high ground quite vehemently in arguing that, by ignoring the dimension of original sin and moral struggle, Pound's hell is vacuous and inconsequential, a mere catalogue of social types that he finds distasteful. Eliot's main objection to this is essentially doctrinal: 'a Hell altogether without dignity implies a Heaven without dignity also. If you do not distinguish between individual responsibility and circumstances in Hell, between essential Evil and social accidents, then the Heaven (if any) implied will be equally trivial and accidental' (Sullivan (ed.), 1970, p. 182). It is true that there are instances of the inconsequential in Pound's hell: why, for example, should 'lady golfers' be so damnable? But, for the most part, the inhabitants of the Hell cantos are perpetrators of evil, exploitative and corrupt. Their sin may not be theologically 'original', but its consequences are neither trivial nor accidental. There is no reason to depict them as dignified or tragic. Dignity and tragedy are the province of their victims. Paradise is, at least in part, an antidote to their influence, their existence, even. Pound's hell and its implications for heaven are, then, wholly secular in Eliot's eyes and therefore anti-Christian in precisely the ways in which he had chosen by 1934 to be Christian.

Eliot also suggests that Pound deals in stereotypes rather than individuals. It is true that there are fairly indiscriminate references to groups of 'unamiable liars', 'usurers squeezing crab-lice' and 'back-scratchers in a great circle', but this may be seen as Dantescan classification. And like Dante, Pound does name names. Some he names in full, such as Calvin and Verres. Others are indexed only by the last letter of their name because, he later explained, they were not worth recording as individuals or they were so corrupt that the last letter of their name was all that was left of them. However, there was probably some element of self-censorship here to avoid possible libel charges. Lloyd George, Woodrow Wilson and Lord Northcliffe are present in this form, as well as one who will represent hell on earth in later cantos:

> Profiteers drinking blood sweetened with shit,
> And behind them ......f and the financiers
>   lashing them with steel wires.

> *(CAN, p. 61)*

The anonymous flagellator is Sir Basil Zaharoff, a notorious arms dealer who along with Maxim and Vickers formed one of the biggest weapons manufacturing conglomerates in the world. Known as 'the merchant of death', he was knighted by the British and honoured by France for his part in supplying arms to the Allies in the First World War. In an article of 1928 Pound suggested that an account of Zaharoff's life would be 'a fascinating document' in the study of the first major cause of war, namely: 'manufacture and high pressure salesmanship of munitions, armaments etc.' (*SP*, p. 192).

The third type of hell I wish to identify in *The Cantos* is, like the first, a pervasive one. Unlike the first, it is neither mythical nor cyclic, but rather an ever-present earthly hell that is both contemporary and caught in a recurrent past. It is peopled and propagated by representatives, real and fictitious, of those groups who inhabit Cantos 14 and 15: arms dealers, murderers, usurers, politicians, warmongers. This hell is more explicitly and extensively dealt with in the first half of the poem as a whole. Pound noted in an interview in 1958: 'There is a turning point in the poem towards the middle. Up to that point it is a sort of detective story, and one is looking for the crime' (Cookson, 1985, p. xxi). However, the crime has its echoes and references more or less to the last, a reminder that the hell we make is never far away.

As if to provide the fascinating document of Zaharoff's life and thereby expose a major aspect of the crime, Pound invents the character Sir Zenos Metevsky. Incidents in Metevsky's life revealed in Cantos 18 and 38 closely parallel those of Zaharoff. The cynical sale of arms to both sides in a South American conflict is exposed at the start of Canto 38. Having told one side of the other's superior firepower and made a sales deal, Metevsky

> went over the border
> and he said to the other side:
> The *other* side has more munitions. Don't buy
> until you can get ours.
>
> (*CAN*, p. 187)

Nor is the hell of corrupt arms deals and industrial chicanery exclusive to Europeans. The first part of Canto 40 outlines the activities of J.P. Morgan, an American financier, one of whose early exploits was a crooked sale of weapons during the American Civil War:

> As to the government's arms: they were bought by
> one government office before they had been sold
> (as condemned) by another ditto (i.e. government office)
> passing through a species of profit sieve.
>
> (*CAN*, p. 198)

It is this 'species of profit sieve' that is particularly obnoxious to Pound, whether related to arms deals or other money manipulations. It is symptomatic of usurious practice, made possible by an economic framework based on usury in its broadest sense, the will to profit. This is the case, the crime, that Pound has spent so much of his energy investigating, since the end of the First World War and his discovery of Douglasite economic theory:

> One half green eye and one brown one, nineteen
> Years on this case, CRIME
> Ov two CENturies, 5 millions bein' killed off
> to 1919
>
> (*CAN*, p. 231)

This rage against hell lived at the behest of usura subsides in the later sets of cantos, but the fight does not cease. In fact, it is celebrated in the manner of Virgil at the boundaries of Cantos 86 and 87:

> Bellum cano perenne . . . [I sing of an eternal war]
> . . . between the usurer and any man who
> wants to do a good job
> (perenne)

without regard to production –
                              a charge
for the use of money or credit.

(CAN, p. 583)

The passage is a particularly good example of Pound's concentrated fragmentism in the later cantos. Everything is an echo. The Latin phrase asserts the epic claim of Pound's enterprise. The next two lines generalize the specifics of the usura cantos 45 and 51, but also remind us of Eliot's dictum: 'No verse is free for the man who wants to do a good job'. 'Perenne' is an immediate resonance of the Latin and reasserts both the everlasting nature of the struggle and the desire to do a good job. The last lines quote from or offer variants of Pound's definition of usury at the end of Canto 45. The layout exemplifies Pound's stated intention of showing the weight and potential realization of each line by spatial means.

PURGATORIES. The Dantescan concept of purgatory is a place of spiritual cleansing where souls are made ready for heaven. As such it is a place of transitoriness through which people move, from which they move on, unlike the damned who are locked in their particular circle of hell. Purgatory is, then, a process rather than a state, and for Dante, a process of expiation and suffering where catharsis makes paradise a possibility. Pound does, I think, take the Dantescan notion of purgatory seriously: his epic poem must, as he said, cross the purgatory of human error. The term 'cross' here not only reinforces the idea of process, but extends that idea to suggest a journey. Given that the arrangement of *The Cantos* avoids Dantescan orderliness, we cannot rely on instances of purgatory following nicely on examples of hell, though there are places where this does happen.

One way of identifying purgatorial elements in the poem is to associate them with journeys, of which there are many in *The Cantos*. There are physical, geographical and historical journeys, but also those which are spiritual or emotional. In most cases these journeys are like the processes of purgatory in that they involve painful discovery, hard-won insight and the context for enlightenment. The most obviously Dantescan purgatorial journey is the poet's escape from the hell of Canto 15. This has quite close parallels with Dante's emergence from the inferno under the guidance of Virgil. Pound's guide is Plotinus, the Neoplatonist philosopher. Unlike Virgil, who cannot be involved in Dante's paradise, Plotinus does not disappear from the poem forever, since his philosophy elsewhere sheds a paradisal light. The purgatory that begins Canto 16 is extremely telescoped. The poet encounters William Blake,

199

naked and howling, as well as Dante himself and St Augustine, but very quickly we are in a Poundian version of the earthly paradise, hardstoned and light-aired:

> and by their fountains, the heroes,
> Sigismundo, and Malatesta Novello,
>> and founders, gazing at the mounts of their cities.
>>>> (*CAN*, p. 69)

Sigismundo, the admired protagonist of the earlier Malatesta cantos, is on the fringe of purgatory, a man of unrealized paradisal vision, who cannot quite take a rightful place in heaven. Like Dante towards the end of *Purgatorio*, Pound falls asleep, but this is not a prelude to rescue in paradise. The voices of sleep plunge him back into hell on earth, wars and revolutions, the 'Liste officielle des morts 5,000,000' (the 'official list of 5 million dead') of his 'case'.

Canto 40, whose hell we looked at in the previous section, provides a good example of the historically attested voyage as purgatorial journey. Following on the depiction of financial greed, shady arms deals and the profligacy of the *nouveau riche* comes the line: 'Out of which things seeking an exit'. This leads directly into an account of part of the voyage of Hanno the Carthaginian, a voyage full of wonders and perils:

> And by day we saw only forest,
>> by night their fires
> With sound of pipe against pipe
> The sound ply over ply; cymbal beat against cymbal,
> The drum, wood, leather, beat, beat noise to make terror.
>>>> (*CAN*, p. 200)

By making different pasts 'simultaneous', the hell of, among other things, nineteenth-century American corruption is purged by the experience of fifth-century BC voyagers. But there is no earthly paradise at the end of it. The experience is marred by the callous slaughter of 'folk hairy and savage' in an act of typically colonial invasiveness:

> Their men clomb up the crags,
> Rained stone, but we took three women
> who bit, scratched, wd. not follow their takers.
> Killed, flayed, brought back their pelts into Carthage.
>>>> (*CAN*, p. 201)

Pound translates, narrates, but does not comment, and with another 'Out of which things seeking an exit' moves on to intimations of paradise, 'the empyrean', 'the ineffable crystal'. In this there does not appear to be any irony. Canto 40, then, constitutes a self-contained Dantescan commedia: hell, purgatory, paradise. Its form and content are fully integrated, its purpose fully realized. However, its failure to relate the slaughter of innocent 'savages', by however culturally different and historically distanced a people, to the financially motivated inhumanity under investigation does detract from Pound's overall indictment.

The purgatories looked at so far have been located within the confines of single cantos. However, it is possible to see whole sections of *The Cantos* as largely purgatorial in intent and content. This idea was used by James Laughlin in 1940 in a pamphlet accompanying the first edition of *Cantos LII–LXXI* which was intended to explain the role of the Chinese history and Adams cantos within the projected structure of *The Cantos* as a whole. The content of the first 51 cantos is mostly the Inferno, while Purgatorio is 'history of money and banking, American Colonial, and Chinese cantos. Material factors' (Homberger (ed.), 1972, p. 344). Paradiso is then allocated to 'the cantos to come'. Although this is too schematic, it does capture a global trend in the structure of the poem, though it could not, of course, in 1940, anticipate *The Pisan Cantos* and the impossibility of constructing any kind of Dantescan paradise in their aftermath. We have, then, three large blocks of cantos that can be seen as largely purgatorial in effect. Each gives a different shape to the purgatorial process by means of journeys that are respectively historical, civic and personal.

Pound's trawl through Chinese civilization from its earliest origins to the eighteenth century presents us with a succession of dynasties, emperors, princes, mandarins. The ever-present contrast is between good government, the well-ordered state under a strong and capable leader, and weak government perpetrated by lax regimes and dissipated rulers. These cantos are a convincing demonstration of the myth of human progress, since their repetitive account of good and bad, rise and fall, renewal and decadence suggests a perpetual limbo, a pattern that can never quite be broken. The historical narrative is, understandably, highly condensed. Its welter of detail can be overwhelming and frustratingly incomplete at the same time. For example, the great Han dynasty, which lasted over 400 years, is dealt with in a few pages and finished off as follows:

> HAN sank and there were three kingdoms
>   and booze in the bamboo grove
> where they sang: emptiness is the beginning of all things.
>
> (*CAN*, p. 281)

The lines work as narrative poetry in terms of sequence, rhythm, alliteration, assonance and the like. My initial reading of them as the depiction of an empire split three ways and marked by dissipation and a sense of nihilism is satisfying enough. However, we need an annotated index to tell us that China was divided into three kingdoms after the fall of the Han dynasty during which period Taoist philosophers promoted the idea that happiness derives from wine and everything originates from the void (Terrell, 1993, p. 219). The unrelenting march of events recounted in the Chinese cantos in this way is cumulatively outwearing, reinforcing the purgatorial nature of human history.

Quite perversely, given the chronologically ordered overview of the Chinese history cantos, it is in one of these that Pound defines his notion of periplum:

> not as land looks on a map
> but as sea bord seen by men sailing.
>
> *(CAN,* p. 324)

The definition is much more applicable to the next block of cantos dealing with the life and works of John Adams. Here the dunes, docklands, coastlines and sea caves of John Adams country are apparently happened upon as the result of a fairly aimless voyage, though a map is provided by Pound's source material. While the content is clearly historically situated, the journey is very much around and into the life and opinions of John Adams and the institutions he influenced. Without chronological markers and other sequential or logical connectives the periplum is purgatorial in presenting a disorientating limbo of fragments to the reader. A brief example will serve as illustration:

> AS of a demonstration in Euclid:
>   system of government
> Immediacy: in order to be of any effect
> perceive taste and elegance are the cry
>   which I have not
>   Libertatem Amicitiam Fidem
>
> *(CAN,* p. 347)

There are three sense units here, all condensed versions of Adams's own words: (a) a statement that the American constitution has the clarity of a Euclidian geometrical proof; (b) a defence of the apparent lack of style in his treatise on the constitution because it was written in haste; and (c) Adams's Latin motto based on a quotation from Tacitus (Terrell, 1993, p. 269). An unsupported reading of this is rather more difficult than anything in the Chinese cantos because the condensation is maximal, the boundaries of the sense units are not obviously signalled by layout or punctuation and the grammatical structure of the central sense unit is unclear. In purging his source material in this way Pound has produced an ironically obscure version of the life and works of someone whose main political goals were civic clarity and rectitude in governance.

The final purgatory I want to look at is the very personal one of *The Pisan Cantos*. Perhaps for the first time in his life Pound experienced 'the dark night of the soul'. Certainly, he alludes to this concept from St John of the Cross on several occasions in the opening canto of the sequence, as in: 'nox animae magna [great night of the soul] from the tent under Taishan' (*CAN*, p. 451). A hill outside Pisa becomes a sacred mountain in China to which Pound makes mental pilgrimage as *The Pisan Cantos* proceed. Unlike a Dantescan cleansing of the soul after death in preparation for heaven, these cantos are more like a purging of the living soul anticipating death:

> the loneliness of death came upon me
> (at 3 P. M., for an instant)
>
> (*CAN*, p. 541)

In this dire circumstance, Pound takes stock of his life. There is a confessional element to the poetry, though this is no parade of magnanimously appropriated guilt, but rather the expression of realized regret:

> Tard, très tard je t'ai connue, la Tristesse,
> [Late, very late I have known you, Sadness]
> I have been hard as youth sixty years
>
> (*CAN*, p. 527)

The quotation from Villon's *Le Testament* suggests that Pound is thinking of the legacy that his hardness may have left and this is the focus of his self-judgement.

In the physically constrained limbo of the Detention Training Centre, a holding place on a journey back to America, trial, likely conviction, possible execution, the poet takes another kind of journey back. Without the usual access to documentation afforded by books and libraries there can be no purgatorial condensation of source material. Memory must be the mechanism. This recall has two aspects. One is nostalgic. Pound scours his mind for details of past life: the little disappointments set against the 'enormous tragedy', minor triumphs, setbacks and vindications, and most of all those who are cherished and lost through separation or death:

> Lordly men are to earth o'ergiven
>   these the companions:
> Fordie that wrote of giants
> and William who dreamed of nobility

> and Jim the comedian singing:
>   'Blarrney castle me darlin''
> you're nothing now but a StOWne'
>
>   (*CAN*, p. 447)

In this way Ford Madox Ford, W.B. Yeats and James Joyce, among many others, are celebrated for what they were by instances of what they did. Throughout his dark night Pound exemplifies the power of memorial detail to purge away the dross and at one point summarizes that power to himself:

>   nothing matters but the quality
> of the affection −
> in the end − that has carved the trace in the mind
> dove sta memoria [where memory lives]
>
>   (*CAN*, p. 471)

There is a very real sense that Pound is not only recalling his past but also reaffirming sensibilities that he had let lapse and which are still under an ongoing threat from outbreaks of rage.

The use in the above passage of a quotation from Cavalcanti's 'Donna mi priegha', translated as Canto 36, illustrates the second aspect of recall in *The Pisan Cantos* and one which Pound used extensively in later sections of the poem: anaphoric or backward-glancing reference to earlier material in *The Cantos*. This intratextuality is, of course, not a new feature of the poem. However, with few other textual sources at his disposal and remembrance of things past on his mind, Pound's use of textual reprise here becomes a shorthand for things, people, emotions and insights from previous cantos, another kind of condensation. Even at the time of writing he was aware of the problems this might pose for the reader. In a letter ironically meant to assure the DTC censor that his poetry was not a message in code, he explained: 'The present Cantos do, naturally, contain a number of allusions and 'recalls' to matter in the earlier 71 cantos already published, and many of these cannot be made clear to readers unacquainted with the earlier parts of the poem' (Cookson, 1985, p. xx). So, in a way that would not interest the censor, these cantos are partly in a code which cryptically digests the previous cantos. This is not just the exercise of a purgatorial mind but the application of a conscious technique. As such, it is a victory for Pound's sense of himself as a poet, even in the purgatory of Pisa, and belies the despairing view of Canto 77:

> in limbo no victories, there, are no victories −
>   (*CAN*, p. 484)

PARADISES. We are told five times in *The Pisan Cantos* that, in the words of Baudelaire, paradise is not artificial: 'Le Paradis n'est pas artificiel.' On each occasion there is comment close by to suggest what this ambiguous, polysemic line might imply. In Canto 74 paradise consists of fragments given to us by nature through our senses: the taste of sausage, the smell of mint, the cat in the night (ibid., p. 452). Canto 76 juxtaposes the line with the statement: 'States of mind are inexplicable to us' (ibid., p. 474), suggesting that a paradisal psychological state cannot be artificially induced, though it may be visited upon us. A repeat of Baudelaire's line occurs on the same page with the reminder that hell is not artificial either, possibly to suggest that paradises are related to hells as mirror images or polar opposites. In Canto 77 the line is followed by the repeated Greek epithet of Aphrodite: 'Cythera, Cythera' (ibid., p. 482). Paradise is the domain of gods. Lastly, in Canto 83, the line precedes an anecdote about Yeats wandering round the cathedral of Notre Dame in Paris and admiring the statuary (ibid., p. 542). Any outline of the way Pound gets paradise into *The Cantos* can only be partial and indicative. With that in mind I take three of the aspects of paradise implied by these responses to Baudelaire's line as the basis for my discussion, the natural, the mythic and the luminous.

In Canto 81's wonderfully sustained passage on 'the vanity of human wishes' we find Pound's clearest statement on the relation between the artist and nature:

> Learn from the green world what can be thy place
> In scaled invention or true artistry
>
> (*CAN*, p. 535)

The implication of this commandment is that nature presents us with so much that is perfectly invented, true to itself in some absolute way, that the artist is not only set an example but also constantly reminded of the imperfections of human artistic endeavour. This may seem a strange tenet to emerge from a poet who often writes about and so much celebrates the artifacts of human artistry in painting, sculpture and architecture. Pound is not a 'nature poet'. Few, possibly none, of his poems are 'about' nature, have nature as the object of some philosophical or phenomenological discussion. Indeed, some of his pronouncements about Victorian and Georgian poetry may be taken as antipathetic statements about nature poetry. Yet, as we have seen from many previous examples, not just in *The Cantos* but in earlier poems as well, Pound's presentation of natural detail is not only achieved with true artistry but is often essential to his poetic argument, the metaphor for a feeling, the metonym of a larger emotional or religious association.

For example, in the context of presenting the seventeenth-century astrologer and alchemist John Heydon's doctrine of intelligent nature, Pound gives us these lines:

> The water-bug's mittens
> > petal the rock beneath,
> The natrix glides sapphire into the rock-pool.
>
> > > > (*CAN*, p. 630)

The details are evidence of close observation. The tips of the water-bug's legs on the surface of the water cast refracted shadows that look like petals on the rock below where the blue water-snake enters the pool. Such details provide and celebrate instances of natural beauty that belie those 'who say there is no road to felicity', the object of Heydon's concern cited in the preceding lines. Felicity in the sense both Heydon and after him Pound use the term is probably one synonym of paradise.

Precisely worded images from nature are even more often the accompaniment of, the context for, divine intervention and numinous presence or, as Pound himself expressed it in a letter to his father in 1927, 'the "magic moment" or moment of metamorphosis, bust thru from quotidien into "divine or permanent world"' (*SL*, p. 210). In this formula ordinary everyday reality is punctured by visitations of a different order. Pound illustrates this very early in *The Cantos* with a remarkable passage in Canto 2 which recounts the coupling of the future queen Tyro and the god Poseidon in the form of a wave. After the 'lithe turning of water' and 'bright welter of wave-cords' which is their sexual passion, there is

> quiet water,
> > quiet in the buff sands,
> Sea-fowl stretching wing-joints,
> > splashing in rock-hollows and sand-hollows
> In the wave-runs by the half-dune
>
> > > > (*CAN*, p. 10)

This is Pound's deployment of imagism in its essential form, neither description nor metaphor, but an equation for intensely felt experience. To the extent that such experience transcends the mundane it presupposes a paradisal dimension.

In 1918 Pound wrote a short catechism entitled 'Religio or The Child's Guide to Knowledge' which sets out in deceptively simple question-and-answer form his pagan polytheism. Gods appear both formed and formlessly, formed to the sense of vision, formless to the sense of knowledge, though we may also sense their presence as if they were standing behind us (*SP*, p. 47). People transform this revealed, intuited or known presence of the gods into myth as a way of dealing with the experience and conveying it to others without ridicule. As we have already seen in several previous examples, the presence of the gods and their encompassing myths are of continuing significance in *The Cantos*. In the last *Drafts and Fragments* Pound reminds us of his long-held belief with a distinct reference to his early poem 'The Return': 'The Gods have not returned. "They have never left us."' (*CAN*, p. 801). The constant presence of the gods, the potential for vision and revelation, makes paradise a possibility, even in the middle of a 'real' purgatory. Aphrodite and the lynxes sacred to Dionysus become a visible presence for the embattled poet in his Pisan cage:

> Cythera, here are lynxes
> Will the scrub-oak burst into flower?
> There is a rose vine in this underbrush
> Red? White? No, but a colour between them
> When the pomegranate is open and the light falls
> half thru it
>
> (*CAN*, p. 504)

Here there is possibility of transformation, the flowering of scrub and vines bursting forth in the undergrowth as they once seemed to do from his fingers in the more obviously paradisal Venetian setting at the beginning of Canto 17. Even so, Pound affirms his belief in the metamorphic power of the gods and makes 'a story woven out of his own emotion, as the nearest equation that he was capable of putting into words' (*LE*, p. 431).

More than anything else, Pound's paradise is an exponent of light. His symbolization of light involves a complex set of resonances between, among other things, neoplatonic thought, mysticism both pagan and Christian, fertility rites, sexual ecstasy, the troubadours and Confucian philosophy. A useful, though necessarily simplifying, approach to this complexity is to identify two aspects of light: emanation and illumination. In the first case light is a shining forth, a luminosity of divine essence. According to neoplatonism, the last version of pagan Greek philosophy, light from the gods shines forth from everyone and everything. Therefore, the soul can find its way to the highest level of being via the divine light in natural objects. For Plotinus, the Hellenic philosopher who founded neoplatonism in Rome in the third century AD, this and other doctrines implied a mystical union with supreme goodness through ecstatic meditation. However, there is also an animist and metamorphic aspect with magical or mythic implications, and for Pound, therefore, a resonance with his own view that the gods have never left

207

us. Plotinus, having escorted Pound from hell in Canto 15, crops up in later cantos, most notably in *Thrones* where extracts from his philosophic works, the *Enneads*, are quoted and his belief that the body inhabits the soul is repeated several times. Although neo-platonism was initially developed as an antidote to Christianity, its philosophical framework was later used to reinforce Christian doctrine. For example, the ninth-century Irish theologian, Johannes Scotus Erigena, attempted to formulate the neoplatonic emanation of light in Christian terms. Significantly, Pound first introduces Erigena in Canto 36, following Cavalcanti's poem 'Donna mi priegha' and links them by juxtaposition to his Latin tag concerning the revelatory power of sex. The mystical element in Erigena's philosophy met with papal disapproval centuries after his death and reputedly his remains were exhumed and burnt for heresy. Pound refers to this in Canto 36 and much later in Pisa in the context of quoting in Latin Erigena's most famous aphorism, 'all things that are are lights', a succinct statement of the neoplatonic idea of emanation:

> omnia, quae sunt, sunt lumina, or whatever
> so they dug up his bones in the time of De Montfort
> (*CAN*, p. 542)

Light, then, is an emanation of divine presence in animate and inanimate natural forms. The mystical experience of such light can beam us up to paradise.

The second aspect of light is illumination, the lighting up of the mind and the enlightened ways of being that are implied by such illumination. This aspect has a more human emphasis, as if Pound wishes to reformulate neoplatonic emanation in specifically human terms. This involves linking two apparently irreconcilable domains: love, including sexually realized love, and Confucian ethics. In the early Confucian Canto 13 the disciples of Kung rehearse their preferred 'ideas into action' and then want to know which of them Confucius thinks has answered correctly:

> And Kung said, 'They have all answered correctly,
> 'That is to say, each in his nature.'
> (*CAN*, p. 58)

We might gloss this last phrase with the more commonplace 'according to his lights', which makes explicit the link between ill-umination and inner conviction. In his translation of Cavalcanti that constitutes most of Canto 36 Pound retains the Italian term *virtu* in respect of love. The word is difficult to gloss in English, but in the context of this poem means something like 'love's power'.

This *virtu* is not a product of reason but feeling: it too is an inner conviction. Light is a major facet of love's power: love is 'Formed like a diafan from light on shade' and 'taken in the white light that is allness' (ibid., pp. 177, 179). The juxtaposition of neoplatonic emanation, Confucian illumination and love's power is achieved later on. For example, in Canto 74 alongside the ideogram 'hsien', meaning radiance or lustre, which is given by Pound as 'tensile light', we have:

> in the light of light is the *virtu*
> 'sunt lumina' said Erigena Scotus
> as of Shun on Mt Taishan
>
> (*CAN*, p. 443)

Shun, one of the most 'virtuous' emperors from the legendary early period of Chinese history, is thus evoked as an embodiment of divine emanation and the luminary power that is *virtu*, a concept most associated by Pound, via Cavalcanti, with love.

In a later *Pisan Canto* Pound makes explicit the essential connection between love and being in his parody of Descartes' famous dictum: 'Amo ergo sum, and in just that proportion' (ibid., p. 507), that is, we only fully exist to the extent that we experience love. So important in Pound's thinking is the sexual realization of love, not only to the poet's *virtu* but also for the sacred illumination it affords, that we might consider Pound's Latin to encompass the meaning: 'I make love, therefore I am'. Pound was in no doubt that there was a profound element of sexual enlightenment in the fertility rites celebrated in homage to the gods 'who have never left us'. Sex was one of the keys that unlocked the mysteries of Eleusis, that allowed their light to emanate. Somehow that light had survived the repressive activity of the Christian church, to live on in the love-cults of the troubadours. In 1930 he stated his own credo on the subject as follows: 'I believe that a light from Eleusis persisted throughout the middle ages and set beauty in the song of Provence and of Italy' (*SP*, p. 53). Pound went further, as we have seen, by relating the light from Eleusis to neoplatonic mysticism. In the late cantos this link between sexual enlightenment and neoplatonic emanation is captured in the image of 'That great acorn of light bulging outward' (*CAN*, p. 769). While this is a symbol of active male sexuality, it also contains the idea of divine light shining forth from a seed with untold potential. This second aspect of the image is the one reprised towards the very end of *The Cantos*, when Pound issues the challenge: 'Can you enter the great acorn of light?' (ibid., p. 809). If so, we can find our way to the highest level of being its divine light will lead to, which Pound labels 'splendour'. This ultimate luminosity is Confucian. Using the Chinese ideograms for 'clear radiance', he gives us 'the light of hsien ming, by the silk cords of the sunlight' (ibid., p. 707). In their own ideogramic way the later cantos make feasible, even if they do not finally reach, the paradise Pound discerned in Canto 52 'Between KUNG and ELEUSIS' (ibid., p. 258).

Conclusion

Pound's long and complexly eventful life was almost unbelievably productive. All questions of quality set aside, the sheer amount of material he produced is hard to credit. Besides the poetry and literary prose, there is substantial writing on music, visual arts, economics and culture in general, as well as thousands of letters, often of high interest as discussions of these topics in their own right. Comparatively, his other artistic activities, such as musical composition, are marginal, but they took time and effort to realize. Alongside all this there is what might be called his entrepreneurial activity on behalf of literature and his fellow writers. While all of this needs to be taken into account in any ongoing evaluation of Pound's stature, my relatively brief conclusion to this preface will focus on a few aspects only.

One way of drawing some conclusions about Pound's life and work is to examine them in relation to the notion of 'tragedy' which is often invoked in this context. Pound was in many respects a highly privileged individual. In ordinary terms he was well off, well-educated, travelled widely from an early age and lived in freedom and comparative comfort most of his life. However, he was also possessed of a wonderful creative talent and the high energy levels needed to exercise it fully. These qualities allowed him to spend his life in the artistic company and friendship of some of the most creatively gifted people of this century. By ordinary standards this hardly constitutes a tragic life. On the other hand, Pound's domestic arrangements and primary relationships cannot have been without personal pain and the legacy of private hurt that entails. In this respect the notion of tragedy is as valid for Pound as for anyone else, no less real for being commonplace and not unique to great poets. The experience of Pisa and the incarceration in St Elizabeth's Hospital were, however, very different. Here Pound's case was unique. There were elements of cruelty and injustice in his treatment and in particular in the length of time he was deprived of his freedom. Nevertheless, those years allowed Pound not only to survive but to produce great work. Assassination or summary execution in Italy would have been real tragedy.

Most commentators, critics and biographers who take the tragic line are, however, more concerned with the supposed dissipation of Pound's poetic talent in politics and economics. The assumption is that his later poetry would have been different, or at the very least that *The Cantos* would have been 'better', if these obsessions had not figured in his life. This hypothesis can, of course, be turned on its head. It is possible to suggest that *The Cantos* only got written at all because they were a way of realizing Pound's political and economic concerns in poetic form. There is an ethical dimension to these speculations, since Pound gave his ideological support not just to Mussolini but to the wider fascist cause and did so in language whose effect was often anti-Semitic. Clearly, in so far as this ideology and its linguistic realization are features of the poetry there is an aesthetic sense in which they disfigure Pound's achievement. Discussing the problems of prejudice in poetry, Stephen Wilson notes: 'Our aesthetic response is disturbed precisely when we find unacceptable content embodied in compelling beauty – our preconceptions are violated' (Wilson, 1989, p. 47). This formulation raises questions of what constitutes unacceptable content and whose perception of that content is taken into account. Even so, the violation done to our preconceptions is surely not just aesthetic, but also ethical. While it is doubtful that a poet's political allegiance, chosen freely and without coercion, could ever be considered tragic, the deployment of that poet's talent in the cause of an evil, and not just a politically disadvantageous, regime is not only an aesthetic disjunction but probably does constitute a moral tragedy.

In 1918 Pound published a short poem in *The Little Review* entitled 'Cantico del Sole'. It mostly consists of three repetitions of the following lines:

> The thought of what America would be like
> If the Classics had a wide circulation
> Troubles my sleep
>
> (*CSP*, p. 183)

The poem is both an ironic response to the censorship that *The Little Review* was then undergoing and a droll lament against philistinism: new serious literature was being suppressed not in the face of the 'classics' but the conservatism of the popular press. The poem and its provenance encapsulate some contradictory features of Pound's artistic stance. There is the fierce desire to 'make it new' and to promote the newness of others. In 1918 and for most of Pound's poetically active life this meant reaching comparatively few people in a way that mass media and information technology have now obviated. Today it is possible to be avant-garde and listened to, read or seen by very large numbers of people. Being modernist probably required the self-defensive sense of exclusivity, the couldn't-care-less elitism that Pound cultivated but which I do not think he wholly believed in. But Pound does not directly castigate the ignorance or suppression of the new. His argument is more roundabout: if people had a grounding in, a familiarity with, the classics, there would be a more receptive climate for the avant-garde. A letter to Margaret Anderson, the editor of *The Little Review*, about the time 'Cantico del Sole' was written sets out his position. It is clear that he sees the classics 'ancient and modern' as an essential foundation, a yardstick for quality and 'the only antiseptics against the contagious imbecility of mankind. I can conceive an intelligence strong enough to exist without them, but I cannot recall having met an incarnation of such intelligence' (*SL*, p. 113). There is, then, probably no other modernist for whom the artistic products of the past are so valuable.

Pound's acute sense of the past makes his place in literary history somewhat paradoxical: the prime mover of modernism as self-professed traditionalist. In *The Pisan Cantos* he claims it was not vanity, usefully thought of as 'empty exercise' in this context, 'To have gathered from the air a live tradition' (*CAN*, p. 536). To the extent that Pound was responsible for, at the very least, bringing to notice a wide range of otherwise esoteric and neglected material, he may be seen to have invented the tradition he was gathering. His invention was not just in interweaving particular strands of western culture, such as Homeric Greek, Classical Latin, the troubadours, Renaissance Italy, revolutionary America, to name only the most prominent. For someone, however misguidedly, implicated in racist ideology, he was perversely unethnocentric. In her discussion of *The Pisan Cantos* Kathleen Woodward judges Pound to be the only great modernist poet 'to believe in what we now call ethnopoetics – the coupling of anthropology and poetry, the opening up of other, nonwestern cultural traditions – both as method and metaphor' (Woodward, 1980, p. 92). Certainly, his adoption and celebration of Chinese, African and other cultures bears this out and makes the tradition that Pound gathered a richly diverse one.

The tradition Pound gathered becomes the basis for the tradition we gather from him. Reading his poetry and prose is a highly educative experience. Even given the chance, he may well not have proved to be a very good teacher in the formal settings of an education system, but there is little doubt about his pedagogic impulse, his urge to inform and expound ideas to others. His prose positively overflows with those ideas, about literature, art, music, history, philosophy, aesthetics, economics and the rest. The overall impression of much of Pound's prose work is twofold: enthusiasm of expression and commitment to the views being relayed. This is especially true in his essays on literary and artistic topics, such

as those supporting fellow writers or trying to outline the theories
of modernist aesthetics and poetics. Such material will, I expect,
remain canonical as expositions of early modernist thought, no
matter how much they are rightly subjected to iconoclastic scru-
tiny. Pound's vitality and exuberance in putting his ideas across
can and do degenerate sometimes into the brow-beating tone of
a convinced and closed mind, most notably in some, but by no
means all, of his prose concerning economics. Two quite different
perspectives on Pound as purveyor of ideas and disseminator of
insights about his gathered tradition are worth citing from con-
temporary sources. When Pound published his great labour of
love, *Guido Cavalcanti Rime*, in 1932, he did so under his initials
only. The French scholar Etienne Gilson reviewed the work as if
it were anonymous and said: 'whoever he may be, I want to as-
sure him that I fully realize what a claim he has on the gratitude
of his readers, even where they feel inclined to disagree with some
of his interpretations' (Homberger (ed.), 1972, p. 273). While this
is specific to a particular work, it has a more general application
to many of Pound's projects which brought to light, made new,
not only single works but whole areas of neglected culture. How-
ever, a more jaundiced view of Pound the promoter occurs in *The
Autobiography of Alice B. Toklas* by Gertrude Stein. She wrote of her
meeting with Pound in Paris in 1921 as follows: 'Gertrude Stein
liked him but did not find him amusing. She said he was a village
explainer, excellent if you were a village, but if you were not, not'
(Stein, 1966, p. 217). This is excellent wit, indeed, and nicely
deflates the tendency to hector in Pound's enthusiasm. But at the
end of a truly devastating century for humankind, perhaps it makes
an unintentionally serious evaluation of Pound and his work. The
world is now, in McCluhan's term turned cliché, 'a global village'.
Pound's poetry and much of the prose work which underpins it
is his attempt to explain that village in the process of going global.
We may disagree with some of the interpretations Pound offers,
but we have to acknowledge and, I think, be grateful for the effort
and skill he put into making them.

As well as the live tradition as he saw it, Pound was very much
concerned to gather a living creativity of the new and excellent.
No conclusion to a book of this sort on Pound could omit to
reaffirm his importance in supporting and promoting other writers
and artists, especially in the crucial period when the work of early
modernists was struggling for recognition. I have referred to the
major figures that Pound influenced, helped and defended, but
there were many more. Some commentators have grudgingly at-
tributed this activity to motives of empire-building and the desire
for reflected glory. I see little evidence for this in Pound's letters,

contemporary accounts or the comments of those who benefited from his generosity. There were literary squabbles, some of which became fairly vociferous rows, but no more than in any other period of literary innovation, past or present. Pound seems to have been almost devoid of literary jealousy, which is relatively rare, though he also put critical honesty before the sensitivities of friendship on occasions, something which can easily be misinterpreted.

What Pound loved well, the literatures and cultures he chose from the past, the works of those he nourished in his present, is only part of his true heritage. Equally important is his lasting effect on the practice of poetry and its role in society. It is impossible to be comprehensive in this respect, since the influence, both immediate and displaced, pervades so much of twentieth-century poetry. I mention only three points that seem particularly significant to me from the many that come to mind. First, there is the immeasurable impact Pound has had on the act and art of poetic translation. In a key statement on Pound's contribution, George Steiner outlines some of the economic and sociological factors that have made the twentieth century a golden age of poetry in translation, then goes on to say:

> As important as all these reasons put together, however, and central to the manner and controversial liberties of the modern form, is the achievement of one man . . . Pound's actual translations play a vital part. They have altered the definition and ideals of verse translation in the twentieth century as surely as Pound's poetry has renewed or subverted modern English and American poetics.
>
> (Steiner (ed.), 1970, p. 32)

Despite their critical reception in some quarters and the debate about Pound's scholarship that still goes on, his single poems, great cycles and translated elements within *The Cantos* have set an example whose basic premise is that the translation should be a poem in its own right and as good a poem as the translator can make it. The impulse not only to make it new but also to make it excellent is nowhere better realized than in Pound's finest translations.

My second point is a very simple one about the sheer quality of much of Pound's poetry, the beauty of so many of his lines, the technique with which they are assembled into poems. This quality often seems to get overlooked in all the debate about Pound's political incorrectnesses. So many books and papers that chew the theoretical and ideological fat about Pound give the impression that they could have been, and perhaps were, written without any care for his poetry, possibly even without it being read. Those who read and endlessly reread his poetry for pleasure or emotional renewal will know that this is a travesty. Those who practise, however ineptly, writing poetry themselves can only benefit from reading his work in terms of the craftsmanship it displays. Pound never wanted anyone to imitate his poetic manner and was always pleased when someone cast off any mannerism that derived from him. In that respect, he would have had little time for poetry that was distinctly Poundian. Nevertheless, given that Steiner is right about Pound's effect on modern poetics, there is a sense in which most poetry in English, and many other languages too, is post-Poundian, not in a straightforwardly chronological way, but in the sense of taking cognizance of the quality he achieved. As with any great art, there will always remain something inexplicable about this quality that no amount of commentary can capture. All the more reason, then, to endorse the view of Pound's friend William Carlos Williams: 'His work shines most in the reading, not in the reading about it' (Homberger (ed.), 1972, p. 227).

My third point, and the one on which I end this book, concerns the status of Pound as a political poet, by which I mean someone who writes poetry that, ulterior to its aesthetic qualities, is motivated by a desire for political change. This has oppositional and explanatory aspects. Pound's anti-war poetry develops from the remotely mythologized, such as 'The Coming of War: Acteon', through the wistful parallelism of *Cathay* and the satiric analogies of *Propertius*, to the irrational howl of anger in *Mauberley*. In *The Cantos*, however, it is much more focused on systems and the individuals who profit from playing those systems. In particular, his fight against the arms trade seems uniquely bold in its time and can be seen to set an example for the oppositional poetry associated with the Vietnam War and other major modern conflicts. This is directly acknowledged by Allen Ginsberg who dedicated his 1967 anti-war poem 'War Profit Litany' to Pound (Ginsberg, 1987, p. 486). Closely allied to this is the poetry of nuclear protest which Pound's oppositional poetry can also be seen to foreshadow. True to his perceived role as explainer, though, Pound was not content merely to protest. This urge to explain in global and historical terms had a formal implication that is best captured by Alfredo Rizzardi, the Italian scholar and first translator of *The Pisan Cantos* into Italian. Referring to Pound's definition of an epic as 'a poem containing history', he says: 'Such an expression needs an interpretation, perhaps a deepening of its meaning... An epic which is also great poetry is a poem which has suffered history. It is a new poetical dimension, the widest horizon of Pound's literary discoveries' (Rizzardi, 1961, p. 156). Perhaps this is the real meaning of 'the great ball of crystal', not *The Cantos* themselves but the challenging precedent they set for poetry. As to who can lift it, I suggest there may only be room for one Ezra Pound per century. If that is the case, then the next poet to reach the widest horizon of Pound's literary discovery is still a child, as yet unaware of what he (though I suspect it will be a she) is likely to achieve.

Part Three
Reference Section

Brief biographies

RICHARD ALDINGTON, 1892–1962. English poet, novelist and biographer. He was among the first poets to be designated an 'Imagiste' by Pound and his first book of poems was actually called *Images 1910–1915*. Aldington married Hilda Doolittle in 1913 but after the First World War they separated and were subsequently divorced. Aldington's *Collected Poems* were published in 1928. His wartime experience gave rise to his bitter anti-war novel *Death of a Hero* (1929) in which a fictional caricature of Pound appears. Aldington produced controversial accounts of the lives of both D.H. Lawrence and T.E. Lawrence (Lawrence of Arabia). His autobiography, *Life for Life's Sake* (1941), is a source for numerous anecdotes about Pound's London years.

MARGARET ANDERSON, 1886–1973. American editor, critic and autobiographer. After contributing to various magazines Anderson founded *The Little Review* in 1914 in Chicago. In 1916 its publication moved to New York. The magazine was significant in promoting avant-garde literature as well as publishing informed discussion of contemporary cultural concerns. Anderson made an arrangement with Pound whereby the poetry and prose of London-based modernist writers was regularly featured in the magazine. Pound's letters to Anderson over the period of the magazine's publication are a rich resource of information and insight about the early years of literary modernism. *The Little Review* became notorious for serializing Joyce's *Ulysses* prior to its publication in book form, for which it was prosecuted and confiscated. The magazine eventually closed in 1929. In 1953 she edited *The Little Review Anthology*, a selection of pieces originally published in the magazine. This prompted Pound to write to her from St Elizabeth's and they briefly renewed their correspondence. Anderson's surviving letters from 1953 reveal something of her own forceful personality and her enduring feeling for Pound. One letter ends: 'Always with affection, and with a lasting gratitude for all that you did for the L.R.' Another begins: 'Ezra – you ARE nice – I loved your letter.' The last, from 1954, ends with a parenthesis: '(I'm doing a job of work that would repulse you as much as your economics do me. Well. . . .) Ever M' (Scott *et al* (eds), 1988, pp. 322, 327, 329). Margaret Anderson wrote three volumes of autobiography, *My Thirty Years War* (1930), *The Fiery Fountains* (1951), *The Strange Necessity* (1969), which are an important source of first-hand detail about the modernist literary movement.

GEORGE ANTHEIL, 1900–59. American composer. In his early career, largely based in Europe, Antheil wrote pieces that were experimental and avant-garde in nature, such as the *Ballet Mécanique* (1926) which incorporates the sounds of aeroplane propellers and motor horns. Antheil became friends with Pound in Paris in the early 1920s and helped him to orchestrate his opera *Le Testament*. Olga Rudge and Antheil gave concerts whose main focus was the performance of his latest compositions and Pound promoted his work, especially in the volume *Antheil and the Treatise on Harmony* (1924). In his turn Antheil wrote an article 'Why a Poet quit the Muses' in praise of Pound's own musical compositions: 'Pound's whole music has a medieval intelligence, a brilliant intelligence although it is not intellectual . . . I am convinced that no other music today is so completely free from the developments of music during the last three or four hundred years, yet the music is as tight and as built up upon inner and strict laws of its own, as if it were built upon hundreds of years of musical tradition' (Shafer (ed.), 1978, p. 513). Antheil's opera *Transatlantic*, whose première Pound attended in Frankfurt in 1930, assimilated elements of jazz. Antheil's later music was more conventional and he also worked in Hollywood as a composer of film music. His autobiography, *Bad Boy of Music*, published in 1945, is an entertaining reflection on his career as an avant-garde composer. Antheil is mentioned fleetingly in Canto 74 in the tangle of memory and sensory impression of the Pisan prison cage (*CAN*, p. 441).

BÉLA BARTÓK, 1881–1945. Hungarian composer. Bartók was a pioneer of musical ethnography, travelling extensively in Eastern Europe and North Africa and making early recordings of authentic folk music. His own compositions incorporated the idioms of such music in a distinctively modernist way, resulting in some of the greatest masterpieces of twentieth-Century music. Pound heard some of his chamber music in concerts in Venice and at Rapallo and was particularly impressed by the Fifth Quartet (1934), which he likened to *The Cantos* as a record of artistic struggle.

HENRI BERGSON, 1859–1941. French philosopher. Professor at the Collège de France in Paris where Hulme attended his lectures. His major areas of inquiry included intuition, memory, creativity and the nature of time. His theories, which incorporated the idea that the past is constantly part of present experience, can be seen to be particularly influential on the structure of *The Cantos*. Bergson's most famous works are *Time and Freewill* (1889), *Matter and Memory* (1896) and *Creative Evolution* (1907).

BASIL BUNTING, 1900–85. English poet. Born in Northumberland with a Quaker background. He was imprisoned during the First World War as a conscientious objector. Bunting was one of Pound's foremost disciples during the Rapallo years. He abandoned his pacifism during the Second World War and served with the British forces in Persia. Later, he worked in Newcastle as a journalist. His masterpiece *Briggflats* (1966) is a long autobiographical poem which synthesizes modernist poetic practice at its best. Bunting's *Collected Poems* first appeared in 1968 and his work continues to influence other modernist poets.

WINSTON CHURCHILL, 1874–1965. British statesman. Following early experience as a soldier and journalist Churchill became a Conservative MP in 1900, but actually rose to government office as a Liberal, becoming Minister of Munitions during the First World War. In 1926 he was Chancellor of the Exchequer during the period of the General Strike and miners' strike and contributed vehemently to their suppression. Churchill's leadership during the Second World War and his implacable resistance to the onslaught of Nazism, characterized by his wartime oratory, made him one of the most famous Englishmen of all time. Nevertheless, he was defeated in the election of 1945 by an incoming Labour government, a fact celebrated by Pound in *The Pisan Cantos*. Churchill continued his political and literary career until very late in life. He was awarded the Nobel Prize for Literature in 1953.

MARY DE RACHEWILTZ (née Rudge), b. 1925. Writer, translator and Pound scholar. Daughter of Olga Rudge and Ezra Pound. Mary Rudge was raised by foster parents in the Italian Tyrol, receiving visits from her parents and grandfather, visiting her mother's home in Venice and later her apartment in Sant'Ambrogio. Alongside her convent education she began to translate *The Cantos* into Italian under her father's direction. Mary married Prince Boris de Rachewiltz in 1946 and set up home in a ruined castle, Brunnenburg, in the Italian Tyrol. On his return to Italy Pound lived intermittently at Brunnenburg Castle with Mary and her family before settling down with Olga Rudge in Venice. Today, the castle is part museum, part centre of Pound scholarship, but still very much the home of an extended family. Mary de Rachewiltz published a fine autobiography, *Discretions*, in 1971. As well as being a poet in her own right, she is also the author of the definitive Italian translation of *The Cantos*.

HILDA DOOLITTLE, 1886–1961. American poet, novelist and auto-biographer. As a young woman in Pennsylvania she was roman-tically involved with Pound. She was already writing poetry during the period of her emigration to London, but her poetic career was given a sharper focus when Pound labelled her work 'H.D. Imagiste'. She retained the abbreviation as a pen-name for the rest of her career. She married Richard Aldington in 1913, but their marriage foundered and she later established a lifelong relationship with the Englishwoman Bryher, a novelist and supporter of the arts. Her first collection of poems, *Sea Garden* (1916), confirmed her as probably the only imagist to realize consistently the tenets of imagism. Her early poetry was brought together in *Collected Poems* (1925). H.D.'s fic-tion was both experimental and autobiographical, including *Palimpsest* (1926) and *Her* (1927), though the latter was not published until 1981. In the 1930s she underwent psychoanalysis with Freud, an experience of major significance for her subsequent writing. H.D. wrote a series of long poems while in London during the Second World War, published as *Trilogy* in 1946. Her later works, influ-enced by Freudian psychoanalysis and surrealism, include a series of unpublished novels as well as *Helen in Egypt* (1961) and *Hermetic Definition* (1972). Her memoir of her relationship with Pound, *End to Torment*, was published posthumously in 1979.

C.H. DOUGLAS, 1879–1952. British economist. After an early career in engineering Douglas became interested in economic solutions to society's problems. He originated the theory of Social Credit, the basis of an economic policy which would give greater purchasing power to consumers. Douglas expounded this theory in *The New Age* magazine where Pound first encountered his ideas. His book, *Economic Democracy*, was published in 1920. Social Credit was given relatively little serious consideration by mainstream economists and its tenets were never adopted at national government level, some-thing which Pound expended enormous energy trying to achieve. Douglasite economics figure largely in Pound's writings after 1920, not only in his prose on the topic but also in *The Cantos*.

T.S. ELIOT, 1888–1965. American poet, dramatist, critic and Nobel Prize winner. During his years as a student at Harvard University Eliot became significantly interested in the work of Jules Laforgue and the French symbolists who influenced his early poetry. Eliot left America in 1914 and eventually settled in London where the rest of his life was based. His early career was substantially sup-ported by Pound artistically, financially and with some degree of collaboration. The result was two successful volumes of poetry, *Pru-frock and other Observations* (1917) and *Poems* (1920).The culmination of this support was Pound's editing of *The Waste Land* which came to be seen as the definitive modernist poem in the aftermath of its publication in 1922. Eliot also made significant contributions to modernist poetics with essays that introduced such concepts as the 'objective correlative', the 'dissociation of sensibility' and the theory of 'impersonality' in poetry. Eliot's increasing preoccupation with High Anglican religion influenced most of his subsequent creative output, as reflected in such poems as 'The Journey of the Magi' and 'Ash Wednesday'. An aside from this high seriousness was provided by *Old Possum's Book of Practical Cats* (1939), which is now a classic of children's verse. Eliot's last major poetic achievement was *Four Quartets*, a meditative cycle begun in 1935 and published complete in 1943. The possibilities of a modernist verse drama, hinted at in *The Waste Land*, were fragmentarily realized in *Sweeney Agonistes* (1932). This was followed by Eliot's most successfully performed play, *Murder in the Cathedral* (1935). After the Second World War he concentrated on a series of verse dramas and further collections of critical and theoretical essays. The conservative nature of Eliot's later beliefs made him an establishment figure rather than a member of the avant-garde. However, his directorship at Faber & Faber gave him substantial influence over the promotion and publication of poetry in Britain. Eliot played an important role in Pound's eventual release from St Elizabeth's in 1958.

JACOB EPSTEIN, 1880–1959. American sculptor. Epstein was born and brought up in New York City, but after two years of study in Paris he settled in London in 1905 and made England his permanent home. Although primarily a portrait sculptor, Epstein became involved in the artistic and literary avant-garde activities associated with Pound, Lewis and Gaudier-Brzeska. One of his most famous modernist pieces, 'The Rock Drill' (1913), dates from this period. Pound was particularly impressed by this work and named a section of *The Cantos* after it. Epstein's later work included monolithic figures, often controversial in their crude depiction of religious themes, and mainly bronze portraiture. He received a British knighthood in 1954.

FORD MADOX FORD, 1873–1939. English novelist and man of letters. He was born Ford Hermann Hueffer and related to the Pre-Raphaelite Rossetti family as well as the painter Ford Madox Brown. His literary thinking, influenced by Pre-Raphaelitism and Impressionism, anticipated modernist trends and in the early 1900s he collaborated on a distinctly modernist agenda with Joseph Conrad. Through his editorship of *The English Review* he supported Pound and other avant-garde writers and was instrumental in helping Pound to reach a less flowery, harder-edged poetic style. *The Good Soldier* (1915), generally considered to be his finest novel, is a subtly experimental fiction of passion and deceit. Ford saw active service during the First World War and was badly wounded. Like Pound, he also said farewell to London after the war, at the same time changing his name. With a more or less new identity he lived in Paris and founded the *Transatlantic Review*, another vehicle for modernist writers. His other major work of fiction, the tetralogy *Parade's End*, was completed in 1928. He wrote several autobiographical memoirs during his final years in America and the south of France, including *Return to Yesterday* (1931) and *It was the Nightingale* (1933). These provide a singular record of the development of early modernism. While teaching in America in the 1930s, Ford lined up a possible teaching post for Pound, but the poet refused. Ford and Pound met in New York in 1939 shortly before Ford was to return to France. Within a few weeks Ford was dead.

HENRI GAUDIER-BRZESKA, 1891–1915. French artist. After studying art in Orleans Gaudier met his future partner, the Polish woman Sophie Brzeska, in Paris in 1910. The couple then settled in London where Pound first saw Gaudier-Brzeska's work at an exhibition in 1913. Pound befriended Gaudier-Brzeska, championed his work in magazine articles and promoted its sale. Together with Wyndham Lewis and his associates, Gaudier-Brzeska was involved in the vorticist movement and his work figured in their exhibitions and publications. His sculpture evolved into fully abstract forms that were influential on later modernist work. Gaudier-Brzeska's massive marble bust, known as the 'Hieratic Head of Ezra Pound', remains an icon of a friendship and an avant-garde movement in art. Gaudier-Brzeska was killed in the trenches of the First World War, curtailing the work of a potential genius of modern sculpture. Pound was deeply affected by this loss and first published his memoir of the artist in 1916. He saw Gaudier-Brzeska's death as a consequence of the callous disregard for human life of politicians, arms dealers and international financiers, a view which prompted his economic and political activism in later years.

THOMAS HARDY, 1840–1928. English novelist and poet. He was born and brought up in Dorset where, except for relatively short periods, he lived the rest of his life. His novels, and many of his poems, are set in a fictional Wessex, based on Dorset and its surrounding counties. Following the increasingly negative reception of his pessimistic fiction which culminated in the scandalized response to *Jude the Obscure* (1895), Hardy gave up writing novels and became a prolific poet over the next 30 years. He was one of the few writers whose professional advice Pound openly acknowledged.

ERNEST HEMINGWAY, 1898–1961. American novelist and short story writer. His youthful experience as a journalist was interrupted by the First World War in which he was a voluntary ambulance worker. Hemingway lived in Paris in the 1920s and associated with Pound at this time, later acknowledging Pound's influence on his style. His novel about the American and British 'lost generation', *The Sun Also Rises* (1926), was based on his years in France. This was followed by, among other things, the collection of short stories *Men without Women* (1927), *A Farewell to Arms* (1929) and *To Have and Have Not* (1937). His work as a war correspondent during the Spanish Civil War led to *For Whom the Bell Tolls* (1940), another of his major novels. Despite the achievement of *The Old Man and the Sea* in 1952 and the recognition of the Nobel Prize, Hemingway committed suicide. His memoir of Paris in the 1920s, *A Moveable Feast*, with its affectionate vignettes about Pound, was published posthumously in 1964.

T.E. HULME, 1883–1917. English philosopher and essayist. His articles in *The New Age* magazine on Bergson and 'Romanticism and Classicism' in the years before the First World War promoted an anti-Romantic ideal of clarity and precision. His study and translation of the work of Bergson led him to develop theories of imagism which were taken up by Pound as well as other writers and artists. Hulme's own imagist poems were published in *The New Age* and subsequently appeared in Pound's *Ripostes* as 'The Complete Poetical Works of T.E. Hulme'. Hulme was killed in action in France. His notebooks were edited after his death, most notably in *Speculations*, published in 1924, and *Notes on Language and Style* (1929).

JAMES JOYCE, 1882–1941. Irish novelist, short story writer and poet. He was born and educated in Dublin, where he graduated from University College in 1902. From then on he spent most of his life in exile, living in Italy, France and Switzerland. Joyce's collection of short stories, *Dubliners*, depicting the emotional and social paralysis of its characters within the context of Irish Catholicism, initially met with resistance from publishers. Pound learned of Joyce's difficulties and began to promote his work, while also providing financial support. Joyce transformed an earlier attempt at an autobiographical novel, *Stephen Hero*, into *A Portrait of the Artist as a Young Man* (1916) and Pound arranged for its serialization in *The Egoist* magazine. The book's linguistic experimentation, themes and central character prefigure the even greater achievement of *Ulysses* (1922). This was also serialized at Pound's instigation in *The Little Review* before the instalments were curtailed by prosecution for obscenity, precipitating its appearance in book form in Paris. Pound's contemporary review of *Ulysses* for *The Dial* rightly placed Joyce in the company of Flaubert, Rabelais, Proust and Henry James as one of the great stylists and innovators. Joyce spent more or less the rest of his creative life writing what was to become *Finnegans Wake* (1939). The extreme complexity and density of Joyce's polyglot stream of consciousness technique renders the book obscure and semantically resistant, yet imbues it with a kind of musicality that is enhanced by reading aloud. Pound was unable, or possibly unwilling, to see connections between Joyce's work and some aspects of his own technique in *The Cantos*. The two writers more or less went their separate artistic, social and political ways, though Pound's memories of Joyce in *The Cantos* affirm his enduring affection.

WASSILY KANDINSKY, 1866–1944. French painter of Russian background. He was one of the first Abstract Expressionist painters and also wrote theoretical works on the nature of modernist art, drawing interesting parallels between visual art and music. Pound is likely to have seen his work at the Allied Artists' Exhibition in London in 1911 and was undoubtedly influenced by Kandinsky's treatise *Concerning the Spiritual in Art* (1910) which he quotes in his 1914 essay on vorticism. In 1912 Kandinsky founded the influential Blaue Reiter group of artists with Franz Marc and Paul Klee. In the 1920s and 1930s he worked at the Bauhaus in Germany.

JAMES LAUGHLIN, b. 1914. American editor, publisher and poet. While still a student at Harvard, Laughlin visited Rapallo where Pound advised him to become a publisher rather than a poet. As a result, in 1936 Laughlin founded New Directions, the publishing company best known for its modernist literature. From 1940 onwards New Directions was the major American outlet for Pound's work. Laughlin carried on writing poetry and his *Selected Poems 1935–1985* were published in 1986.

WYNDHAM LEWIS, 1882–1957. English artist and novelist. Born of an American father and English mother, Lewis studied art in London and Paris, where he was first known as a painter. His works were characterized by dynamic lines and geometric forms on which he based the concept of vorticism in the visual arts. Together with Pound he published the magazine *Blast*. This 'Review of the Great English Vortex' was supposed to be a periodical, but its publication was curtailed by, among other things, the outbreak of the First World War. While Lewis was on active service during the war,

Pound promoted his literary career by having his first novel, *Tarr* (1918), serialized. This novel has some of the stylistic and thematic characteristics of Lewis's later works, impetuous narrative and hectic colloquial dialogue, satire on the manners and morals of society, scepticism about humanity, misogyny. Lewis's satirical and semi-autobiographical fiction also included *The Apes of God* (1930) and *Self-condemned* (1954). Actual autobiography is to be found in *Blasting and Bombardiering* (1937) which is a source of reminiscence about Pound, Joyce, Eliot and the modernist movement, among other things. Lewis drew or painted Pound's portrait several times. The drawings of 1919 and 1920 are very different: in the former, Pound stares penetratingly at the viewer, while the latter is monolithic with Pound's sightless face like a marble statue in half-profile. On his visit to London in 1938 Pound sat for a portrait at Lewis's studio in Notting Hill. The result is the oil painting now in the Tate Gallery in which Pound leans back with closed eyes, more sleeping volcano than restful poet. Lewis also wrote numerous books of philosophical or political comment, such as *The Art of Being Ruled* (1926). These promote an authoritarian, anti-democratic view that is sceptical of the achievements of liberal society and anticipate his initial support for Hitler. This was particularly damaging to his literary and artistic reputation before the Second World War, even though he revised his views in *The Hitler Cult* (1939). Lewis spent the war years in North America. He suffered from a brain tumour in his latter years, remaining artistically active as long as his ensuing blindness would allow, something Pound refers to in Canto 115 of the *Drafts and Fragments* (*CAN*, p. 808).

AMY LOWELL, 1874–1925. American poet. Her first book of poems, *A Dome of Many-colored Glass*, was published in 1912. She visited London, became an active member of the early imagist group of poets and was represented in the *Des Imagistes* anthology of 1914. Pound disagreed with her over what he saw as a dilution of imagist principles in later anthologies which she produced without his support. Their ideological differences were unresolved at her death. She has subsequently been seen not only as a champion of modernist American poetry but also as someone promoting a feminist voice in the male-dominated poetry world of her time. Her *Complete Poetical Works* were not published until 1955.

HARRIET MONROE, 1860–1936. American poet and editor. She was already a well-published poet when she founded the magazine *Poetry* in Chicago in 1912 and edited it for the rest of her life. *Poetry* played a significant part in promoting new poets who subsequently became major figures in twentieth-century American poetry, such as Carl

Sandburg, Robert Frost, Wallace Stevens, Marianne Moore and Edna St Vincent Millay. Pound was the magazine's European correspondent in its early years and recommended the work of Eliot, H.D. and others for publication. Monroe's own poetry culminated in the collection *Chosen Poems* in 1935. She also published a collection of critical essays, *Poets and their Art* (1932). Her autobiography, *A Poet's Life: Seventy Years in a Changing World*, appeared posthumously in 1937 and gives an informed overview of developments in American poetry during her lifetime.

MARIANNE MOORE, 1887–1972. American poet and woman of letters. Her work is highly distinctive and characterized by a cryptic and ironic mode of expression. Among other things her work develops a metapoetic stance, exploring the aesthetics of poetry itself in linguistically rich and unconventional ways. Pound was an early admirer of Moore's modernist qualities, promoted her work in his capacity as literary editor of several magazines and succeeded in getting her first book, *Poems* (1921), published by the Egoist Press. Moore was also a perceptive critic and essayist to which her *Complete Prose*, collected posthumously in 1986, testifies. Her reviews of Pound's work and assessment of his poetic talents are consistently favourable, though balanced by a healthy dismissal of some of his more extreme theories. Moore built up an outstanding body of poetry over a long period, winning the Pulitzer prize for her *Collected Poems* (1951).

BENITO MUSSOLINI, 1883–1945. Italian politician and dictator. In his early career Mussolini was a socialist, but became disenchanted with Italian socialism during the First World War. He founded the Italian Fascist Party in 1919 and, following his march on Rome in 1922, became prime minister, then dictator of Italy. Pound met Mussolini in 1933, an audience which probably led him to support the fascist cause. Mussolini's policies led to the invasion of Abyssinia, political isolation, an alliance with Hitler's Germany and eventually war against the Allies. He was overthrown in 1943, but set up by the Germans in the puppet Salo Republic in northern Italy. He was assassinated by Italian partisans. Pound remained loyal to Mussolini or, perhaps, the idealized version of 'the Boss' that he had built up, and refers to him with admiration, affection and sadness in *The Cantos*.

CHARLES OLSON, 1910–70. American poet. Following a political career under President Roosevelt, Olson chose to become a writer. He also taught at Black Mountain College where he wrote his influential essay 'Projective Verse' in 1950, advocating experimental forms of poetic composition. The Black Mountain school of poets developed from this. Olson visited Pound in the early years of his time in St Elizabeth's, torn between admiration for the poet and his work and dismay at his fascist views. These emotions are movingly captured in a journal of his visits which was published posthumously in 1975. Olson's major poetic work, *The Maximus Poems*, began to emerge in 1953, though a complete edition was not published till 1983. A distinctly post-Poundian epic, the work explores place and time through the voice of Maximus, the poet's persona, in the confines of a small American town. It is generally regarded as one of the chief works of postmodernist American poetry.

DOROTHY POUND (née Shakespear), 1887–1973. Wife of Ezra Pound. She met Pound at her London home in 1909 when he came to visit her mother, Olivia Shakespear, friend and former lover of W.B. Yeats. They were married in 1914. Dorothy Pound was an accomplished artist and designed covers for Pound's *Ripostes* and the *Catholic Anthology* in 1915. She had a son, Omar, in 1926 in Paris. Throughout the St Elizabeth's years she lived in an apartment near the hospital in Washington D.C. She was appointed a one-person committee to look after Pound's business affairs and officially he was released from St Elizabeth's into her custody. Following the domestic tensions and problems that arose during the early years of Pound's return to Italy, she began to spend more time in England and saw little of Pound in the final years of his life. Dorothy Pound died in a nursing home near Cambridge in December 1973.

OMAR SHAKESPEAR POUND, b. 1926. Son of Dorothy Pound. He was born in Paris and adopted by his grandmother, Olivia Shakespear. Having spent his childhood and early youth at Felpham in Sussex, Omar Pound was educated at the English public school, Charterhouse. As a registered American citizen, he joined the US Army in 1945 and served in Europe where he met Mary de Rachewiltz for the first time at Rapallo. He visited Pound in Howard Hall and subsequently maintained contact throughout the St Elizabeth's years. Omar Pound took degrees in anthropology and Islamic studies. After holding teaching posts in Boston and Tangier, he settled with his family in Cambridge.

JOHN QUINN, 1870–1924. American patron of the arts. Quinn met Pound in 1910 in New York. During Pound's London years Quinn bought the work of Gaudier-Brzeska, Lewis and Epstein at Pound's recommendation. In a letter to Quinn in 1915 Pound wrote: 'If a patron buys from an artist who needs money, the patron then makes himself equal to the artist: he is building art into the world; he creates' (*SL*, p. 50). Quinn also financed Pound's contribution to *The Little Review* and supported Eliot during the period when he was writing and publishing *The Waste Land*. He was the initial recipient of the manuscript of the poem. Quinn visited Pound in Paris in 1923 to arrange what turned out to be his final act of patronage, the financing of a new magazine, the *Transatlantic Review*, founded and edited by Ford Madox Ford.

F.D. ROOSEVELT, 1882–1945. American statesman. Roosevelt pursued a career in politics, despite his polio-induced disability, as a senator and governor before becoming president of the United States in 1933. He instituted the so-called New Deal to counteract economic stagnation and unemployment. At this stage Pound was interested in trying to persuade Roosevelt to apply Douglas's Social Credit in America, but in subsequent years he developed a strong disaffection for Roosevelt's policies. Because of his successive re-elections Roosevelt was in office throughout the years leading up to and during the Second World War. Pound was convinced that Roosevelt's policies and tactics throughout this period were unconstitutional and his attacks on the president became vehemently personal. Roosevelt did not live to see the final result of leading America through the war, dying a few weeks before the surrender of Germany.

OLGA RUDGE, 1895–1996. American violinist and musicologist. In the early decades of the century she toured Europe, playing both the standard repertoire and works by contemporary composers. Rudge met Pound in Paris in the early 1920s where she took part in a series of concerts to promote Antheil's avant-garde compositions and Pound's own musical efforts, including the première of his opera *Le Testament*. Pound and Rudge began a lifelong relationship and in 1925 they had a daughter, Mary. Although she maintained her own home in Venice, during the Rapallo years Rudge helped to organize and was a major performer at Pound's annual series of concerts. She spent considerable time cataloguing the Vivaldi manuscripts in the National Library in Turin and subsequently became a leading Vivaldi scholar in Siena where she founded the Centre for Vivaldi Studies. Following Pound's return to Italy after his release from St Elizabeth's the couple spent his remaining years together. In her final years Rudge left Venice to live in the care of her daughter at Brunnenburg Castle, Merano, Italy, where she celebrated her 100th birthday in April 1995. Olga Rudge died at Brunnenburg in March 1996. She is the dedicatee of *The Cantos*.

MAY SINCLAIR, 1863–1946. English novelist. After the publication of several early novels Sinclair's radical views led to her involvement in the suffragist movement, and her later novels expose the repression of women in Victorian and Edwardian England. She was acquainted with Pound from an early stage in his London years and introduced him to Ford Madox Ford. Her best-known books are the psychological novels, such as *Mary Oliver* (1919) and *The Life and Death of Harriet Frean* (1922), which explore the hidden motives and suppressed desires of their characters in a subtle form of 'stream of consciousness' technique.

WILLIAM BROOKE SMITH, 1884–1908. Pound's 'first friend'. Smith was a student at Philadelphia College of Art and graduated with a Diploma in 1905. He then became a freelance designer with a studio in his aunt's mansion. Pound met Smith in his first year at the University of Pennsylvania in 1901 and was influenced by his knowledge of contemporary art and literature, particularly the poets of the Nineties and their aestheticism. The friendship clearly meant a lot to Pound who dedicated his first book of poems *A Lume Spento* to Smith's memory.

GERTRUDE STEIN, 1874–1946. American novelist and woman of letters. Although she lived in America for nearly half her life, Stein is best known for her life of exile in Paris where she lived with her companion, Alice B. Toklas, from 1907. Stein's prose is characterized by an idiosyncratic and experimental use of language which can now be seen to have been highly influential on other modernist writers. One of her best known books in this vein is *Tender Buttons* (1914). Her home became a meeting place for avant-garde artists such as Braque, Gris and Picasso, as well as expatriate writers like Hemingway and Fitzgerald. In this way Pound met her in the early 1920s during his stay in Paris. This gave rise to Stein's much-quoted 'village explainer' remark in her most famous work, *The Autobiography of Alice B. Toklas* (1933), a third person account of her own life supposedly from her companion's point of view. Stein was a prolific writer across the genres. One of her plays, *Four Saints in Three Acts* (1929), was the basis of an opera by the American composer Virgil Thompson. She also wrote critical works, such as *Composition as Explanation* (1926), and memoirs, most notably *Wars I Have Seen* (1945).

HARRIET SHAW WEAVER, 1876–1961. English editor and political activist. A former social worker who inherited considerable wealth, Weaver rescued *The New Freewoman* from financial collapse in 1913, after which it was renamed *The Egoist*. Pound became its literary editor and persuaded Weaver to publish Joyce's *Portrait of the Artist as a Young Man* in serial form. Weaver subsequently became Joyce's main source of financial security for the rest of his life, a sounding board for his literary endeavours and ultimately his literary executor. In later life Weaver became a staunch communist and continued her political activism into old age.

WILLIAM CARLOS WILLIAMS, 1883–1963. American poet and man of letters. Williams qualified as a doctor and spent his working life as a general practitioner in his home town of Rutherford, New Jersey. His poetry is distinctively modernist in style, making innovative use of rhythmic units and typographical layout. His early work was represented in *Des Imagistes*, Pound's first imagist anthology, in 1914. Williams's dictum 'No ideas but in things' could well stand as another tenet of imagism and has some affinity with Pound's 'Imagiste' warning to 'Go in fear of abstractions'. Williams also wrote literary essays and fiction, including a substantial body of short stories and several novels. His first major novel, *The Voyage to Pagany* (1928), was dedicated to 'the first of us all, my old friend Ezra Pound'. His large output of poetry culminated in *Paterson*, a poem of epic proportions in several books, which conflates personal and public history by means of textual montage. Williams himself said of the poem: 'I had known always that I wanted to write a long poem but I didn't know what I wanted to do until I got the idea of a man identified with a city ... I called my protagonist Mr Paterson. When I speak of Paterson throughout the poem, I speak of both the man and the city' (Williams, 1967, pp. 81, 83). Williams's last collection, *Pictures from Bruegel and Other Poems* (1962), posthumously received the Pulitzer prize. Williams's friendship with Pound was severely tested by Pound's political views and allegiances, which he found difficult to comprehend, though he rallied to Pound's support during the St Elizabeth's years. He never lost his admiration for Pound's technical facility and ear for poetry which he frequently praised in reviews of his work. Pound obliquely salutes Williams's objectivist ideals in Canto 78:

> and as for the solidity of the white oxen in all this
> perhaps only Dr Williams (Bill Carlos)
> will understand its importance,
> its benediction. He wd/ have put in the cart.
> (*CAN*, p. 497)

W.B. YEATS, 1865–1939. Irish poet and dramatist. Yeats's career straddled the late nineteenth and early twentieth centuries in a significant way. His distinctly Irish affiliations, Celtic revivalism and nationalism, were offset by his involvement in the Rhymers' Club in London and French symbolism in Paris. Yeats's interest in theosophy, rosicrucianism and other aspects of the occult also provided him with a philosophical and symbolic framework. His early work, including love poetry inspired by his adoration of Maud Gonne, culminated in *The Wind among the Reeds* (1899). In the first decade of the twentieth century Yeats was heavily involved in the establishment of a distinctively Irish theatre. Besides writings plays, such as *Cathleen Ni Houlihan* (1902), he was also a joint director of the Abbey Theatre in Dublin. This was the Yeats who so impressed Pound in his student years and more than any other writer prompted Pound's exile to London. The two poets became close friends and colleagues. It is arguable that Yeats was the greater beneficiary. His drama was significantly influenced by Japanese Noh plays brought to his attention by Pound, and the development of his later poetic style can be traced from Pound's critical readings of the poems leading up to the collection *Responsibilities* (1914). Yeats's later work included major collections of poems, such as *The Tower* (1928) and *The Winding Stair* (1933), which contain complex and powerful reflections on the personal and political. The friendship between Pound and Yeats came under great strain in the 1930s when they quarrelled about the quality of their most recent work. This seems to have been resolved when Pound saw Yeats for the last time in 1938 a few months before the latter's death. Of the people Pound knew, Yeats is one of the most frequently mentioned in *The Cantos*. There is an extended passage in Canto 80 relating to Yeats's involvement in the Irish Senate in the 1920s. Yeats subsequently advised Pound not to attempt to become a senator himself. In this canto Pound responds to 'old Billyum' as follows:

> If a man don't occasionally sit in a senate
> how can he pierce the darrk mind of a
> senator?
> (*CAN*, p. 510)

LOUIS ZUKOFSKY, 1904–78. American poet. Zukofsky's early work appeared in Pound's magazine, *The Exile*, in 1928 and he visited Pound in Rapallo during the 1930s. Zukofsky founded the Objectivist school of poetry and edited *An Objectivists' Anthology* in 1932. His own work is distinctively modernist, innovative, dense, yet characterized by refreshingly witty use of language. In 1940 he began a long poem called *A* which was published in its complete form in 1978. His *All the Collected Short Poems* appeared in 1966. Despite his Russian Jewish background, Zukofsky wrote in Pound's defence during the St Elizabeth's years.

Gazetteer

England

LONDON. Pound first visited London on a sight-seeing tour in 1898 with his wealthy Aunt Frank. He returned in 1902 in the company of his father, on which occasion they visited the Royal Mint at its now redeveloped site in Tower Hill. He visited the city again in 1906 during the European trip funded by his university fellowship. These were to be probes into a place that became his home and venue for artistic endeavours from 1908 to 1920. From October 1908 Pound lived in a boarding house at 48 Langham Street and established a working relationship with Elkin Matthews who sold and later published his books from his shop in Vigo Street. He found some artistic solidarity in T.E. Hulme's literary group which met at the Tour Eiffel restaurant in Soho and also attended Yeats's Monday evenings in Woburn Buildings, now Woburn Walk. The Polytechnic in Regent Street was the scene of his series of lectures on the troubadours. During this period Pound moved to 10 Church Walk, Kensington, where he lived until the summer of 1910. Following trips to America and Europe, Pound eventually returned to Church Walk in 1911 and felt that he came to know Kensington 'stone by stone'. In 1914 he married Dorothy Shakespear at St Mary Abbots, Church Street, Kensington. For the next five years they lived at 5 Holland Place Chambers, Kensington, in an apartment whose living room was pentagonal. In the short-lived vorticist period Pound frequented the Rebel Art Centre in Great Ormond Street and the Dieudonne restaurant, much mentioned in *The Cantos*, the scene of an imagist dinner and a vorticist celebration of *Blast*. As the music critic William Atheling he preferred recitals and chamber music at the Aeolian Hall, New Bond Street, now partly occupied by Sotheby's, and the Wigmore Hall, Wigmore Street, rather than the larger orchestral venues. Pound was clearly very fond of London, but came to hate what it stood for as the capital of the British Empire and establishment conservatism. These attitudes are reflected in his 'farewell to London', *Hugh Selwyn Mauberley*, and even more so in the Hell cantos, which were meant to depict specific figures in a London setting. After his permanent departure in 1920 Pound returned to London on two occasions. In 1938 a visit was prompted by the death of Olivia Shakespear, his mother-in-law, during which he took the opportunity to meet Yeats. In 1965 he attended the memorial service for T.S. Eliot in Westminster Abbey.

STONE COTTAGE, COLEMAN'S HATCH, SUSSEX. W.B. Yeats rented this dressed stone cottage, which still overlooks the heathland of Ashdown Forest in East Sussex, for three consecutive winters between 1913 and 1916. Pound was initially enlisted as Yeats's secretary, despite some uncertainty about his personality, but the relationship between the two poets became one of mutual artistic support and refreshment. Dorothy Shakespear already knew the village of Coleman's Hatch from visits to her uncle's cottage nearby. When she and Pound were married in 1914, the couple spent their honeymoon at Stone Cottage and Dorothy accompanied her husband on the subsequent winters with Yeats. In the nostalgia of Pisa Pound recalls his time with Yeats in Canto 83 as follows:

> at Stone Cottage in Sussex by the waste moor
> (or whatever) and the holly bush
>   who would not eat ham for dinner
> because peasants eat ham for dinner
>   despite the excellent quality
> and the pleasure of having it hot
>
> (*CAN*, p. 548)

United States of America

CRAWFORDSVILLE, INDIANA. Pound held a short-lived teaching post here at Wabash College, a long-established Presbyterian institution. Although he made some acquaintances of his own kind, he soon became disenchanted and homesick. Within a few months he was dismissed from his post on the pretext that he had behaved improperly in accommodating a stranded actress in his rooms. The official history of Wabash College, published in 1932, notes that the authorities 'were content to use the occasion to make an arrangement about their contract that encouraged Mr Pound to shake the dust of a small middle-western Presbyterian college forever from his feet, and content to rejoice in his subsequent triumphs in poetry' (Stock, 1970, p. 43).

HAILEY, IDAHO. In 1884 this town in central Idaho, on the Bigwood River, was a mining community in Idaho Territory and still very much a frontier town. Homer and Isabel Pound settled there in a newly built house that was probably its best residence. According to Pound, in his early family history, *Indiscretions*, Hailey consisted of 'one street lined with saloons' (*PD*, p. 29). Homer had been appointed to establish a government land office in Hailey where miners could register their claims. Ezra Pound was born at home the following year. The Pounds did not stay long in Hailey and within a year Ezra left the town for good. Pound was very proud of the fact that he left Hailey during a blizzard 'behind the First Rotary Snow-plough' (ibid., p. 41).

NEW YORK. Pound was first taken to New York as an infant on his way back from Idaho. He stayed at his Aunt Frank's boarding house on East 47th Street, Manhattan. Further visits were quite frequent throughout his childhood and youth. Pound spent several months in the city during his return to America in 1910, toying with business at the Nassau Street office of James Bacon, the 'Baldy Bacon' of Canto 12. Among other addresses he lived at 270 Fourth Avenue (now Park Avenue South). While in New York he met Jack B. Yeats, the painter and father of W.B. Yeats, who wrote a very favourable report of Pound in a letter to his son. It was not until 1939 that Pound revisited New York on his ill-fated visit to America a few months before the outbreak of the Second World War. He stayed some of the time with the poet E.E. Cummings in Patchin Place. Pound's only other real stay in New York was in 1969 when he returned for the exhibition of the rediscovered manuscript of Eliot's *The Waste Land* at the Public Library.

PHILADELPHIA, PENNSYLVANIA. From 1889 onwards Pound's childhood and youth were spent in Philadelphia, where his father had a post at the United States Mint. The family made several moves in the Philadelphia area. Their first permanent home was at 417 Walnut Street, Jenkintown, a suburb north of the city. Two years later they finally settled in the suburb of Wyncote at 166 Fernbrook Avenue. Following attendance at public elementary school, Pound went to Cheltenham Military Academy, a private boys' school, in 1897. Four years later, at the premature age of sixteen, he began his higher education at the University of Pennsylvania in west Philadelphia. Hilda Doolittle lived in the nearby suburb of Upper Darby and this was the main venue for her courtship with Pound, particularly the tree-house in the grounds of her father's house. After a brief stay in a cottage in Swarthmore outside Philadelphia in the summer of 1910, Pound did not return to the city of his youth until 1958. While waiting to leave for Italy after his release from St Elizabeth's he actually stayed the night at 166 Fernbrook Avenue as a guest of the current occupants. In a memoir of his own visit to Wyncote Donald Davie noted: 'It is still an attractive place, preserved almost in a time-capsule, pre-1914, though much more leafy and umbrageous now than when the poet's father, Homer Pound, set up house there. His house is virtually unchanged, and kept that way – as a sort of shrine – by the present occupant, who entertained Pound there in 1958' (Alexander and McGonigal (eds), 1995, p. 28).

WASHINGTON D.C. Pound visited the American capital for a few weeks in 1939 on his desperate trip to the United States just before the outbreak of the Second World War. He stayed with friends in the Georgetown area of the city and attended sessions of Congress. It was on one of these occasions that he had his much recalled confrontation with Senator William Borah who, in response to Pound's offer to help keep America out of the war to come, told him: 'am sure I don't know what a man like you would find to *do* here' (*CAN*, p. 551). Pound's application to see the president was inevitably rejected and he left Washington in great disappointment. When he was repatriated to America in 1945 to face trial for treason, his plane had to land at Bolling Field, a military airstrip within the District of Columbia, in order to ensure Federal jurisdiction over his case. At first he was kept in the District prison on 19th Street, but later removed to Gallinger Hospital for observation. Finally he was transferred to St Elizabeth's Federal Hospital for the Insane, where he was at first kept on the punishment block known as Howard Hall. After his insanity plea had been upheld, he was eventually moved to Cedar Ward. In 1948 he was transferred to Chestnut Ward where, in the relative privilege of a small single room, he spent the next ten years.

France

PARIS. Pound made numerous trips to Paris in the years before the First World War, beginning with his visit in 1898 on a European tour with his aunt. Probably the most significant of these visits was that in the spring of 1911 when, at La Concorde station, he apparently had the experience from which he derived 'In a Station of the Metro', his archetypal imagist poem. Several visits in the aftermath of the war led to Pound and his wife settling in Paris in 1921, their eventual home being an apartment at 70 bis Rue Notre Dame des Champs in Montparnasse. Pound frequented Sylvia Beach's bookshop, Shakespeare and Company, which first published Joyce's *Ulysses* in 1922. In the relatively short time he lived in Paris Pound was particularly hyperactive. He wrote a regular newsletter for *The Dial* magazine, composed an opera, *Le Testament*, translated de Gourmont's *Physique de l'Amour* and wrote substantial parts of his first batch of cantos. He also edited Eliot's

The Waste Land, supported the musician Antheil and befriended
Hemingway and the sculptor Brancusi. In 1923 he met the violin-
ist Olga Rudge who later performed his compositions at the Salle
Pleyel. They established a relationship that was to last the rest of
his life. Nevertheless, Paris was ultimately a disappointment to Pound
and he left in October 1924. He returned on several occasions, not-
ably in 1926 for the first performance of Antheil's *Ballet Mécanique*
at the Théâtre des Champs-Elysées and his own opera at the Salle
Pleyel. Dorothy Pound's son, Omar, was born at the American
Hospital in Paris in September the same year. Pound visited Paris
on a number of occasions following his return to Europe in 1958.
In 1965 he saw a performance of Beckett's *Fin de Partie* [Endgame]
there and renewed his acquaintance with the author.

Italy

BRUNNENBURG, TIROLO DI MERANO. This castle in the Italian Tyrol
is the family home of Mary de Rachewiltz, the daughter of Olga
Rudge and Ezra Pound. Schloss Brunnenburg was in ruins when
Mary and her husband Prince Boris de Rachewiltz made it their
home in 1948. Pound lived at the gradually renovated castle on
his return to Italy in 1958 following his release from St Eliza-
beth's. Many of Pound's papers and possessions were lodged at
the castle and it has become an important centre for Pound stud-
ies. Part of the castle is open to the public as a major cultural venue
in the region.

PISA. The site of the Disciplinary Training Centre (DTC), where
Pound was imprisoned for six months during 1945 while awaiting
his return to America, was outside Pisa on the road to Viareggio.
The DTC was a camp for American military personnel who were
convicted criminals. It was here that Pound wrote *The Pisan Cantos.*
One recurrent aspect of these is reference to the Italian landscape,
natural features and people outside the perimeter of the camp. In
particular, a prominent hill visible from the camp is likened to the
sacred Chinese mountain Taishan.

RAPALLO. Pound made initial visits to this small resort on the
Italian Riviera, east of Genoa, in 1922 and 1923. In 1925 he and
Dorothy settled there in a sixth-floor apartment at Via Marsala
12. Notable visitors from Pound's London and Paris years stayed
in Rapallo, including Yeats who noted, among other things, Pound's
care for the town's cats. However, Pound's Rapallo also attracted
numbers of disciples and became the first so-called 'Ezuversity'. In
1928 Pound's parents visited Rapallo and decided to retire there,

moving into an apartment of their own. In 1929 Olga Rudge began to live in Sant'Ambrogio, a village high above the town, in an apartment at Casa 60. Together they instituted the annual series of concerts from 1933 onwards, with Olga as a prominent soloist. In 1944 Pound and Dorothy were forced by wartime circumstances to move into Olga's apartment and it was from Casa 60 that Pound was arrested by Italian partisans in May 1945. After his return to Italy Pound spent some time in Rapallo in 1959. From 1962 onwards he divided most of his time with Olga between Sant'Ambrogio and Venice.

ROME. Although Pound visited Rome on at least one of his early European trips and stayed there briefly in 1923, the city did not have major significance in his life either as cultural symbol or artistic venue. His association with Rome is rather more political. He met Mussolini there in 1933 at the Palazzo Venezia and also visited the city during the crisis caused by Italy's invasion of Ethiopia. In 1939 Pound made his first enquiries about speaking on the radio, but it was not until 1941 that he began his broadcasts for Rome Radio. Following the Allied bombing of Rome and the deposition of Mussolini in 1943, Pound made his way from the city to the Tirol to see his daughter Mary and did not see Rome again until his return to Italy after St Elizabeth's. Donald Hall's interview of Pound for the *Paris Review* in 1960 took place in Rome, where the poet was staying with friends on a convalescent visit. A similar visit took place the following year, but Pound had serious depressive illness problems and had to be rescued from a nursing clinic by Olga Rudge.

SIRMIONE. This resort on Lake Garda in the Italian Alps inspired great affection in Pound and he made repeated trips there throughout his life in Europe. In 1910, staying at his favourite hotel, the Eden, he was joined by Olivia and Dorothy Shakespear and this probably marks the beginning of his relationship with his wife. Sirmione seems to have been a place which Pound found conducive to writing, composing, for example, 'The Seafarer' there in 1911. Pound's celebrated first encounter with James Joyce and his son Georgio took place in Sirmione in 1920. During Pound's St Elizabeth's years the resort was the venue for a meeting between Archibald MacLeish and Mary de Rachewiltz to discuss plans for her father's release. In 1959 Pound revisited Sirmione, a place associated by him in both his early poems and *The Cantos* with paradise.

VENICE. Pound first visited Venice in 1898 on his European tour with Aunt Frank. Writing in 1923, he said: 'Venice struck me as

241

an agreeable place – as, in fact, more agreeable than Wyncote, Pa., or "47th" and Madison Avenue. I announced an intention to return. I have done so. I do not know quite how often. By elimination of possible years: 1898, 1902, 1908, 1910, 1911, 1913, 1920' (*PD*, p. 6). Of these visits the one in 1908, when Pound stayed in the Ponte San Vio and 'sat on the Dogana's steps', was notable for the publication of Pound's first book of poems, *A Lume Spento*, but it was probably also the occasion when Venice became more than just an agreeable place and began to be an urban symbol of earthly paradise. After the First World War Pound resumed his frequent trips to Venice, but the city took on another significance once Olga Rudge had acquired a house there in the Calle Querini, since it became his home for some weeks each year during much of the time he lived in Rapallo. In her autobiography *Discretions* their daughter Mary vividly recalls her visits to Venice during this period before it was shattered by war. It was not until the early 1960s that Pound was able to live with Olga in Venice again and the house in Calle Querini became another venue for disciples to visit. Despite his retreat into silence and periodic depression, Pound appears to have found some measure of peace in his last Venetian years with 'gods in the azure air'. He died in Venice and is buried in the cemetery of San Michele. Today, despite public directions to the appropriate section, the actual plot remains unobtrusive. In a place of complete tranquillity a flat stone bearing only his name is surrounded by flowers and overlooked by a laurel tree, as most befits a great poet. His plea, 'Oh let an old man rest', seems properly fulfilled.

Bibliography

Works by Ezra Pound

The following is not a comprehensive list of Pound's works. It only gives the titles of works quoted from in this book. The date of first publication is given in parenthesis after the title. The edition I have referred to is given by publisher and date. Each title is preceded by the abbreviation I have used in the text for ease of reference.

ABC: *ABC of Reading* (1934). Faber 1961

CAN: *The Cantos* (1925–69). 4th collected edn; Faber 1987

CON: *The Classic Anthology as Defined by Confucius* (1954). Faber 1974

CSP: *Personae: Collected Shorter Poems of Ezra Pound* (1926). Faber 1984

FEN: *The Chinese Written Character as a Medium for Poetry* by Ernest Fenollosa (1920). Stanley Nott 1936

GB: *Gaudier-Brzeska, A Memoir* (1916). The Marvell Press 1960

GK: *Guide to Kulchur* (1938). Peter Owen Ltd 1966

INS: *Instigations* (1920). Books for Libraries Press 1969

LE: *Literary Essays of Ezra Pound* ed. T.S. Eliot (1954). Faber 1960

PD: *Pavannes and Divagations* (1958). Peter Owen Ltd 1960

RG: Rémy de Gourmont, *The Natural Philosophy of Love* trans. with a postscript by Ezra Pound (1922). Trans. and with an Introduction by Ezra Pound, Quartet Books 1992

SL: *The Selected Letters of Ezra Pound 1907–1941* ed. D.D. Paige (1950). New Directions 1971

SP: *Selected Prose 1909–1965* ed. William Cookson (1973). Faber 1973

SR: *The Spirit of Romance* (1910). Peter Owen Ltd 1952

TEP: *The Translations of Ezra Pound* ed. Hugh Kenner (1953). Faber 1970

WT: Sophocles, *Women of Trachis* A Version by Ezra Pound (1954). Faber 1969

Recordings

Pound's idiosyncratic delivery of his own poetry can be sampled on the following recordings:

EPR: *Ezra Pound Reading His Poetry* Vols 1 and 2 (1960). Caedmon Cassettes 1960. These recordings from Pound's St Elizabeth's days in the 1950s contain almost the whole of *Hugh Selwyn Mauberley*, 'The Exile's Letter' from *Cathay*, and a selection of *The Cantos*, including numbers 1, 4, 36, 51, 84 and 99.

PV: The Poet's Voice: poets reading aloud and commenting upon their works selected and ed. Stratis Haviaras. Harvard University Press 1978. This recording brings together material Pound recorded in 1939 and includes 'The Seafarer', the explosive version of 'Sestina: Altaforte' and Canto 45 '(With Usura)'.

Other references

The following is a list of all works edited or written by other authors which I have referred to or quoted from in this book.

Ackroyd, Peter 1980. *Ezra Pound and his World*. Thames and Hudson

Alexander, Michael and McGonigal, James 1995. *Sons of Ezra (British Poets and Ezra Pound)*. Editions Rodopi B.V.

Axelrod, Stephen G. 1978. *Robert Lowell: Life and Art*. Princeton University Press

Barthes, Roland 1990. *S/Z*. Basil Blackwell

Bell, Ian F.A. 1981. *Critic as Scientist (The modernist poetics of Ezra Pound)*. Methuen

Blonsky, Marshall (ed.) 1985. *On Signs*. Basil Blackwell

Brendon, Piers 1984. *Winston Churchill, A Brief Life*. Secker and Warburg

Brooker, Peter 1979. *A Student's Guide to the Selected Poems of Ezra Pound*. Faber

Bunting, Basil 1978. *Collected Poems*. Oxford University Press

Burke, Sean 1995. *Authorship: From Plato to the Postmodern*. Edinburgh University Press

Butler, Christopher 1994. *Early Modernism*. Oxford University Press

Carpenter, Humphrey 1990. *A Serious Character: The Life of Ezra Pound*. Dell Publishing

Chaytor, H.J. 1970. *The Troubadours*. Kennikat Press

Cookson, William 1985. *A Guide to The Cantos of Ezra Pound*. Croom Helm

Cory, Daniel 1968. Ezra Pound, a memoir. *Encounter*, May 1968

Davie, Donald 1991. *Studies in Ezra Pound*. Carcanet

Dick, Kay (ed.) 1972. *Writers at Work: interviews from the Paris Review*. Penguin

Doob, Leonard W. 1978. *'Ezra Pound Speaking': Radio Speeches of WW2*. Greenwood Press

Edwards, J.H. and Vasse, W.W. 1957. *The Annotated Index to the Cantos of Ezra Pound: Cantos 1-84*. University of California Press

Eliot, T.S. 1965. *To Criticize the Critic*. Faber

Eliot, Valerie (ed.) 1971. *T.S. Eliot 'The Waste Land': A Facsimile.* Faber

Ellmann, Richard (ed.) 1975. *Selected Letters of James Joyce.* Faber

Gilbert, Sandra M. and Gubar, Susan 1988. *No Man's Land Vol. 1 (The War of the Words).* Yale University Press

Ginsberg, Allen 1987. *Collected Poems 1947–1980.* Penguin

Gordon, David M. (ed.) 1994. *Ezra Pound and James Laughlin: Selected Letters.* W.W. Norton and Co.

Grant, Michael (ed.) 1982. *T.S. Eliot, The Critical Heritage* Vol. 1. Routledge

Hamilton, Ian 1982. *Robert Lowell: A Biography.* Faber & Faber

Hanscombe, Gillian and Smyers, Virginia L. 1987. *Writing for their Lives, The Modernist Women 1910–1940.* The Women's Press

Harwood, John 1993. Pound, Eliot and *The Waste Land.* In Andrew Gibson (ed.) 1993. *Pound in Multiple Perspective.* Macmillan

Hemingway, Ernest 1977. *A Moveable Feast.* Granada

Heyman, C. David 1976. *Ezra Pound: The Last Rower.* Faber

Homberger, Eric (ed.) 1972. *Ezra Pound: The Critical Heritage.* Routledge

Kandinsky, Wassily 1947. *Concerning the Spiritual in Art.* George Wittenborn

Kenner, Hugh 1972. *The Pound Era.* Faber

Lidderdale, Jane and Nicholson, Mary 1970. *Dear Miss Weaver.* Faber

Livi, Grazia 1979. The poet speaks: *Paideuma,* Vol. 9, Pt 2

Longenbach, James 1988. *Stone Cottage: Pound, Yeats and Modernism.* Oxford University Press

Lunn, Eugene 1985. *Modernism and Marxism.* Verso

McDougal, Stuart Y. 1972. *Ezra Pound and the Troubadour Tradition.* Princeton University Press

Materer, Timothy (ed.) 1991. *The Selected Letters of Ezra Pound to John Quinn 1915–1924.* Duke University Press

Meyers, Jeffrey 1980. *The Enemy. A Biography of Wyndham Lewis.* Routledge

Nicholls, Peter 1984. *Ezra Pound, Politics, Economics and Writing.* Macmillan

Nicholls, Peter 1995. *Modernisms.* Macmillan

Norman, Charles 1969. *Ezra Pound.* Macdonald

Pearson, Norman Holmes and King, Michael (eds) 1980. *End to Torment: a Memoir of Ezra Pound by H.D..* Carcanet

Pound, Omar and Spoo, Robert 1988. *Ezra Pound and Margaret Cravens: A Tragic Friendship 1910–1912.* Duke University Press

de Rachewiltz, Mary 1971. *Discretions.* Faber

Read, Forrest (ed.) 1969. *Pound/Joyce: The Letters of Ezra Pound to James Joyce.* Faber

Reck, Michael 1968. A conversation between Ezra Pound and Allen Ginsberg. *Evergreen Review* No. 57

Rizzardi, Alfredo 1961. The Mask of Experience: A Chapter upon Ezra Pound's Pisan Cantos. *Studi Urbinati di Storia Filosofia e Letteratura,* Anno 35, Nuova Serie B, No. 2

Robinson, Janice S. 1982. *H. D. The Life and Work of an American Poet.* Houghton Mifflin Co.

Ruthven, K.K. 1969. *A Guide to Ezra Pound's Personae 1926.* University of California Press

Schulman, Grace (ed.) 1974. *Ezra Pound: A Collection of Criticism.* McGraw Hill

Scott, Bonnie Kyme (ed.) 1990. *The Gender of Modernism.* Indiana University Press

Scott, Thomas L. *et al* (eds) 1988. *Pound/The Little Review: The Letters of Ezra Pound to Margaret Anderson.* Faber

Seelye, Catherine (ed.) 1975. *Charles Olsen and Ezra Pound, An Encounter at St Elizabeth's.* Grossman Publications

Shafer, R. Murray (ed.) 1978. *Ezra Pound and Music.* Faber

Shepherd, W.G. 1985. *Propertius, The Poems.* Penguin

Showalter, Elaine 1991. *Sexual Anarchy: Gender and Culture at the Fin de Siècle.* Bloomsbury

Stead, C.K. 1986. *Pound, Yeats, Eliot and the Modernist Movement.* Macmillan

Stein, Gertrude 1966. *The Autobiography of Alice B. Toklas* (1933). Penguin

Steiner, George (ed.) 1970. *Poem into Poem.* Penguin

Stock, Noel 1970. *The Life of Ezra Pound.* Routledge

Stock, Noel 1989. Ezra in exile. *Phoenix Review,* Spring (1989)

Sullivan, J.P. (ed.) 1970. *Ezra Pound: Penguin Critical Anthology.* Penguin

Terrell, Carroll F. 1993. *A Companion to the Cantos of Ezra Pound.* University of California Press

Tillyard, S.K. 1988. *The Impact of Modernism.* Routledge

Torrey, E. Fuller 1984. *The Roots of Treason.* Sidgwick and Jackson

Tytell, John 1987. *Ezra Pound: The Solitary Volcano.* Bloomsbury

Wagner, Linda W. 1976. *Interviews with W.C. Williams.* New Directions

Wilhelm, James J. 1990. *The letters of William Brooke Smith to Ezra Pound.* Paideuma, Spring (1990)

Williams, William Carlos 1967. *I Wanted to Write a Poem: The Autobiography of the Works of a Poet* reported and ed. Edith Heal (1958). Jonathan Cape

Willis, Patricia C. (ed.) 1987. *The Complete Prose of Marianne Moore.* Faber

Wilson, Stephen 1989. Prejudice in poetry. *Encounter* Vol. 73

Woodward, Kathleen 1980. *At Last, The Real Distinguished Thing.* Ohio State University Press

Yeats, W.B. 1969. *A Vision.* Macmillan

Further reading

The poems

Pound's major poetic output is collected in two essential volumes: *Collected Shorter Poems* (1926) (Faber, 1984) and *The Cantos* (1925–69) (Faber, 1987). Both exist in several editions. I have referred to the latest paperback editions. In the case of the shorter poems, this is a reprint of the 1949 edition and differs in pagination from the 1968 hardback edition which is held by many libraries, though the content is very similar. In the case of *The Cantos* the latest edition contains the Italian poems and other additional fragments. Most critical works and commentaries still refer to the 1975 edition which differs in pagination from Canto 72 onwards by a fairly consistent fourteen pages.

Guides to the poems

For those who want to read the poetry independently, but supported by a guide to Pound's many references and allusions, the following books provide definitions, translations, glossaries and background information.

William Cookson, *A Guide to The Cantos of Ezra Pound* (Croom Helm, 1985). A useful combination of glossary and minimal critical material.

K.K. Ruthven, *A Guide to Ezra Pound's Personae 1926* (University of California Press, 1969). A helpfully arranged key to the *Collected Shorter Poems* that works independently of whichever edition is used.

Carroll F. Terrell, *A Companion to the Cantos of Ezra Pound* (University of California Press, 1993). An encyclopedic key to *The Cantos*, with many entries of critical as well as purely informational interest.

The prose

Pound wrote a vast amount of prose over a wide range of literary and non-literary topics. The following is a minimal selection for further reading:

ABC: *ABC of Reading* (1934) (Faber, 1961). Pound's 'gradus ad Parnassum, for those who might like to learn' retains a freshness of insight in its brief, aphoristic overview of poetics and poetry.

Further reading

LE: *Literary Essays of Ezra Pound*, ed. T.S. Eliot (1954) (Faber, 1960). A more or less definitive selection, containing essential articles on a wide range of literary topics from the troubadours to James Joyce.

SL: *The Selected Letters of Ezra Pound 1907–1941* ed. D.D. Paige (1950) (New Directions, 1971). Although there are numerous more specialized selections of letters, some of which I have included in the references above, this remains an essential selection that charts many important events of the early modernist period.

SP: *Selected Prose 1909–1965* ed. William Cookson (1973) (Faber, 1973). A helpfully arranged selection of mainly non-literary prose. Particularly useful for those who wish to try and understand Pound's economic views.

R. Murray Shafer (ed.), *Ezra Pound and Music* (Faber, 1978). A comprehensive collection of all Pound's writings on music, collated and contextualized with scholarly commentary.

The life

There is an enormous amount of biographical material about Pound, ranging from personal memoirs, sketches and anecdotes to full-scale biographies. Some of this material is over-sensational or seems designed to present Pound in the worst possible light for the writer's own purposes. The following biographies for the most part present a balanced picture:

Peter Ackroyd, *Ezra Pound and his World* (Thames and Hudson, 1980). A delightful book for the wealth of illustration. The necessarily brief treatment demanded by the format is nevertheless an excellent starting point for students of Pound's life.

Humphrey Carpenter, *A Serious Character: The Life of Ezra Pound* (Dell Publishing, 1990). The most comprehensive account of Pound's life. The detail is not always luminous or free of sensationalism, but a balanced appraisal is achieved.

Mary de Rachewiltz, *Discretions* (Faber, 1971). The autobiography of Pound's daughter. Essential for its authentic detail and finely written personal perspectives.

Noel Stock, *The Life of Ezra Pound* (Routledge, 1970). The first full-length biography, written by someone closely involved with Pound in the years following his release from St Elizabeth's. A major source of authentic detail.

John Tytell, *Ezra Pound: The Solitary Volcano* (Bloomsbury, 1987). A compact synthesis of Pound's life and work, written from the perspective of literary scholarship.

Critical works

The 'Pound industry' has generated a large number of critical and theoretical works about both the poetry and the ideas associated with it, some of which is reflected in my references above. This literature can be complex and contentious in its own right and sometimes unnecessarily obscure. The following brief selection of works is partly guided by their usefulness in compiling this *Preface*.

Michael Alexander and James McGonigal, *Sons of Ezra (British Poets and Ezra Pound)* (Editions Rodopi B.V., 1995). An excellent collection of essays which surveys, through personal testimony and informed commentary, the Poundian tradition in British poetry.

Donald Davie, *Studies in Ezra Pound* (Carcanet, 1991). The collected writings about Pound by a major British scholar. The way Davie's thinking about Pound developed over a long period of time is useful to chart in itself.

Eric Homberger (ed.), *Ezra Pound: The Critical Heritage* (Routledge, 1972). A very useful source of original reviews and criticism as it emerged in response to Pound's published work.

Peter Jones (ed.), *Imagist Poetry* (Penguin, 1972). An illustrative selection of poetry from the early imagist anthologies and after, accompanied by useful commentary and extracts from imagist manifesto material.

Hugh Kenner, *The Pound Era* (Faber, 1972). More or less a classic of Pound criticism and commentary. Densely detailed and full of insight across the whole range of Pound's work.

James Longenbach, *Stone Cottage: Pound, Yeats and Modernism* (Oxford University Press, 1988). Despite the apparent specificity of its title, this book provides valuable insights about the development of early modernism in general.

Stuart Y. McDougal, *Ezra Pound and the Troubadour Tradition* (Princeton University Press, 1972). Scholarly treatment of the topic, particularly useful for its clear and accessible readings of Pound's poetry.

J.P. Sullivan (ed.), *Ezra Pound: Penguin Critical Anthology* (Penguin, 1970). As well as significant early criticism by others, this volume brings together many essential extracts from Pound's own prose and letters.

Index

General Index

Adams, John, 167, 176, 179, 180, 181, 183, 202
Aldington, Richard, 27, 28, 221, 224
Anderson, Margaret, 41, 213, 221
Antheil, George, 7, 8, 50–1, 222, 240
Anti-Semitism, 63, 65, 70, 78, 112–15, 179
Apollonius of Tyana, 184

Barthes, Roland, xi, 95, 165–6
Bartok, Bela, 61, 87, 172, 183, 222
  Fifth Quartet, 172, 222
Beach, Sylvia, 42, 44, 239
Bergson, Henri, 27, 222
Blast, 6, 35–8, 40, 42, 96, 228, 236
Browning, Robert, 3, 16, 18, 19, 83, 84, 85, 169
  'Home Thoughts from Abroad', 183
  'My Last Duchess', 83
  'Two in Campagna', 83
  Sordello, 169
Brunnenburg, 71, 76, 223, 240
Bunting, Basil, 8, 54, 55, 164, 223
  Briggflatts, 55, 223
  Collected Poems, 55; 223
  'On the Fly-leaf of Pound's Cantos', 164
Burne-Jones, Edward, 160
  'Cophetua and the Beggar Maid', 160

Catullus, 16, 31, 150
Cavalcanti, Guido, 8, 16, 56, 57, 85, 181, 190, 209
  'Donna mi priegha', 57–8, 177, 204, 208
Chomsky, Noam, 152, 156
Churchill, Winston, 9, 11, 65, 107, 109, 181, 223
Confucius, 31, 56, 100, 103–5, 167, 174, 183
Crawfordsville, Indiana, 22, 237
Criterion, The, 47, 54

cummings, e. e., 43, 238
Cunard, Nancy, 58

Daniel, Arnaut, 47, 130
Dante, ix, 16, 167, 192, 193, 194, 195, 197, 199, 200
  Divine Comedy, 192, 193, 194
  Inferno, 130, 195
  Paradiso, 177, 185
  Purgatorio, 200
de Born, Bertran, 19, 24, 26, 130–3, 170
de Gourmont, Remy, 117, 119–21, 161
  Physique de L'Amour, 120–1, 239
de Rachewiltz, Mary, 7, 11, 53–4, 65, 67, 70, 71, 73, 76, 223, 231, 240, 241
  Discretions, 11, 54, 71, 73, 77, 223, 242
de Saussure, Ferdinand, 95
Des Imagistes, 5, 29, 100, 229, 234
Dial, The, 44, 47, 54, 228, 239
Doolittle, Hilda (H.D.), 4, 5, 10, 21–2, 23, 27–8, 33, 121, 221, 224, 230, 238
Douglas, C. H., 6, 39, 110–12, 198, 224

Egoist, The, 6, 33, 37, 40, 116, 117, 227, 233
Eleusinian mysteries, 57, 118, 177, 194, 209
Eliot, T. S., 3, 6, 10, 11, 33, 38, 39–41, 42, 45–9, 71, 72, 98, 135, 142, 145, 153, 196, 197, 199, 224–5, 229, 230, 237
  After Strange Gods, 196
  Ezra Pound: His Metric and Poetry, 40
  Four Quartets, 9, 45, 225
  'Lovesong of J. Alfred Prufrock, The', 39–40, 135
  Poems 1920, 41, 224
  'Preludes', 40

251

Index

Odysseus, 167, 173, 175, 177, 179,
182, 190, 192, 193, 194
Olson, Charles, 10, 38, 69–70,
230–1
Orage, A. R., 26
Ovid, 16, 161
Metamorphoses, 104

Paris, 3, 4, 7, 15, 42, 43, 45, 49,
51, 140, 222, 225, 226, 227,
228, 231, 232, 233, 235,
239–40
Periplum, 166, 193, 194, 202
Persona, 82–5, 132, 147, 152, 158,
163
Phanopeoia, 98–9, 102
Philadelphia (including Wyncote), 3,
14, 23, 75, 113, 233, 238–9
Pisa, 10, 12, 13, 45, 181, 182, 183,
203, 211, 237, 240
Plotinus, 199, 207, 208
Poetry, 27, 40, 41, 100, 119, 229
Pound, Dorothy (née Shakespear), 5,
9, 24, 27, 30, 32, 53, 67, 70,
71, 231, 236, 237, 241
Pound, Homer, 8, 9, 14, 53, 66, 237,
239
Pound, Isabel, 8, 10, 70, 71, 237
Pound, Omar Shakespear, 7, 53,
231, 240
Pre-Raphaelites, The, 21, 131, 160,
225
Propertius, Sextus Aurelius, 16, 132,
146–51, 158

Quinn, John, 35, 41, 47, 123,
231–2

Rapallo, 7, 8, 12, 32, 52, 60, 67,
76, 172, 228, 232, 235, 240–1
Rome, 64, 67, 241
Rome Radio, 9, 64, 78, 114, 181,
241
Roosevelt, F. D., 8, 9, 10, 60, 63,
64, 65, 181
Rossetti, Dante Gabriel, 22, 85, 160
Rudge, Olga, 7, 9, 11, 50–2, 53,

59, 61, 67, 70, 73, 77, 78, 79,
223, 232, 240, 241, 242

St. Elizabeth's Hospital, 10, 13, 23, 38,
68–75, 105, 184, 211, 221, 225,
231, 234, 235, 238, 239, 240
Schoenberg, Arnold, 86, 88, 93
Shakespear, Olivia, 24, 53, 231, 236,
241
Sinclair, May, 24, 124, 233
Sirmione, 42, 45, 241
Smith, William Brooke, 4, 18–20,
34, 233
Stein, Gertrude, 8, 214, 233
Steiner, George, 148, 215, 216
Stone Cottage, 29–32, 160, 169, 237
Swinburne, Algernon Charles, 16, 19,
85

Troubadours, 16, 26, 85, 117–18,
130–3, 169, 170, 174, 195, 209

Upward, Allen, 100
'Scented Leaves from a Chinese
Jar', 100

Venice, 3, 4, 15, 53, 77, 79, 174,
175, 189, 223, 232, 241–2
Villon, Francois, 16, 50, 69, 85, 203
Vivaldi, Antonio, 51, 61, 232
Vorticism, 6, 34, 35, 39, 42, 89, 97,
102–3, 129, 139, 192

Washington, 10, 68, 239
Weaver, Harriet Shaw, 33–4, 233–4
West, Rebecca, 6, 33
Williams, William Carlos, 4, 11,
20–1, 28, 33, 54, 62, 72, 75,
129, 216, 234

Yeats, W. B., 3, 5, 7, 9, 11, 16, 23,
24, 29–32, 54, 85, 121, 134,
160, 204, 205, 234–5, 236, 237,
240

Zukofsky, Louis, 8, 54, 55, 113, 235

Index

Index of references to Pound's works